RÉGION ET DÉVELOPPEMENT

n° 40-2014

Advances in spatial econometrics

REVUE RÉGION ET DÉVELOPPEMENT

Revue fondée en 1995 par Gilbert Benhayoun et Maurice Catin

Revue semestrielle référencée dans ECONLIT et dans IDEAS (REPEC)

Site web : www.regionetdeveloppement.org
ISSN 2117-0843

5-7, rue de l'Ecole polytechnique, 75005 Paris

http://www.harmattan.fr
diffusion.harmattan@wanadoo.fr
harmattan1@wanadoo.fr
ISBN : 978-2-343-06436-9
EAN : 9782343064369

Région et Développement

n° 40 - 2014

Advances in Spatial econometrics

Guest edited by
Alexandra SCHAFFAR

INTRODUCTION
AVANCEES RÉCENTES EN ÉCONOMÉTRIE SPATIALE

Alexandra SCHAFFAR *

En notant que le voisinage géographique de certains phénomènes économiques est susceptible de générer des situations de corrélation semblables à celles qui surgissent lorsque l'on considère la succession de ces phénomènes dans le temps, Student (1914) initie une réflexion sur la prise en considération des interdépendances spatiales dans l'analyse économique moderne (Le Gallo, 2002). Cependant, Student (1914) referme aussitôt la brèche ouverte en soulignant que, sur un plan méthodologique, l'étude des corrélations spatiales s'avère hautement plus problématique que celle des corrélations temporelles. Vingt ans plus tard, Stephan (1934) observe que les données concernant les unités géographiques régionales semblent attachées comme « *une grappe de raisins* » ; il est, donc, impératif d'intégrer la dimension spatiale des observations dans le processus de construction des bases de données statistiques ou alors de corriger les éventuels effets d'autocorrélation spatiale.

Bien que les principales théories d'économie spatiale émergent dans les années qui précèdent et succèdent la deuxième guerre mondiale, il faut attendre le travail séminal de Paelinck (1963) sur la comparaison des processus de développement des différentes régions belges pour assister à une première étude d'économétrie spatiale. Les pionniers de cette discipline sont les chercheurs flamands en *regional science* (Paelinck, Klaasen, Brandsma et Nijkamp) et les géographes quantitatifs britanniques (Bivand, Cliff, Fingleton), tandis qu'en France, Lebart (1969) explore l'utilisation de l'indicateur de Geary à l'échelle départementale.

En 1972, Cliff et Ord (1972) publient le premier article qui combine des méthodes économétriques classiques et une analyse spatiale ; quelques années plus tard, Paelinck et Klaassen (1979) produisent une étude synthétique des principes et des techniques de l'économétrie spatiale. En 1990, Paelinck tente une première revue de littérature en économétrie spatiale dans la Revue Européenne des Sciences Sociales, intitulée *Econométrie spatiale : contributions récentes après 20 ans d'histoire*. Il énumère les cinq principes fondateurs de cette discipline :

* LEAD-LIA CNRS, Université de Toulon, E-mail: schaffar@univ-tln.fr

- *l'interdépendance spatiale*, c'est-à-dire l'absence d'indépendance entre les observations géographiques des phénomènes ou des comportements économiques ;
- *l'asymétrie spatiale* des spécifications considérées, c'est-à-dire la différentiation spatiale des phénomènes et des comportements observés ;
- *l'allotopie* qui prend en considération l'influence à distance de variables exogènes dans les choix et les comportements des agents économiques ;
- *la différentiation des interactions ex-post et ex-ante*, ce qui implique l'influence des choix (spatiaux) de certains agents sur les choix d'autres agents ;
- *le caractère topologique* des modèles économiques, c'est-à-dire l'introduction de mesures de l'espace physique dans les différents modèles économique utilisés.

La parution de l'ouvrage de Anselin (1988) *Spatial econometrics, methods and models* représente une étape majeure dans la construction de l'économétrie spatiale avec une bifurcation à la fois épistémologique et disciplinaire dans la décennie suivante, caractérisée par l'adoption des nouveaux questionnements en économie spatiale et régionale par les chercheurs en économétrie classique (Bera, Durlauf, LeSage, Kelejian, Prucha). En 2001, Baltagi intègre la dimension spatiale dans la deuxième édition de son ouvrage *Econometric analysis on Panel data*.

Sur un plan théorique, les années quatre-vingt-dix sont marquées par l'introduction des filtres spatiaux (Getis, 1995), par le recours à l'utilisation des statistiques bayesiennes (LeSage, 1997), par le développement des approches par les moments généralisés (Kelejian et Prucha, 1998), par l'amélioration du traitement des petits échantillons (Anselin et Florax, 1995).

Sur un plan méthodologique, les instituts statistiques nationaux accordent une importance grandissante à la dimension spatiale des informations recueillies, tandis que sur le plan du traitement des données apparaissent les premiers logiciels spécialisés (SpaceStat, Anselin et Hudak, 1992) avant que les logiciels classiques (Matlab, Stata) n'intègrent des *toolboxes* permettant de traiter les modèles en économétrie spatiale. Plus tard, Bivand (2006) participent à l'intégration des modèles et des tests en économétrie spatiale dans les logiciels *open source* de type *R*.

Sur un plan institutionnel, la discipline commence à identifier ses contours. En 2002, démarre une série de workshops internationaux annuels sur l'économétrie et les statistiques spatiales, organisés en France ; en 2006 est créée la *Spatial Econometrics Association* (SEA) à Rome dont le premier colloque aura lieu en 2007 à l'Université de Cambridge ; en 2010, Anselin publie *Thirty years of spatial econometrics* dans les *Papers in Regional Science*, en résumant les avancées significatives de cette discipline dans l'économie moderne.

Le numéro 40 de *Région et Développement* comprend une série d'articles sélectionnés lors du 13ème International *Workshop on Spatial Econometrics and Statistics* organisé à l'Université de Toulon, les 15 et 16 Avril 2014, par le Laboratoire d'Economie Appliquée au Développement (LEAD). L'objectif de ce workshop était de réunir en deux journées un ensemble de chercheurs dont les travaux récents, méthodologiques et/ou appliqués, contribuent à l'avancement de cette discipline.

L'objectif de l'article de James LESAGE est, avant tout, méthodologique. James Lesage développe différentes fonctions du logiciel MATLAB permettant de comparer des modèles spatiaux sur des données de panel en s'appuyant sur les méthodes bayésiennes. Sa contribution s'inscrit dans la continuité du travail de Lesage et Pace (2009) sur les procédures de sélection du modèle spatial le plus adéquat sur données de panel.

L'article de Badi BALTAGI, Bernard FINGLETON et Alain PIROTTE s'appuie sur un modèle autorégressif spatial qui utilise des données de panel aléatoirement relevées afin d'étudier la variation annuelle des prix immobiliers entre 2000 et 2007 dans 353 districts locaux en Angleterre. Badi Baltagi, Bernard Fingleton et Alain Pirotte proposent d'utiliser un estimateur nouveau calculé à partir des approches qui intègrent des variables instrumentales dans les modèles autorégressifs spatiaux.

L'article de Julie LE GALLO et de Jan MUTL se focalise sur les distributions asymptotiques de l'estimateur des Moindres Carrés Ordinaires et de l'estimateur des Moindres Carrés Généralisés dans un modèle comportant une autocorrélation spatiale des erreurs et une erreur de mesure affectant la variable explicative. Julie Le Gallo et Jan Mutl montrent que la présence simultanée de l'autocorrélation spatiale et d'une erreur de mesure sur la variable explicative conduit à un arbitrage entre le biais et la variance.

Dans leur article sur la pertinence de la définition des matrices de poids, Davide FIASCHI et Angela PARENTI reviennent sur la définition des matrices de poids, en rappelant les questions soulevées par Anselin (2010) selon lequel l'économétrie spatiale peut être considérée comme une option de l'économétrie des réseaux (Dow, 1984). L'objectif de cet article est de montrer la pertinence de l'utilisation d'une matrice d'interconnection dans l'étude de l'autocorrélation spatiale entre des régions institutionnelement définies. Ce travail est illustré par l'étude de la volatilité des taux de croissance annuels du PIB par habitant dans 199 régions européennes (NUTS2), enregistrés durant la période 1981-2008.

Dans un article qui se focalise davantage sur des aspects empiriques, Stéphane GREGOIR et Tristan-Pierre MAURY examinent l'impact de la création de zones industrielles et de zones commerciales sur les prix immobiliers dans l'agglomération parisienne. Stéphane Gregoir et Tristant-Pierre Maury s'appuient sur une méthodologie originale qui utilise des techniques semi-paramétriques pour étudier l'influence différenciée de trois types de zones industrielles, définies selon leur caractéristiques institutionnelles et fonctionnelles (ZUS, ZRU et ZFU), sur l'évolution des prix des appartements à Paris.

De leur côté, Davide FIASCHI, Lisa GIANMOENA et ANGELA PARENTI admettent l'hypothèse que les dynamiques spatiales peuvent être représentées comme un vecteur aléatoire dans le diagramme de Moran, ce qui leur permet d'analyser les effets de causalité de ces dynamiques par un test de dépendance spatiale. Leur travail est appliqué aux Etats-Unis et permet de prédire la future distribution de revenus, en tenant compte des effets de dépendance spatiale.

Enfin, dans un travail méthodologique, Huyen DO VAN, Christine THOMAS-AGNAN et Anne VANHEMS utilisent une base de données démographiques disponible dans le package de R intitulé 'US census 2010' dans le but de tester plusieurs méthodes basées sur la régression dans le cas de données liées à des comptages. Par ce biais, elles comparent l'approche extensive et l'approche intensive pour une variable qui est un rapport de deux variables de comptage.

L'ensemble de ces contributions permet de dessiner les contours des évolutions récentes en statistiques et économétrie spatiales, sur un plan théorique, méthodologique ou empirique. Les enjeux futurs de la discipline sont nombreux : parmi ceux-ci, il convient de citer l'exploration approfondie des applications possibles aux modèles spatio-temporels sur données de panel, l'amélioration des techniques informatiques et la construction systématisée de bases des données statistiques à dimension spatiale. A côté de ces approfondissements, il est nécessaire que la discipline continue à fournir des outils simples et performants, manipulables par un grand nombre de chercheurs en sciences économiques et en sciences régionales.

REFERENCES

Anselin L., 1988, *Spatial Econometrics : methods and models*, Kluwe Academic Publishers, The Netherlands.

Anselin L., Hudak S., 1992, Spatial econometrics in practice : a review of software options, *Regional Science and Urban Economics*, 22, 509-536.

Anselin L., Florax R., 1995, *New directions in Spatial econometrics*, Springer-Verlag.

Anselin, L., 2010, Thirty years of spatial econometrics, *Papers in Regional Science,* 89, 3-25.

Baltagi B.H., 2001, *Econometric Analysis of Panel Data*, 2nd edition. Wiley, Chichester.

Bivand R., 2006, Implementing spatial data analysis software in *R. Geographical Analysis*, 38, 23-40.

Cliff A., Ord J., 1972, Testing for spatial autocorrelation among regression residuals, *Geographical analysis*, 4, 267-284.

Dow M., 1984, A biparametric approach to noetwork correlation : Galton's problem, *Sociological methods and Research*, 13, 201-217.

Getis A., 1995, Spatial filtering in a regression framework : examples using data on urban crime, regional inequality and government expenditures, in Anselin L. Florax R., 1995, *New Directions in spatial econometrics*, 172-185, Springer-Verlag.

Kelejian H., Prucha R. 1998, A generalized spatial two-stage least squares procedure for estimating a spatial autoregressive model with autoregressive disturbances, *Journal of Real Estate Finance and Economics* 17, 99-121.

Le Gallo J., 2002, Econométrie spatiale : l'autocorrélation spatiale dans les modèles de régression linéaire, *Economie et Prévision*, 155, 4, 139-158.

Lebart, L., 1969, *Analyse statistique de la contiguité*, Publications de l'Institut de Statistique de l'Université de Paris, 18, 81-112.

LeSage J., Pace R., 2009 *Introduction to Spatial Econometrics*, CRC Press Taylor & Francis Group, Boca Raton.

LeSage J., 2014, Spatial econometric panel data model specification: A Bayesian approach, *Spatial Statistics* 9, 122-145.

Paelinck, J., 1963, La teoría del desarrollo regional polarizado, *Revista Latino-americana de Economía*, 9, 175-229.

Paelinck J., 1990, Vingt ans d'économétrie spatiale: contributions récentes, *Revue Européenne des Sciences Sociales*, XXVIII (88), 1-16.

Paelinck J., Klaassen L., 1979, *Spatial econometrics*, Saxon House.

Stephan F., 1934, Sampling errors and interpretation of spatial data ordered in time and space, in Ross F., *Proceedings of the American Statistical Journal, New Series*, 185, Suppl ; 165-166.

Student, 1914, The elimination of spurious correlation due to position in time and space, *Biometrika*, 5, 351-360.

SOFTWARE FOR BAYESIAN SPATIAL MODEL COMPARISON

James P. LESAGE*

Abstract - *Taking a Bayesian perspective on model comparison for cross-sectional and static panel data models considerably simplifies the task of selecting an appropriate model. A wide variety of alternative specifications that include various combinations spatial dependence in lagged values of the dependent variable, spatial lags of the explanatory variables, as well as dependence in the model disturbances have been the focus of a literature on various statistical tests used by practitioners to distinguishing between alternative specifications. LeSage and Pace (2009) make a theoretical argument that implies the task of model selection can be simplified by focusing on only two model specifications, one reflecting theoretical situations involving global spillovers (the spatial Durbin model, SDM) and the other theoretical scenarios involving local spillovers (the spatial Durbin error model, SDEM). LeSage (2014) extends this theoretical argument to the case of static panel data models. MATLAB software functions for carrying out Bayesian cross-sectional and static spatial panel data model comparisons is described here along with a number of illustrative applications.*

Keywords - STATIC SPACE-TIME PANEL DATA MODELS, BAYES FACTORS, LOCAL VERSUS GLOBAL SPATIAL SPILLOVERS

Classification JEL - C11, C23, O47, O52

* Fields Endowed Chair ; Texas State University-San Marcos, Department of Finance & Economics, San Marcos, TX 78666; E-mail: jlesage@spatial-econometrics.com

1. INTRODUCTION

LeSage and Pace (2009) define spatial spillovers for a causal relationship between characteristics/actions of entity/agent (X_i) located at position i in space and the outcomes/decisions/actions (Y_j) of an agent/entity located at position j as a situation where: $\partial Y_j / \partial X_i \neq 0$.

LeSage and Pace (2014) argue that practitioners should focus on a theoretical motivation for either *local* or *global* spatial spillovers, which would facilitate choice of an appropriate spatial regression specification. If locations j are neighbors to location i, we have a *local* spatial spillover, whereas situations involving locations j that include not only neighbors to i, but neighbors to neighbors of i, neighbors to neighbors to neighbors, and so on, are defined as *global* spillover.

Two of the most popular spatial regression specifications are: 1) global spillover models that include a spatial lag of the dependent variable, and 2) local spillover models that include spatial lags of the explanatory variables but not the dependent variable. LeSage (2014) shows that practitioners need logically only consider the single SDM global spillover model versus the SDEM local spillover specification. The logic behind his argument is that other specifications such as the spatial autogressive (SAR) and spatial error (SEM) are subsumed by these two, as is the spatially lagged explanatory variables (SLX) specification from LeSage and Pace (2009).

2. TESTING FOR SLX, SDM VERSUS SDEM IN CROSS-SECTIONAL MODEL SPECIFICATIONS

There is a large literature on various statistical tests that can be used to distinguish between alternative spatial model specifications. For example, the (robust) LM tests developed by Anselin et al. (1996) for cross-sectional data to test whether spatial interaction effects ($\rho(I_T \otimes W)y$) should be included in the model. Elhorst (2010) extends these tests to the case of static panel data models. Another alternative has been to estimate a model that includes spatial interaction effects and test whether the model can be simplified to one that excludes these effects using Wald or Likelihood ratio tests. These tests and the numerical outcomes for a widely used panel data set on cigarette demand (Baltagi, 2001) are illustrated in Elhorst (2012).

LeSage and Pace (2014) point out that before engaging in statistical tests to determine an appropriate model specification, the theoretical context might point to either a local or global specification. For example, if the substantive (or theoretical) aspects of our applied modeling situation point to *local* spillovers as the only reasonable possibility, there should be no need for statistical tests. LeSage (2014) points out that there are cases where theory is ambiguous regarding the question of local versus global spillovers. As a concrete illustration, he points to the case of spillovers from state-level cigarette taxes, noting that substantial commercial smuggling activity could produce global spillovers, whereas mere cross-border shopping by consumers suggests local spillovers (see LaFaive and Nesbit, 2013).

LeSage and Pace (2009) describe calculation of Bayesian posterior model probabilities for cross-sectional spatial regression models based on work of LeSage and Parent (2007). LeSage (2014) sets forth the theoretical underpinnings for calculation of Bayesian posterior model probabilities for the SLX, SDM and SDEM spatial panel data model specifications. Our focus here is on describing a set of MATLAB functions that implement these approaches to Bayesian model comparison that produce model probabilities. Applied examples are provided that should assist practitioners with intelligent use of these functions.

2.1. The lmarginal_cross_section() function

A single MATLAB function named *lmarginal_cross_section* was constructed to carry out Bayesian posterior model probabilities that compare the three relevant cross-sectional spatial regression models, SLX, SDM and SDEM. In a cross-sectional spatial regression, an $N \times 1$ vector y contains the dependent variable for N regions, an $N \times k$ matrix X contains explanatory variable vectors, and an $N \times N$ matrix W holds the spatial weight matrix.

A call of the function using these model data with no options produces a *results structure variable* with a 3×1 vector of log marginal magnitudes (these form the basis for Bayesian model comparison) and a 3×1 vector of posterior model probabilities for the three models, SLX, SDM and SDEM. Since no input options were specified, these results are based on default values used by the function. We can print out the results using the *mprint* function from the toolbox.[1]

1.0

```
result = lmarginal_cross_section(y,X,W);
in.cnames = strvcat('log-marginal','model probs');
in.rnames = strvcat('model','slx','sdm','sdem');
in.fmt = '%10.4f';
out = [result.lmarginal result.probs];
mprint(out,in);
```

The results printed are shown below, where we see that all three models exhibit similar log-marginal likelihoods and posterior model probabilities. This type of result will occur when spatial dependence in the dependent variable for the SDM model and the disturbances of the SDEM model is low. Note that in the presence of no spatial dependence, all three models collapse to the same specification (the SLX).

[1]All references to the toolbox are to the Spatial Econometrics Toolbox for MATLAB available for free at www.spatial-econometrics.com

```
model log-marginal model probs
slx    -1088.6072    0.3686
sdm    -1088.8197    0.2980
sdem   -1088.7077    0.3334
```

This should be clear from examining equations for the three model specifications, where ρ is the scalar parameter reflecting the strength of spatial dependence. As $\rho \rightarrow 0$, all specifications collapse to the SLX. The sample data vector y in this example was in fact generated using the SLX specification, so the posterior probabilities produced by the model comparison method are correct.

$$\text{SDEM: } y = X\beta + WX\gamma + u, \;\; u = \rho W u + \varepsilon \tag{1}$$

$$\text{SDM: } y = \rho W y + X\beta + WX\gamma + \varepsilon \tag{2}$$

$$\text{SLX: } y = X\beta + WX\gamma + \varepsilon \tag{3}$$

$$\varepsilon \sim N(0, \sigma_\varepsilon^2 I_N)$$

As with all functions in the *Spatial Econometrics Toolbox*, typing 'help lmarginal_cross_section' in the MATLAB Command Window will show documentation for the function.

```
>> help lmarginal_cross_section
PURPOSE: Bayesian log-marginal posterior for cross-sectional spa-
tial regression models
      no priors on beta, sige
      uniform prior on rho, lambda over eigenvalue bounds
-------------------------------------------------------------
USAGE: results = lmarginal_cross_section(y,x,W,info)
where:
  y = dependent variable vector (N x 1)
  x = independent variables matrix, WITHOUT INTERCEPT or W*x
      variables
  W = N by N spatial weight matrix (for W*y and W*e)
  info.lflag = 0 for full lndet computation (default = 1,fastest)
             = 1 for MC lndet approximation (fast for large
                 problems)
  info.order = order to use with info.
                lflag = 1 option (default = 50)
  info.iter = iterations to use with info.
               lflag = 1 (default = 30)
  info.rmin = (optional) minimum value of rho in search
              (default = -1)
  info.rmax = (optional) maximum value of rho in search
              (default = +1)
  info.eig  = 0 for default rmin = -1,rmax = +1,
            = 1 for eigenvalue calculation of these
-------------------------------------------------------------
 RETURNS: a structure:
   results.meth   = 'lmarginal_cross_section'
   results.nobs   = # of cross-sectional observations
   results.y      = N x 1 vector of y from input
   results.nvar   = # of variables in x-matrix
   results.rmin   = minimum value of rho used (default +1)
   results.rmax   = maximum value of rho used (default -1)
   results.lflag  = lflag value from input (or default value used)
```

```
   results.eig  = 0,1 from input (or default value used)
   results.lmarginal = a 3 x 1 column-vector with [log-marginal]
      [ logm_slx logm_sdm logm_sdem ]'
   results.probs = a 3 x 1 column-vector with model probs
   results.logm_slx
   results.logm_sdm
   results.logm_sdem
 ---------------------------------------------------
```

This documentation shows that when calling the function an $N \times k$ explanatory variables matrix without an intercept is used, since the function adds the intercept term as well as the spatially lagged explanatory variables WX. These spatial lags of X are part of all three model specifications being compared. The user-controlled options are input using a structure variable (named 'info' here) that allow for various choices that influence the speed and accuracy of the computations involved.[2] Generally, faster computational speed is accompanied by slightly lower numerical accuracy, for example one can use the default (info.eig = 0) which uses the range of $-1 < \rho < 1$ for the spatial dependence parameter rather than the true range of $1/\omega_{\min} < \rho < 1/\omega_{\max}$, where $\omega_{\min}$ and $\omega_{\max}$ denote the smallest (i.e., most negative) and largest characteristics roots of the matrix W. Calculating a minimum eigenvalue can take time for problems involving a large number of observations N.

An example of the trade-offs between speed and accuracy is shown below, where an SLX model was generated using 605 observations (reflecting Ohio school districts). Despite the difference in accuracy, one should draw the same inference that an SLX model is the specification most consistent with the sample data from both sets of results.

```
results for defaults (no info input arguments)
uses -1, 1 interval and lndetmc
true model is SLX
time taken is:       0.1720 seconds
model log-marginal model probs
slx   -1088.6072     0.4447
sdm   -1089.1336     0.2627
sdem  -1089.0255     0.2927
results for info.lflag = 0, info.eig = 1
true model is SLX
time taken is:       8.2840 seconds
model log-marginal model probs
slx   -1088.6072     0.3686
sdm   -1088.8197     0.2980
sdem  -1088.7077     0.3334
```

2.2. Comparing models and spatial weight matrices

The log-marginal values returned in the function *lmarginal_cross_section* result structure variable can be viewed as a common denominator for comparing a number of alternative SLX, SDM, SDEM models based on varying spatial

[2] Users can rely on any structure variable name, for example options.lflag = 0 would work, with the name 'options' entered in place of 'info'.

weight matrices. Note that these cannot be used to compare models with differing sets of explanatory variables (see LeSage and Parent, 2007 regarding this type of comparison). To illustrate this, we use the per capita income growth rates over the 1987 to 1993 period for $N = 3{,}111$ US counties (in the lower 48 states plus the district of Columbia) as the dependent variable y and the initial period (1987) logged income level and logged population level as explanatory variables to form the matrix X.

A series of nearest neighbor spatial weight matrices are compared along with the three model specifications using a loop, with the code shown below.

```
   latt = uscounties(:,2); % extract latt-long coordinates
long = uscounties(:,3); % from the dataset
lmarginals = []; % empty matrix for storing results
neighbors = [];
for ii=5:16; % loop over varying nearest neighbors W-matrices
W = make_neighborsw(latt,long,ii);
neighbors = [neighbors ii];
result = lmarginal_cross_section(pci_growth,xmatrix,W);
% extract log-marginals and put them into a matrix
lmarginals = [lmarginals
       result.lmarginal']; % we transpose the 3 x 1 vector
       % each column is a different model (column 1 = slx,
       %                            column 2 = sdm column 3 = sdem)
end;
% calculate model probabilities for each column (model)
nmodels = length(lmarginals);
adj = max(lmarginals);
madj = matsub(lmarginals,adj);
xx = exp(madj);
% compute posterior probabilities
psum = sum(xx);
probs = [neighbors matdiv(xx,psum)];
in.fmt = strvcat('%10d','%16.4f','%16.4f','%16.4f');
in.cnames = strvcat('#neigbhors','slx','sdm','sdem');
mprint(probs,in);
```

Since the log-marginals require exponentiation, we use a normalization that subtracts the 1×3 vector of maximum values from each column of the 8×3 matrix (returned by the MATLAB *max* function) using the *matsub* function from the toolbox. This function performs non-conformable matrix subtraction allowing us to subtract the 1×3 vector of column maximum values from each row of the matrix. This normalization avoids numerical over- and under-flows that may arise from exponentiation, but does not alter the posterior probability results.

The results which took 9.8 seconds to calculate are shown below, where we see that for all three models a 14 nearest neighbors weight matrix W has the highest probability.[3] The probabilities sum to unity down the columns, since the 8 different weight matrices are being compared for each model here.

---

[3] When using the default MC determinant option, info.lflag = 1, every run of the program will produce slightly different results because a Monte Carlo approximation to the log-determinant calculation is being used, (see Barry and Pace, 1999).

Changing the input options to the function to produce the most accurate but slowest results produced the second set of results shown, and took 2,786 seconds. It should be apparent that in cases where the sample size is large, the default input options produce reasonably accurate results.[4]

	default options results (no info structure input)			most accurate options results (info.lflag = 0, info.eig = 1)		
#neig	slx	sdm	sdem	slx	sdm	sdem
5	0.0000	0.0000	0.0000	0.0000	0.0000	0.0000
6	0.0000	0.0000	0.0000	0.0000	0.0000	0.0000
7	0.0126	0.0000	0.0000	0.0126	0.0000	0.0000
8	0.0168	0.0000	0.0000	0.0168	0.0000	0.0000
9	0.0109	0.0000	0.0000	0.0109	0.0000	0.0000
10	0.0050	0.0000	0.0000	0.0050	0.0000	0.0000
11	0.0289	0.0000	0.0000	0.0289	0.0000	0.0000
12	0.0501	0.0044	0.0000	0.0501	0.0098	0.0001
13	0.0814	0.0232	0.0028	0.0814	0.0310	0.0037
14	0.7646	0.8901	0.9683	0.7646	0.8710	0.9815
15	0.0210	0.0112	0.0021	0.0210	0.0056	0.0008
16	0.0086	0.0711	0.0268	0.0086	0.0826	0.0139

There is still the question of which specification (SLX, SDM, SDEM) is most consistent with this sample data. As noted, log-marginal likelihoods can be viewed as a common denominator for comparing models, so the following code re-normalizes the log-marginals using the maximum element of the entire 8×3 matrix, not just the maximum of each column. This produces posterior model probabilities that compare all 24 model specifications such that the 24 probabilities sum to unity.

Interestingly, the results point to the SDEM specification (and a weight matrix based on 14 nearest neighbors) as most consistent with the sample data for this simple county-level spatial growth regression. Most empirical studies in the spatial growth regression literature use the SAR or SDM specification which are global spillovers models, in contrast to the local spillovers SDEM pointed to here. These results indicate that spatial spillovers at the county level do not extend (on average over the sample of counties) beyond first-order (contiguous) counties, and that the spillovers are the result of *contextual effects*, not *endogenous interaction* (see LeSage and Pace, 2014 for detailed discussion of these issues).

```
% find best model, slx, sdm, sdem
adj2 = max(max(lmarginals)); % maximum element of the matrix
madj2 = lmarginals-adj2;
% calculate probabilities across all models and weight matrices
xx2 = exp(madj2);
psum2 = sum(vec(xx2));
probs2 = [neighbors xx2./psum2];
mprint(probs2,in);
```

[4] The SLX model results are identical because no numerical integration is required to calculate the log-marginal likelihood in this case. Varying degrees of accuracy in numerical integration are what explains the difference in results (see LeSage, 2014 for details regarding this.)

#neig	default options results (no info structure input) slx	sdm	sdem	most accurate options results (info.lflag = 0, info.eig = 1) slx	sdm	sdem
5	0.0000	0.0000	0.0000	0.0000	0.0000	0.0000
6	0.0000	0.0000	0.0000	0.0000	0.0000	0.0000
7	0.0000	0.0000	0.0000	0.0000	0.0000	0.0000
8	0.0000	0.0000	0.0000	0.0000	0.0000	0.0000
9	0.0000	0.0000	0.0000	0.0000	0.0000	0.0000
10	0.0000	0.0000	0.0000	0.0000	0.0000	0.0000
11	0.0000	0.0000	0.0000	0.0000	0.0000	0.0000
12	0.0000	0.0000	0.0001	0.0000	0.0000	0.0001
13	0.0000	0.0000	0.0064	0.0000	0.0000	0.0037
14	0.0000	0.0004	0.9468	0.0000	0.0002	0.9812
15	0.0000	0.0000	0.0024	0.0000	0.0000	0.0008
16	0.0000	0.0002	0.0437	0.0000	0.0000	0.0139

A discussion of the way in which the levels of spatial dependence, and number of observations which impact signal-to-noise in spatial regression models impacts the accuracy of Bayesian model comparison methods can be found in LeSage and Pace (2009, Chapter 6).

3. PANEL DATA MODELS

Taking the same approach used to integration of the model parameters LeSage (2014) extended the cross-sectional approach to the case of a panel data model setting. The function *lmarginal_static_panel* can be used to compare static panel data specifications for SLX, SDM and SDEM.[5] A static panel model does not contain variables and parameters that allow for time dependence (see Parent and LeSage, 2012 for an example of a dynamic spatial panel data model specification).

A vector of panel data observations for N regions over T time periods should be organized such that the first N elements of the vector y represent the first time period, the next N elements the second time period, and so on. The $NT \times k$ explanatory variables matrix X is organized in the same fashion, with the intercept excluded. For the moment, we ignore the issue of fixed or random effects as part of the model, with this issue discussed later. In addition to the $NT \times 1$ vector y and $NT \times k$ explanatory variables matrix X, we assume a single spatial configuration between the N regions for all time periods, and let W be an $N \times N$ row-standardized spatial weight matrix.

The local spatial spillover specification for the case of static panel data models is the *spatial Durbin error model* (SDEM) shown in (4), where ν represent fixed effects and ψ_t time period specific effects.

[5] LeSage (2014) shows that these three models subsume other models such as SAR and SEM as special cases, following the same logic as set forth in LeSage and Pace (2009).

$$y_t = X_t\beta_1 + WX_t\beta_2 + \nu + \psi_t + u_t$$
$$u_t = \rho W u_t + \varepsilon_t \qquad t = 1, \dots, T \tag{4}$$
$$\varepsilon_t \sim N(0, \sigma_\varepsilon^2 I_N), \qquad t = 1, \dots, T$$

The model allows for local spillovers to immediately neighboring observations through spatial lag terms for the explanatory variables: WX_t, which have been labeled *contextual effects* in the social networking literature. To differentiate these from the *endogenous interaction* arising from spatial lags of the dependent variable, they have also been labeled *exogenous interaction effects*.

As in the case of cross-sectional models, as the spatial dependence parameter $\rho \to 0$, both the SDM and SDEM collapse to the panel data SLX specification. All three specifications are shown below using matrix notation, where the vector y is $NT \times 1$, the matrix X has dimension $NT \times k$, and we use F_S, F_T to denote spatial and time period fixed effects, and $\otimes$ is the Kronecker product.

$$SLX: y = X\beta_1 + (I_T \otimes W)X\beta_2 + F_S + F_T + \varepsilon \tag{5}$$
$$SDM: y = \rho(I_T \otimes W) + X\beta_1 + (I_T \otimes W)X\beta_2 + F_S + F_T + \varepsilon \tag{6}$$
$$SDEM: y = X\beta_1 + (I_T \otimes W)X\beta_2 + F_S + F_T + u \tag{7}$$
$$u = \rho(I_T \otimes W)u + \varepsilon$$

Both SDM and SDEM can be viewed as *encompassing models* for the SLX, since they nest this model. Because of this, when ρ takes a value of zero, the sample data provide no basis for selecting between these three models. In this circumstance, the log-marginal likelihoods (and associated model probabilities) should approach equality. If fact, despite our interest in comparing the SDM versus SDEM models, practitioners would be interested in knowing when the level of spatial dependence in the data is low enough to allow use of the simpler SLX specification.

Lee and Yu (2010) have proposed a transformation procedure to eliminate both space and time fixed effects from the model. A MATLAB function *demeanF* written by Elhorst can be used to accomplish this task, and the documentation (shown below) for the function *lmarginal_static_panel* indicates that it is the user's responsibility to carry out this transformation. There is also a new input option, 'info.iflag' to indicate that this type of transformation has been used prior to inputting the (transformed) data vector $\tilde{y}$, (transformed) data matrix $\tilde{X}$ and (transformed) weight matrix $\widetilde{W}$.

```
>> help lmarginal_static_panel
PURPOSE: Bayesian log-
marginal posterior for static spatial panel models
user should eliminate fixed effects using differencing transfor-
mations
      no priors on beta, sige
      uniform prior on rho, lambda over eigenvalue bounds
 ---------------------------------------------------------
```

```
 USAGE: results = lmarginal_static_panel(y,x,W,N,T,info)
 where:
  y = dependent variable vector (N*T x 1)
  x = independent variables matrix, WITHOUT INTERCEPT TERM
  W = N by N spatial weight matrix (for W*y and W*e)
  N = # of cross-sectional units
  T = # of time periods
  info.lflag = 0 for full lndet computation (default = 1,fastest)
         = 1 for MC lndet approximation (fast for large problems)
  info.order = order to use with info.lflag = 1 option
               (default = 50)
  info.iter = iterations to use with info.lflag = 1(default = 30)
  info.rmin = (optional) minimum value of rho in search
              (default = -1)
  info.rmax = (optional) maximum value of rho in search
              (default = +1)
  info.iflag = 0 for conventional W-matrix
  info.iflag = 1 for transformed W-matrix (using dmeanF())
---------------------------------------------------------
RETURNS: a structure:
  results.meth  = 'lmargainal_static_panel'
  results.nobs  = # of cross-sectional observations
  results.ntime = # of time periods
  results.y     = N*T x 1 vector of y from input
  results.nvar  = # of variables in x-matrix
  results.rmin  = minimum value of rho used (default +1)
  results.rmax  = maximum value of rho used (default -1)
  results.lflag = lflag value from input (or default value used)
  results.iflag = iflag value from input (or default value used)
  results.lmarginal = a 3 x 1 column-vector with [log-marginal]
      [ logm_slx logm_sdm logm_sdem ]'
  results.probs = a 3 x 1 column-vector with model probs
  results.logm_slx
  results.logm_sdm
  results.logm_sdem
 --------------------------------------------------------
```

An example of using the transformation function *demeanF* is shown below, where 'ted=0' is an input option to request only spatial fixed effects, and 'ted=1' both space and time-period fixed effects. The example represents a data-generated y −vector based on $T = 30$ years and $N = 49$ states plus District of Columbia.

```
ted = 0;
[yf,Xf,No,To,Wf]=demeanF(y,X,N,T,ted,W);
info.iflag = 1;
result1 = lmarginal_static_panel(yf,Xf,Wf,No,To,info);
in.cnames = strvcat('log-marginal','model probs');
in.rnames = strvcat('model','slx','sdm','sdem');
in.width = 10000;
in.fmt = '%10.4f';
out = [result1.lmarginal result1.probs];
mprint(out,in);

true model is SLX
model log-marginal model probs
slx   -2896.3385    0.3182
sdm   -2895.9531    0.4679
sdem  -2896.7358    0.2139
```

The time taken to produce these results was round 0.2 seconds on an Intel i7-4510U CPU, 64-bit operating system with MATLAB version 8.3.0.532 (R2014a). We interpret these results to indicate that the SLX model (not the SDM) is the correct specification, and the data-generated y −vector was indeed created to follow the SLX specification. A lack of high probability in favor of the SDM or SDEM specifications should always be interpreted as evidence in favor of the SLX specification. In the face of low levels of spatial dependence, this is the correct inference regarding the alternative model specifications. LeSage (2014) reports results of a Monte Carlo experiment assessing performance of this Bayesian approach to static panel data model comparison with regard to changes in levels of spatial dependence and sample size. LeSage (2014) summarizes the Monte Carlo results by indicating that for the purpose of drawing inferences regarding the SDM versus SDEM specifications low-to-moderate levels of spatial dependence ($\rho \geq 0.3$) will produce results that identify the correct specification.

As an illustration, we compare SLX, SDM and SDEM specifications for the case $N = 49, T = 30$ and two matrices W, one based on first-order contiguity of the states and the other based on lengths of border miles in common between each state and its neighbors. A data-generated y-vector was constructed based on $\rho = 0.3$, with the true weight matrix being that based on border miles in common. Results for the case where the true specification was SDM when comparing three specifications (SLX, SDM and SDEM) based on each weight matrix as as follows:

In this comparison the sum of the three model probabilites in each column is one, and the higher log-marginal values for the W_m miles weight matrix points to these three models as superior to those based on the W_c contiguity matrix. However, use of the W_c matrix produces the wrong inference regarding SLX, SDM, SDEM, erroneously pointing to the SDEM as the correct specification. Results are also shown for the case where $\rho = 0.6$, and here we see that even in the case of the wrong W_c matrix, the correct SDM specification is identified. Intuitively, it is difficult to draw inferences regarding the correct spatial weight matrix when there is low or moderate spatial dependence.

```
true model is SDM Wm (rho = 0.3)
model     log-marginal   model probs          log-marginal   model probs
slx Wm    -2952.5556     0.0000     slx Wc    -3043.9501     0.0000
sdm Wm    -2916.6129     0.8251     sdm Wc    -3014.6607     0.0372
sdem Wm   -2918.1642     0.1749     sdem Wc   -3011.4081     0.9628
```

```
true model is SDM Wm (rho = 0.6)
model     log-marginal   model probs          log-marginal   model probs
slx Wm    -3263.9848     0.0000     slx Wc    -3344.8898     0.0000
sdm Wm    -2992.2356     1.0000     sdm Wc    -3138.2277     1.0000
sdem Wm   -3038.2632     0.0000     sdem Wc   -3155.8827     0.0000
```

For a comparison of all six models such that the model probabilities sum to one, we use the two 3×1 vectors of log-marginals based on the two different W matrices to construct new probabilities as follows:

```
  % find best W-matrix using a 6 x 1 vector of log-marginals
lmarginals = [results1.lmarginal  % 3 x 1 vector based on Wm
              results2.lmarginal]; % 3 x 1 vector based on Wc

nmodels = length(lmarginals);
adj = max(lmarginals(:,1));
madj = matsub(lmarginals,adj);
xx = exp(madj);
% compute posterior probabilities
psum = sum(xx);
probs = [matdiv(xx,psum)];
in2.fmt = strvcat('%16.4f');
in2.rnames = strvcat('models','slx Wm','sdm Wm','sdem Wm','slx Wc
','sdm Wc','sdem Wc');
mprint(probs,in2);

models   (rho = 0.3)
slx Wm        0.0000
sdm Wm        0.8251 % true model
sdem Wm       0.1749
slx Wc        0.0000
sdm Wc        0.0000
sdem Wc       0.0000
```

Here the posterior model probabilities identify the true SDM specification based on W_m, even in the case of low levels of spatial dependence ($\rho = 0.3$).

4. CONCLUSIONS

A set of MATLAB functions for calculating log-marginal likelihoods for comparing SLX, SDM and SDEM model specifications for both cross-sectional and static panel data scenarios was described here. The calculations are fast and Monte Carlo results reported in LeSage (2014) indicate that they should work well provided that moderate levels of spatial dependence exist (levels of the scalar dependence parameter $\rho \geq 0.3$.)

The functions can be used to draw inferences regarding local versus global spatial spillover specifications in cases where theoretical aspects of the modeling exercise do not clearly indicate an appropriate specification. Applied examples also show how to use these functions to compare alternative spatial weight matrices in an effort to find a weight matrix most consistent with the sample data.

An important caveat is that the model comparison approach illustrated here should not be used to compare model specifications based on differing sets of explanatory variables. For this type of model comparison, Parent and LeSage (2007) set forth an approach for spatial regression models similar to that of Fernandez, Ley, and Steel (2001) for non-spatial regression that have become popular in the Markov Chain Monte Carlo Model Comparison ($MCMC^3$) literature. Comparing specifications based on different sets of explanatory variables requires assigning a Bayesian prior distribution (for example, the g −prior from Fernandez, Ley, and Steel, 2001) to parameters in the model, and future work should examine the effectiveness this and other related priors in the case of spatial regression models (see Han and Lee, 2013).

REFERENCES

Anselin L., A.K. Bera, R. Florax and M.J. Yoon (1996) Simple Diagnostic Tests for Spatial Dependence, *Regional Science & Urban Economics,* 26, 77-104.

Baltagi B.H. (2001) *Econometric Analysis of Panel Data*, 2nd edition. Wiley, Chichester.

Barry, R.P. and R.K. Pace (1999) A Monte Carlo Estimator of the Log Determinant of Large Sparse Matrices, *Linear Algebra and its Applications*, 289, 41-54.

Elhorst, J.P. (2010) Applied spatial econometrics: raising the bar, *Spatial Economic Analysis*, 5, 928.

Elhorst J.P. (2012) Matlab Software for Spatial Panels, *International Regional Science Review*, DOI: 10.1177/0160017612452429.

Fernandez, C., E. Ley, and M.F.J. Steel (2001) Benchmark priors for Bayesian model averaging. *Journal of Econometrics,* 100, 381-427.

Han, X. and L. Lee (2013) Bayesian estimation and model selection for Spatial Durbin Error Models with Finite distributed lags, *Regional Science & Urban Economics*, 43, 816-837.

LaFaive, M.D. and T. Nesbit (2013) Higher Cigarette Taxes Create Lucrative, Dangerous Black Market, *Mackinac Center For Public Policy*, www.mackinac.org/18128;

Lee, L.F. and J. Yu (2010) Some recent developments in spatial panel data models, *Regional Science & Urban Economics*, 40, 255-271.

LeSage J.P. (2014) Spatial econometric panel data model specification: A Bayesian approach, *Spatial Statistics,* 9, 122-145.

LeSage, J.P. and O. Parent (2007) Bayesian Model Averaging for Spatial Econometric Models, *Geographical Analysis*, 39, 3, 241-267.

LeSage, J.P. and R.K. Pace (2009) *Introduction to Spatial Econometrics*, CRC Press Taylor & Francis Group, Boca Raton.

LeSage, J.P. and R.K. Pace (2014) Interpreting Spatial Econometric Models, in *Handbook of Regional Science*, M. M. Fischer and Peter Nijkamp (Eds.) Springer, Berlin, 1535-1552.

Parent, O. and J.P. LeSage (2012) "Spatial dynamic panel data models with random effects," *Regional Science & Urban Economics*, 42: 4, 727-738.

SOFTWARE POUR LA COMPARAISON DES MODÈLES SPATIAUX BAYÉSIENS

Résumé - *L'analyse bayésienne a permis d'améliorer sensiblement la comparaison et la sélection des modèles spatiaux statiques sur des données de panel. Durant, ces dernières années, les statisticiens et les économètres se sont focalisés, plus particulièrement, sur l'étude et la comparaison d'un ensemble de spécifications alternatives des modèles spatiaux existants, permettant de combiner des effets de dépendance spatiale sur la variable expliquée, sur les variables explicatives, voire même sur le terme d'erreur. Sur un plan théorique, LeSage et Pace (2009) montrent que les procédures de sélection du modèle spatial le plus adéquat peuvent être simplifiées, si l'on considère une hypothèse binaire dans laquelle soit on observe des effets d'autocorrélation spatiale sur un plan global (appréhendés par le modèle Durbin spatial) soit on observe des effets d'autocorrélation spatiale dont le caractère est purement local (appréhendés par le modèle Durbin spatial à erreurs). Lesage (2014) introduit cette hypothèse également dans la sélection des modèles spatiaux sur des données de panel. L'objectif de cet article est de présenter la programmation de la comparaison des modèles spatiaux sur des données de panel, en s'appuyant sur les méthodes bayésiennes. Cette programmation est faite sous MATLAB, agrémentée de nombreuses applications empiriques.*

Mots-clés - MODÈLES SPATIAUX STATIQUES SUR DES DONNÉES DE PANEL, FACTEURS BAYÉSIENS, EFFETS GLOBAUX OU LOCAUX D'AUTOCORRÉLATION SPATIALE

MULTILEVEL AND SPILLOVER EFFECTS ESTIMATED FOR SPATIAL PANEL DATA, WITH APPLICATION TO ENGLISH HOUSE PRICES

Badi H. BALTAGI[a] **, Bernard FINGLETON**[b]* **and Alain PIROTTE**[cd]

Abstract - *This paper estimates a nested random effects spatial autoregressive panel data model to explain annual house price variation for 2000-2007 across 353 local authority districts in England. The paper applies a newly-proposed estimator based on the instrumental variable approach for the cross-sectional spatial autoregressive model.*

Keywords - HOUSE PRICES, PANEL DATA, SPATIAL LAG, NESTED RANDOM EFFECTS, INSTRUMENTAL VARIABLES, SPATIAL DEPENDENCE

JEL classification - C33

[a] Syracuse University, Department of Economics and Center for Policy Research.
[b] University of Cambridge, Department of Land Economy.
[c] CRED-TEPP (CNRS), University of Panthéon-Assas Paris II.
[d] IFSTTAR-DEST, French Institute of Science and Technology for Transport, Development and Networks.
* Corresponding author. Bernard Fingleton. E-mail: bf100@cam.ac.uk

1. INTRODUCTION

In this paper, we focus on the estimation of a theoretical house price model in which spatio-temporal variations in house prices are driven by supply and demand conditions, with spatial effects coming from two distinct sources. One is the direct dependence of house prices in a given locality on house prices in nearby localities. The other is *via* hierarchical error components typical of multilevel models. Direct dependence is the net effect of what we refer to as displaced demand and displaced supply. Displaced demand occurs where, ceteris paribus, high prices nearby cause demand to increase, because the negative relationship between prices and demand leads to purchasers switching away from high price locations nearby. Displaced supply occurs where high prices nearby cause supply to fall as a result of suppliers of housing switching to where higher prices give better investment returns. The supply and demand equations lead to a reduced form in which prices depend directly on prices nearby. We refer to this as a spillover effect.

The second source of spatial heterogeneity comes from the presence of hierarchical error components which represent the impact of local (district) effects embedded within wider (county) effects. Intuitively, local effects can be thought of as postcode effects, where particular postcodes are associated with more or less prestige. Likewise we envisage an independent county effect (a number of districts together are nested within a county). County A, which is a prestigious address, will tend to be associated with higher prices than less prestigious county B. The difference between these two sources of spatial heterogeneity in house prices is that the hierarchical district and county effects are constant within counties and districts, and terminate abruptly at county or district boundaries. In contrast, the spillover effects have an autoregressive specification, so that they extend across space with diminishing effect as distance increases. Thus spatial heterogeneity and autocorrelation is partly accounted for by the discrete non-overlapping effects of the components of the hierarchical level, and partly by spatial dependence operating, *via* the spatial autoregressive process, simultaneously across all areas.

Our solution to the problem of estimating the panel data model with spatial spillover effects and random hierachical effects, which we refer to as a nested random effects spatial autoregressive panel data model, is to propose a novel methodological approach. While the focus of the paper is squarely on the theory and application in relation to house prices, this has been introduced elsewhere in the literature. In contrast, our proposed estimator as set out intially in Baltagi et al (2014) is new. Recent developments in econometrics allow us to take into account cross-sectional correlation in a panel data context, as demonstrated for example by Elhorst (2003, 2010*a*), Anselin, Le Gallo and Jayet (2008), Anselin (2010) and Baltagi (2011). Early work on hierarchical panels was carried out by Fuller and Battese (1973), Montmarquette and Mahseredjian (1989), Antweiler (2001) and Baltagi, Song and Jung (2001, 2002), among others. The contribution here combines both hierarchical and spatial panel approaches, building on the sparse earlier literature which suggests combining nested models and spatial autoregressive processes in a cross-sectional context (see Corrado and Fingleton, 2011, 2012).

From the purely spatial perspective, a common way to proceed is to apply Maximum Likelihood methods. However, Maximum Likelihood procedures are often challenging when the sample size is large. Moreover, they call for explicit distributional assumptions. In fact, this is why Kelejian and Prucha (1998) and Lee (2003) proposed an Instrumental Variable (IV) procedure for the cross-sectional spatial autoregressive model, which is computationally simple and less restrictive regarding the distribution of the disturbances. In this paper, we extend this cross-sectional IV approach to the nested random effects spatial autoregressive panel data model[5].

The plan of the paper is as follows: Section 2 describes the spatial autoregressive model with nested random effects, Section 3 briefly summarises an IV procedure to estimate this model (details of which are given in Baltagi et al, 2014) and Section 4 describes the house price data. Section 5 discusses the empirical results and Section 6 gives our concluding remarks.

2. THE SPATIAL LAG MODEL INCLUDING NESTED RANDOM EFFECTS

Based on a theoretical framework that assumes the existence of equilibrium housing supply and demand functions, details of which are given in Baltagi et al(2014), we arrive at an empirical specification that allows for a exogenous effects on house prices, spatial spillover of price levels across districts, and nested random effects attributable to districts nested within counties, thus

$$y_{ijt} = \rho \sum_{g=1}^{N} \sum_{h=1}^{M_g} w_{ij,gh} y_{ght} + \mathbf{x}_{ijt}\beta + \varepsilon_{ijt}, \qquad (1)$$

where $i = 1, \dots, N$, $j = 1, \dots, M_i$ and $t = 1, \dots, T$. The dependent variable y_{ijt} denotes the average house price of district j in county i at time period t. $\mathbf{x}_{ijt}$ is a $(1 \times K)$ vector of explanatory (exogenous) variables, namely income within commuting distance (Y_{ijt}^{c}) and the available stock of dwellings (Λ_{ijt}). ρ is a scalar and β is a $(K \times 1)$ vector of parameters to be estimated. The weight $w_{ij,gh} = w_{k,l}$ is the $(k = ij, l = gh)$ element of the matrix $\mathbf{W}_S$ with ij denoting district j within county $i, i = 1, \dots, N, j = 1, \dots, M_i$ and similarely for gh.Thus $k, l = 1, \dots, S$ where $S = \sum_{i=1}^{N} M_i$ and $\mathbf{W}_S$ is an $(S \text{ x } S)$ matrix of known spatial weights denoting inter-district connectivity, which has zeros on the main diagonal and is row-normalised so that for row $k, \sum_{g=1}^{N} \sum_{h=1}^{M_g} w_{k,gh} = 1$. We assume that ρ is bounded numerically to ensure spatial stationarity, i.e., $e_{\min}^{-1} < \rho < 1$ where $e_{\min}$ is the minimum real characteristic root of $\mathbf{W}_S$. The nested random effects are introduced via the remainder term ε_{ijt} which follows an error component structure :

[5] In a similar spirit, Baltagi and Liu (2011) derived an IV estimator in the context of spatial autoregressive random effects panel data model. However, this estimator does not deal with the unbalancedness or the nested structure of the panel data.

$$\varepsilon_{ijt} = \alpha_i + \mu_{ij} + v_{ijt}, \tag{2}$$

where α_i denotes an unobservable *county* specific time-invariant effect which is assumed to be i.i.d.$(0,\sigma_\alpha^2)$. μ_{ij} is the nested effect of *district j* within the ith county which is assumed to be i.i.d.$(0,\sigma_\mu^2)$, and v_{ijt} is a remainder disturbance which is also assumed to be i.i.d.$(0,\sigma_v^2)$. The α_i's, μ_{ij}'s and v_{ijt}'s are independent of each other and among themselves. In contrast to the classical literature on panel data, grouping the data by periods rather than units is more convenient when we consider the spatial dependence. In matrix notation, for a cross-section, the model (1) corresponds to

$$\mathbf{y}_t = \rho \mathbf{W}_S \mathbf{y}_t + \mathbf{X}_t \beta + \varepsilon_t, \tag{3}$$

where $\mathbf{y}_t$ is of dimension $(S \times 1)$, $\mathbf{X}_t$ is an $(S \times K)$ matrix of explanatory variables.

The assumption that the nested error components are independent of each other and among themselves is a standard assumption in the literature. While it would be interesting to attempt to take account of possible interdependencies in a nested random effects context, this is something very much on the research horizon and beyond the scope of the present paper. Additionally, as is typical in random effects specifications, we are assuming the independence of the compound errors and the explanatory variables leading to consistent estimation, but as pointed out by Baltagi (2008), there is no entirely satisfactory test of this assumption. Typically, following Hausman (1978), in a general panel setting one would compare estimates from a fixed effects specification with the estimates from a random effects specification. Unfortunately, although this test is very popular in the literature, it is conditional on an assumption that the fixed effects estimates are consistent, something which cannot be guaranteed.

Against this there are some advantages of a random effects specification. For example, with 353 districts, there would be a considerable loss of degrees of freedom by invoking fixed effects. In addition, random effects allows one to obtain estimates taking account of permanent cross-section or between variation. In comparison fixed effects focuses on short term variation (Partridge (2005), Baltagi (2008), Elhorst (2010*b*)). So while correlation of the random effects with exogenous regressors may induce inconsistency, there will be compensation in the form of enhanced precision of the estimates. Higgins, Levy and Young (2006) use county-level data to analyze growth and convergence across the US, and with 3000 counties and only 3 time periods, the within variation is small and uninteresting compared with the between. Likewise Barro (1997) criticizes fixed effects panel data methods that rely purely on time series information, arguing that the conditioning variables often vary slowly over time, so that the most important information is lost.

3. ESTIMATION

The key to understanding our estimation procedure is the covariance matrix of ε, which is denoted by $\mathbf{\Omega}$. This captures the nested random effects attributable to the influence of counties, districts nested within counties, and the remainder. The paper by Baltagi et al (2014) gives the technical detail of how this is accomplished.

Stacking the T periods, the model (3) becomes

$$\mathbf{y} = \rho\mathbf{W}\mathbf{y} + \mathbf{X}\beta + \varepsilon \tag{4}$$

$$= \mathbf{B}^{-1}(\mathbf{X}\beta + \varepsilon), \tag{5}$$

where $\mathbf{B} = \mathbf{I}_T \otimes \mathbf{B}_S$, $\mathbf{B}_S = \left(diag\left(\mathbf{I}_{M_i}\right) - \rho\mathbf{W}_S\right)$ and $\mathbf{W} = (\mathbf{I}_T \otimes \mathbf{W}_S)$.

It is well known that the spatially lagged dependent variable $\mathbf{Wy}$ is correlated with the disturbances ε and therefore, the Ordinary Least Squares estimator will be inconsistent. Let $\mathbf{Z} = (\mathbf{X}, \mathbf{Wy})$ and $\delta = (\beta, \rho)^T$, the model (5) can be written as

$$\mathbf{y} = \mathbf{Z}\delta + \varepsilon. \tag{6}$$

In the cross-section, Kelejian and Prucha (1998) suggested a Two-Stage Least Squares spatial estimator (S2SLS) for the spatial lag model model, advising that the instrument set should be kept to a low order in order to avoid linear dependence and retain full column rank for the matrix of instruments. We therefore use the recommended instrument set $[\mathbf{X}, \mathbf{WX}, \mathbf{W}^2\mathbf{X}]$.

Premultiplying by $\mathbf{\Omega}^{-1/2}$ gives

$$\mathbf{y}^* = \mathbf{Z}^*\delta + \varepsilon^*, \tag{7}$$

where $\mathbf{y}^* = \mathbf{\Omega}^{-1/2}\mathbf{y}, \mathbf{Z}^* = \mathbf{\Omega}^{-1/2}\mathbf{Z} = \mathbf{\Omega}^{-1/2}(\mathbf{X}, \mathbf{Wy})$ and $\varepsilon^* = \mathbf{\Omega}^{-1/2}\varepsilon$. Applying the Kelejian and Prucha (1998) 2SLS procedure to (7), we obtain our nested random effects spatial Two-Stage Least Squares estimator (NRE-S2SLS) of δ, given by

$$\hat{\delta}_{NRE-S2SLS} = \left(\mathbf{Z}^{*^T}\mathbf{P}_{\mathbf{H}^{**}}\mathbf{Z}^*\right)^{-1}\mathbf{Z}^{*^T}\mathbf{P}_{\mathbf{H}^{**}}\mathbf{y}^*, \tag{8}$$

where $\mathbf{H}^{**} = \mathbf{\Omega}^{-1/2}\mathbf{H}$ and $\mathbf{P}_{\mathbf{H}^{**}} = \mathbf{H}^{**}(\mathbf{H}^{**T}\mathbf{H}^{**})^{-1}\mathbf{H}^{**T}$.

Although we have derived a NRE-S2SLS estimator, in Baltagi et al (2014) we also go one stage further and obtain a (very closely related) nested best spatial 2SLS estimator (NB-S2SLS) estimator, following Lee (2003). This is omitted here to save space.

4. DATA DESCRIPTION

The house price data give p_{ijt}, $i = 1, \dots, N; j = 1, \dots, M_i; t = 1, \dots, T$, which is the average selling prices by local authority district (of which there are 353 covering England). Our modeling is based on $T = 8$ years of data observed over the period 2000 to 2007. While these data may appear fixed (at least until boundary changes occur), we do not regard them as a population, but rather as a realization taken from an infinite number of posisble realizations or super-population. We can think of the remainder disturbance in our model capturing unpredictable unmodelled variance across space and time as a driver of different realizations. We are interested in the underlying process that could have generated different realizations and which has generated the data we observe, and use the 'sample' data to make inferences about this process.

Figure 1 maps the data for a single snapshot of time, the year 2001, clearly showing a heterogeneous and spatially correlated mean house price distribution across districts (the other 7 years show similar patterns).

Figure 1. Mean residential property price (all types) in English districts 2001

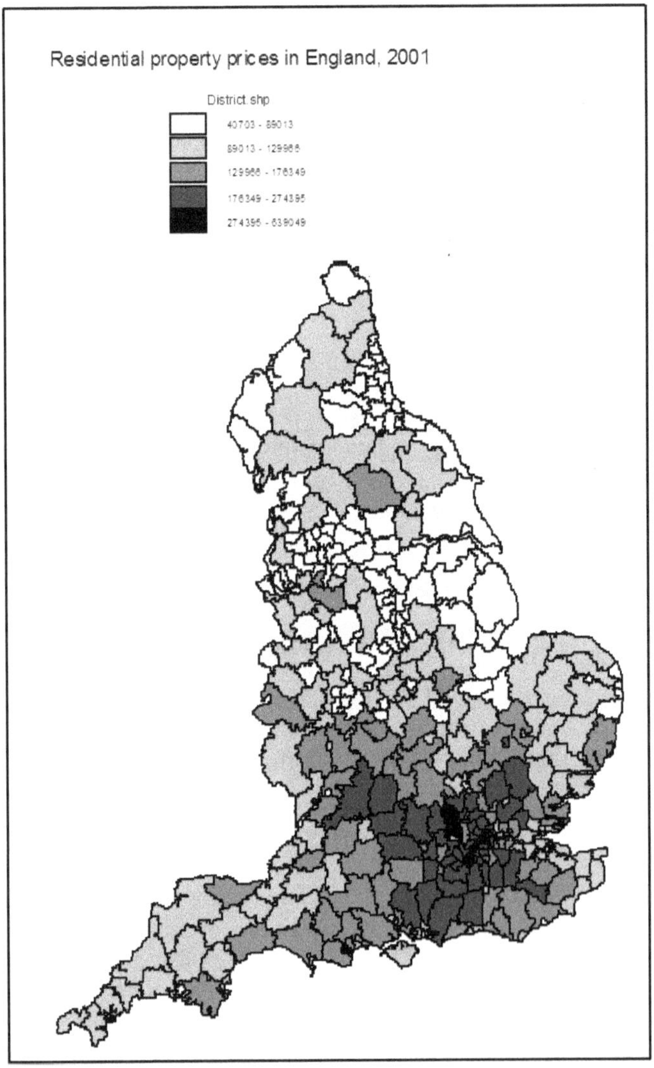

The data are organised by districts nested within counties. Figure 1 gives the distribution of districts, while Figure 2 gives the counties within which districts are nested. The district and county definitions are not immutable, having changed over time typically for administrative reasons. Likewise we choose to change the definition of counties, thus increasing county-level variance, by merging all counties lying outside the South East of England. The rest of England is therefore treated as a single super-county, while the South Eastern counties remain as separate sources of variance. The 16 counties which are 'not merged', with the brackets containing the number of nested districts, are Bedfordshire (4), Berkshire (6), Buckinghamshire (5), East Sussex (6), Essex (14), Hampshire and the Isle of Wight (14), Hertfordshire (10), Kent (13), Oxfordshire (5), Surrey (11), West Sussex (7), Cambridgeshire (6), Norfolk (7), Suffolk (7), Inner London (14), Outer London (19). The remaining 30 counties are merged as one 'super county' nesting the remaining 205 districts.

Figure 2. English counties

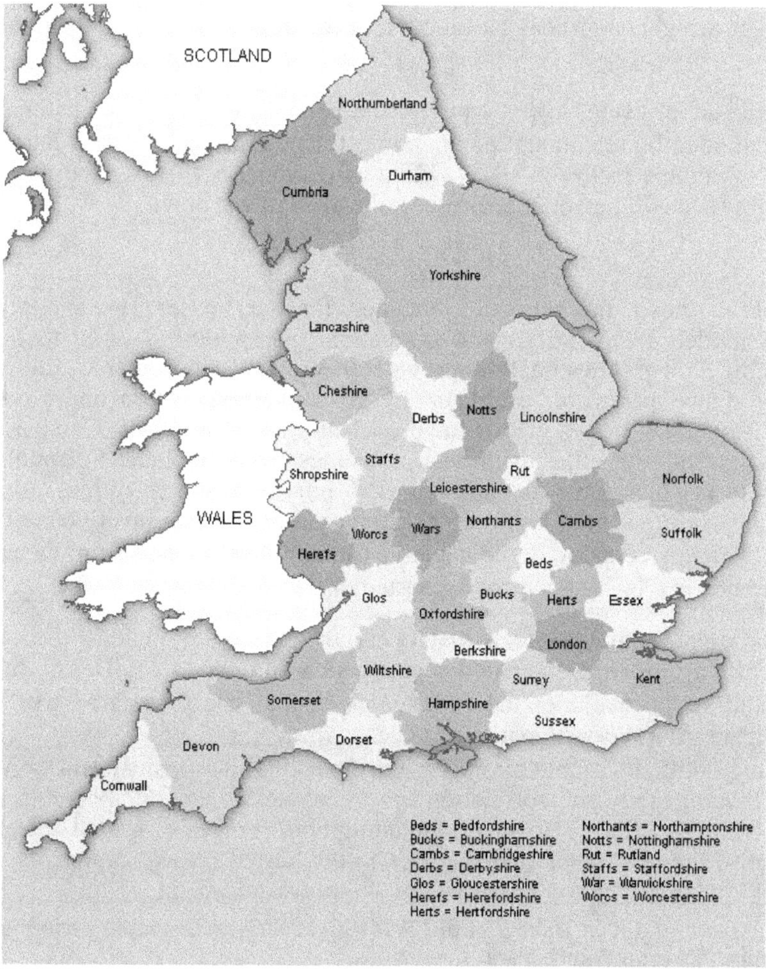

Income by district for each year (Y_{ijt}) is based on data from the UK's Office of National Statistics.

The Office of National Statistics also provides a matrix of inter- and intra-district commuting frequencies (d^*) from the UK 2001 census.

Using these commuting frequencies, we calculate income within commuting distance Y_{ijt}^c, applying less weight to districts with relatively few commuters and most weight is applied to local income with large within-district commuting flows. Thus each district's income is weighted by its row normalized commuting frequency.

The spatial lag matrix $\mathbf{W}_S$ is also based on commuting (subsequently row-normalized to give $\mathbf{W}_S$), but rather than d^* we commence with δ,which is d^* with the main diagonal cells set to zero. Thus the vector $\mathbf{W}_S\mathbf{y}_t$ comprises weighted averages of 'nearby' districts. The rationale here is that inter-district commuting is an appropriate indicator of inter-district proximity or connectivity. The weights matrix $\mathbf{W}_S$ a function of the larger values (> 50) in the cells of δ.

On the supply side, Λ_{ijt} is equal to the annual dwelling stock estimates by district divided by the annual population estimates for each district, data which are also available from the UK's Office of National Statistics. The number of dwellings (per 100 persons) respresents the available supply.

5. MODEL ESTIMATES

Table 1 shows the estimates obtained for our house price model using various model specifications and estimators. Our preferred estimates are the NRE-S2SLS. These estimators provide theoretically acceptable and appropriately signed parameter estimates[6]. OLS estimation, which omits both the spatial lag and the nested error structure, clearly introduces bias. Comparing the OLS estimates with other estimation outcomes which include the endogenous spatial lag **Wy** highlights its omission as an important source of bias. Although it controls for the spatial lag, S2SLS estimation produces a positive coefficient on Λ_{ijt} which is contrary to the negative estimate antici-pated from theory. We attribute this to a lack of control for nested district and county effects.

The nested random effects (ANOVA) estimates do include district and county effects and the anticipated negative sign on the Λ_{ijt} coefficient, but here the model set up excludes the endogenous spatial lag. Compared with NRE-S2SLS, the ANOVA estimates of β_1, β_2, σ_α^2, σ_μ^2, and σ_v^2 are very different, indicating omitted variable bias. This illustrates that it is insufficient to pick up spatial heterogeneity and correlation simply via nested error components and to ignore spillover effects. However, including both sources of spatial correlation, that due to the spatial lag and that due to the nested error components, elimi-

[6] Appendices 2 and 3 in Baltagi et al (2014) gives the small sample performance of these estimators using Monte Carlo simulations.

nates this source of bias and gives us the preferred NRE-S2SLS, which gives outcomes that one would anticipate from theory, with a highly significant estimate of ρ pointing to the importance of the simultaneous spatial interaction of price levels. Also in line with theory is the significant positive coefficient for income within commuting distance Y^c_{ijt}, and significant negative coefficient for the number of dwellings (per 100 persons) Λ_{ijt}.

Table 1. Various parameter estimates for the house price model

	OLS	S2SLS	SML	RE-S2SLS	RE-SML	NRE	NRE-S2SLS	NRE-SML	NB-S2SLS
Income within Comm. Distance (Y^c_{ijt})	**1.1318**	**0.3631**	**0.2536**	**0.5057**	**0.4641**	**6.4756**	**0.4869**	**0.4649**	**0.4975**
s.e.	(0.0355)	(0.0368)	(0.0363)	(0.0732)	(0.0810)	(0.0917)	(0.0724)	(0.0894)	(0.0641)
t-ratio	(31.882)	(9.845)	(6.975)	(6.907)	(5.727)	(70.617)	(6.722)	(5.201)	(7.760)
Supply (Λ_{ijt})	**1391.90**	**2125.303**	**2100.05**	**-730.4573**	**-724.167**	**-2747.29**	**-741.3797**	**-733.5315**	**-744.557**
s.e.	(432.4)	(299.405)	(370.92)	(105.442)	(568.42)	(230.86)	(105.502)	(528.706)	(105.534)
t-ratio	(3.220)	(7.098)	(5.66)	(-6.927)	(-1.274)	(-11.90)	(-7.027)	(-1.387)	(-7.055)
Spatial Lag of House Prices ($p^{W_S}_{ijt}$)	-	**0.5781**	**0.6107**	**0.8489**	**0.7961**	-	**0.8732**	**0.8078**	**0.8713**
s.e.	-	(0.0207)	(0.0150)	(0.0124)	(0.0171)	-	(0.0112)	(0.0301)	(0.0111)
t-ratio	-	(27.8744)	(40.508)	(68.2956)	(46.531)	-	(77.7798)	(26.8258)	(78.7695)
$\hat{\sigma}^2_\alpha$	-	-	-	-	-	0.2533	0.0562	0.1066	(*)
$\hat{\sigma}^2_\mu$	-	-	-	0.2114	0.2482	0.3337	0.1738	0.0973	(*)
$\hat{\sigma}^2_v$	0.4927	0.2343	0.3615	0.0132	0.4892	0.0647	0.0132	0.4707	(*)

(*) *This estimator uses the same consistent estimates of* σ^2_α, σ^2_μ *and* σ^2_v *as those used for NRE-S2SLS.*

With regard to the county effects operating via the error components, we anticipate that there will be discernable county-level impacts in the South and East of England especially, resulting from the inter-county status differences that are perceived by some, even if they are stereotypical rather than being objective reality. Some supposed reputational differences between Essex and the Royal county of Berkshire are caricatured by the entries in Table 2.

District effects can also be envisaged, and are at their most potent in the so-called 'London postcode wars'. For example, people living in parts of the leafy and affluent district of Richmond-Upon-Thames are angry that their postcode is the one used in the more deprived borough of Hounslow. According to the property valuation website Zoopla, in 2013 the average house in Hounslow was worth £ 294,020, while the average house in Richmond was £ 423,982. to According to one newspaper report, a resident said " I don't know anyone who would turn down the offer of a Richmond postcode instead of a Hounslow one", given that it would suddenly increase the value of their home by such a large amount.

Table 2. County comparisons (stereotypes !)

Essex	Berkshire
• one of the country's most distinct reputations - and probably the worst • Simon Heffer, wrote about "Essex Man". Described as a bit "brutish", "culturally barren" and "breathtakingly right-wing", Essex Man quickly became shorthand for the successes - and excesses - of Thatcher's Britain. • big hair, big cars and big wads of cash • tanning salons, nail bars and nightclubs • Numerous private car number plates, such as MON EY1 or UR2 FAT or OOOO7 • TV show The Only Way Is Essex. Like Footballers Wives, this TV series stereotypes those from Essex	• known as the Royal County of Berkshire • Windsor castle • Eton (England's poshest school) • Thames Valley or M4 corridor full of IT firms such as Cable and Wireless, Hewlett-Packard, Microsoft, Sharp Telecommunications, Oracle Corporation, Sun Microsystem, Vodaphone, Cisco, Xerox, accounting firms Deloitte, KPMG, Ernst and Young, and PricewaterhouseCoopers • Ascot Racecourse : thoroughbred horse racing. The course is closely associated with the British Royal Family, being approximately six miles from Windsor Castle • Suppliers of silk top hats are saying demand is out-stripping supply as the Queen gently suggests that she likes to see men wearing them in the Royal Enclosure

The estimates of σ_α^2, σ_μ^2 and σ_v^2 which partition the error into components representing county, district and remainder variance, highlight the relative importance of the district component. With regard to the county-level variance $\hat{\sigma}_\alpha^2$, which is the outcome of dividing counties into two groups, there is discernable contrast between the South and East of England and elsewhere, with inter-county variation within the South East reflecting the (relatively minor) role of county-level factors operating to distinguish, for example, Essex from Berkshire. In the rest of England, we see much less inter-county variation. If we undo the bloc construction so as to introduce inter-county variation also within the rest of England, the NRE-S2SLS estimator gives $\hat{\rho} = 0.855105$ ($t = 70.63$), $\hat{\beta}_1 = 0.545864$ ($t = 7.20$) and $\hat{\beta}_2 = -752.1513$ ($t = -7.11$), and $\hat{\sigma}_\alpha^2$ is equal to 0.013932 ($\hat{\sigma}_\mu^2 = 0.17992$, $\hat{\sigma}_v^2 = 0.013185$) as a consequence of the influence on the estimates of the comparatively smaller inter-county variation in the rest of England.

6. CONCLUSION

The paper analyzes house price data observed in 353 English districts over 8 years. We show that, in line with theoretical expectation, income within commuting distance has a positive effect on prices, and the stock of housing has a negative effect, and that there is a significant spatial lag term indicating postive correlation between prices locally and prices in 'nearby' districts. Also we model additional price heterogeneity using nested error components attributable to district and county effects, showing that these and the spatial lag are both necessary elements of our house price model. Our Monte Carlo analysis detailed in Baltagi et al. (2014) indicates that for realizations of an artificial data generating process with both spatial lag effects and hierarchical error components, our estimators (NRE-S2SLS and NB-S2SLS) are superior to a number of alternatives.

To sum up, the spatial econometrics literature is almost totally devoid of hierarchical models, as pointed out by Corrado and Fingleton (2012). Moreover, the spatial panel literature makes no reference to spatial interaction effects in a nested context. In the presence of both sources of spatial dependence, omission of one or both from the estimator can lead to incorrect inference and an improper understanding of true causal mechanisms.

REFERENCES

Anselin, L., 2010, Thirty years of spatial econometrics, *Papers in Regional Science* 89, 3-25.

Anselin, L., J. Le Gallo and H. Jayet, 2008, *Spatial Panel Econometrics*, Chapter 19 in L. Mátyás and P. Sevestre, eds., The Econometrics of Panel Data: Fundamentals and Recent Developments in Theory and Practice, Springer-Verlag, Berlin, 625-660.

Antweiler, W., 2001, Nested random effects estimation in unbalanced panel data, *Journal of Econometrics* 101, 295-313.

Baltagi, B.H., 2008, *Econometric Analysis of Panel Data* (Wiley, Chichester).

Baltagi, B.H., 2011, *Spatial Panels*, Chapter 15 in *The Handbook of Empirical Economics and Finance*, Aman Ullah and David E.A. Giles, editors, Chapman and Hall, 435-454.

Baltagi, B.H. and L. Liu, 2011, Instrumental variable estimation of a spatial autoregressive panel model with random effects, *Economics Letters* 111, 135-137.

Baltagi, B.H., S.H. Song and B.C. Jung, 2001, The unbalanced nested error component regression model, *Journal of Econometrics* 101, 357-381.

Baltagi, B.H., S.H. Song and B.C. Jung, 2002, Simple LM tests for the unbalanced nested error component regression model, *Econometric Reviews* 21, 167–187.

Baltagi, B.H., B. Fingleton and A. Pirotte, 2014, Spatial Lag Models with Nested Random Effects: an IV procedure with application to English house prices, *Journal of Urban Economics* 80, 76-86.

Barro, R.J., 1997, *Determinants of Economic Growth: A Cross-Country Empirical Study* (Cambridge, MA: MIT Press).

Corrado, L. and B. Fingleton, 2011, Multilevel modelling with spatial effects, *Discussion paper n°11-05*, University of Strathclyde.

Corrado, L. and B. Fingleton, 2012, Where is the economics in spatial econometrics?, *Journal of Regional Science* 52, 210-239.

Elhorst, J.P., 2003, Specification and estimation of spatial panel data models, *International Regional Science Review* 26, 244-268.

Elhorst, J.P., 2010*a*, *Spatial Panel Data Models*, Chapter 2 in M.M. Fischer and A. Getis, eds., Handbook of Applied Spatial Analysis, Berlin Springer-Verlag, 377-405.

Elhorst, J.P., 2010*b*, Applied spatial econometrics: raising the bar, *Spatial Economic Analysis* 5, 9-28.

Felsenstein, D., M. Beenstock and D. Feldman, 2012, Testing for unit roots and cointegration on spatial cross section data, *Spatial Economic Analysis* 7, 203-222.

Fuller, W.A. and G.E. Battese, 1973, Transformations for estimation of linear models with nested error structures, *Journal of the American Statistical Association* 68, 626-632.

Hausman, J., 1978, Specification tests in econometrics, *Econometrica* 46, 1251-1271.

Higgins, M.J., D. Levy and A.T. Young, 2006, Growth and convergence across the United States: Evidence from county-level data, *Review of Economics and Statistics* 88, 671–681.

Kelejian, H.H. and I.R. Prucha, 1998, A generalized spatial two-stage least squares procedure for estimating a spatial autoregressive model with autoregressive disturbances, *Journal of Real Estate Finance and Economics* 17, 99-121.

Lee, L.-F., 2003, Best spatial two-stage least square estimators for a spatial autoregressive model with autoregressive disturbances, *Econometric Reviews* 22, 307-335.

Montmarquette, C. and S. Mahseredjian, 1989, Does school matter for educational achievement? A two-way nested-error components analysis, *Journal of Applied Econometrics* 4, 181-193.

Partridge, M.D., 2005, Does income distribution affect U.S. state economic growth?, *Journal of Regional Science* 45, 363-394.

UNE ESTIMATION DES EFFETS DE DÉBORDEMENT MULTI-NIVEAUX POUR DES MODÈLES SPATIAUX AVEC DES DONNÉES DE PANEL - UNE APPLICATION AUX PRIX IMMOBILIERS EN ANGLETERRE

Résumé - *Le travail présenté dans cet article s'appuie sur un modèle autorégressif spatial qui utilise des données de panel aléatoirement relevées, afin d'étudier la variation annuelle des prix immobiliers durant la période 2000-2007 dans 353 districts locaux en Angleterre. L'originalité de l'article repose sur l'utilisation d'un nouvel estimateur basé sur l'approche des variables instrumentales dans les modèles autorégressifs spatiaux.*

Mots-clés - PRIX IMMOBILIERS, DONNÉES DE PANEL, DÉCALAGE SPATIAL, VARIABLES INSTRUMENTALES, DÉPENDANCE SPATIALE

AUTOCORRÉLATION SPATIALE DES ERREURS ET ERREURS DE MESURE : QUELLES INTERACTIONS ?

Julie LE GALLO*[*] et Jan MUTL*[**]

Résumé - *Dans cet article, nous dérivons les distributions asymptotiques de l'estimateur des Moindres Carrés Ordinaires (MCO) et de l'estimateur des Moindres Carrés Généralisés (MCG) dans un modèle comportant une autocorrélation spatiale des erreurs et une erreur de mesure affectant la variable explicative. Nous spécifions analytiquement la forme du biais asymptotique relatif et de l'efficience asymptotique relative entre les deux estimateurs compte tenu de la structure du modèle. Ceci nous permet de montrer que la présence simultanée de l'autocorrélation spatiale et d'une erreur de mesure sur la variable explicative conduit à un arbitrage entre le biais et la variance. Une estimation par les MCG permet de réduire le biais mais de façon très limitée. Cependant, il existe de nombreuses combinaisons de paramètres pour lesquelles cette réduction du biais se fait au détriment d'une perte d'efficience.*

Mots-clés - AUTOCORRÉLATION SPATIALE, ERREURS DE MESURE, PROPRIÉTÉS ASYMPTOTIQUES

Classification JEL - C13, C21

*CRESE, Université de Franche-Comté, France, jlegallo@univ-fcomte.fr

** EBS Business School, Allemagne, jan.mutl@ebs.edu

1. INTRODUCTION

Les modèles en coupe transversale sur données géoréférencées sont très souvent caractérisés par un phénomène d'autocorrélation spatiale (Anselin, 1988 ; Le Gallo, 2002 ; LeSage et Pace, 2009 ; Le Gallo, 2014). Cette dernière peut être la conséquence d'interactions spatiales ou d'effets de pairs entre individus géographiquement proches ou encore provenir d'un problème de spécification du modèle, comme la présence de variables omises spatialement autocorrélées ou une mauvaise spécification de la forme fonctionnelle. Les méthodes d'estimation et d'inférence des modèles comportant une autocorrélation spatiale sous la forme d'une variable endogène décalée ou d'une autocorrélation spatiale des erreurs sont maintenant bien établies (voir Arbia, 2014 ; Dubé et Legros, 2014 ; Elhorst, 2014 ; Fisher et Nijkamp, 2014 pour des manuels récents).

D'autres problèmes économétriques sont fréquents dans les modèles en coupe transversale. Ainsi, une variable explicative peut être endogène si elle est corrélée avec le terme d'erreur. L'endogénéité des variables explicatives peut avoir plusieurs sources : biais de simultanéité, variables omises corrélées avec les variables présentes dans le modèle ou encore erreurs de mesure. Si les conséquences de l'endogénéité de variables explicatives sont bien connues, la présence simultanée d'autocorrélation spatiale et de variables endogènes n'a que récemment fait l'objet d'études spécifiques. Ainsi, Fingleton et Le Gallo (2007, 2008) proposent une méthode d'estimation basée sur les moments généralisés pour des modèles comportant à la fois des variables explicatives endogènes et une autocorrélation spatiale sous la forme d'une variable spatiale décalée et/ou d'une autocorrélation spatiale des erreurs. Les propriétés asymptotiques de cette méthode d'estimation sont dérivées par Drukker et al. (2013). A travers des simulations, Fingleton et Le Gallo (2009) montrent que le modèle de Durbin spatial est à même de limiter les biais liés à la présence de variables endogènes. Enfin, Jin et Lee (2013) et Liu et Lee (2013) s'intéressent au cas où de nombreux instruments existent.

Dans cet article, nous nous attachons au cas spécifique de l'endogénéité provenant d'une erreur de mesure. Ces dernières sont fréquentes en économétrie appliquée. Par exemple, Temple (1998) a montré que les paramètres estimés dans les modèles de convergence et notamment la vitesse de convergence étaient très sensibles aux problèmes d'erreurs de mesure sur les données de revenu par tête. Lorsque l'erreur de mesure affecte uniquement la variable dépendante, elle est absorbée par le terme d'erreur et n'a pas d'effet sur la convergence des estimateurs des paramètres inconnus. Cependant, lorsqu'une variable explicative est mesurée avec erreur, alors les estimateurs des MCO obtenus en utilisant la variable observée sont affectés d'un biais d'atténuation : ils sont asymptotiquement sous-estimés. Les autres coefficients du modèle peuvent également être affectés : c'est le biais de contamination (Greene, 2011).

La question des erreurs de mesure dans le cadre des modèles d'économétrie spatiale reste aujourd'hui très largement inexplorée. Le Gallo et Fingleton (2012) ont analysé les effets d'une erreur de mesure sur le biais et l'efficience de différents estimateurs dans des modèles d'économétrie spatiale. Sur la base de simulations de Monte-Carlo, ils ont montré que les erreurs de mesure combinées à un processus spatial sur les erreurs, peuvent être, de façon quelque peu paradoxale, mieux traitées par une méthode d'estimation ignorant l'autocorrélation spatiale. Ces résultats font écho à ceux obtenus par Dagenais (1994) qui, dans un cadre de séries temporelles, montre théoriquement que dans certaines circonstances, le biais de l'estimateur des Moindres Carrés Ordinaires (MCO) pouvait même être amélioré par la présence de corrélation sérielle dans les termes d'erreurs.

Dans ce contexte, l'objectif est de revenir sur les propriétés asymptotiques des estimateurs en présence d'erreurs de mesure dans un cadre spatial. Nous nous concentrons dans cet article sur le cas d'une autocorrélation spatiale affectant les termes d'erreurs d'une régression. Notre objectif est alors de dériver les probabilités limite et la distribution asymptotique des estimateurs des MCO et des Moindres Carrés Généralisés (MCG) en présence d'autocorrélation spatiale des erreurs et d'erreur de mesure sur la variable expliquée afin d'évaluer comment ces deux effets interagissent.

Cet article est organisé de la façon suivante. Dans une première partie, nous présentons le modèle et les hypothèses. Ensuite, nous dérivons les distributions asymptotiques des estimateurs des MCO et des MCG. Enfin, nous comparons les biais et l'efficience asymptotiques de ces deux estimateurs à l'aide de représentations graphiques. La dernière section conclut et offre quelques perspectives de recherche futures.

2. LE MODÈLE ET LES HYPOTHÈSES

Dans un premier temps (2.1.), nous précisons la spécification et les hypothèses du modèle avec autocorrélation spatiale des erreurs. Dans un second temps, nous introduisons une erreur de mesure sur la variable expliquée (2.2.).

2.1. Le modèle avec autocorrélation spatiale des erreurs

Sans perte de généralité, on considère un modèle de régression linéaire avec une seule variable explicative :

$$\mathrm{y}_n = \mathrm{X}_n\beta + \mathrm{u}_u \qquad (1)$$

où n est le nombre d'observations en coupe transversale ; y_n est le vecteur de dimension $(n,1)$ comportant les observations sur la variable expliquée ; X_n est le vecteur de dimension $(n,1)$ comportant les observations sur la variable explicative et u_n est le vecteur de dimension $(n,1)$ des termes d'erreurs. Les termes d'erreurs suivent un processus spatial autorégressif (SAR) à l'ordre 1 :

$$\mathrm{u}_n = \lambda \mathrm{W}_n \mathrm{u}_n + \varepsilon_n \qquad (2)$$

où W_n est une matrice carrée de dimension n et qui représente la structure de connectivité entre les observations.

On pose les hypothèses suivantes :

Hypothèse 1 - *sur* ε_n

Les éléments de ε_n *sont identiquement et indépendamment distribués avec des moments absolument finis d'ordre* $4+\delta_\varepsilon$ *pour un* $\delta_\varepsilon > 0$. *En outre,* $E(\varepsilon_n) = \sigma_\varepsilon^2 > 0$.

Hypothèse 2 - *sur* W_n

Les éléments de la matrice de poids W_n *sont non-stochastiques avec :*

(a) $w_{ii,n} = 0$

(b) *Les sommes absolues en ligne et en colonne des matrices* W_n *et* $\left(\mathrm{I}_n - \lambda \mathrm{W}_n\right)^{-1}$ *sont uniformément bornées en valeur absolue, i.e.* $\sum_{i=1}^{n} \left|a_{ij}\right| \leq k \leq \infty$, *où k ne dépend pas de n (mais peut dépendre des paramètres du modèle, i.e.* λ*) et* a_{ij} *dénotent les éléments des matrices* W_n *et* $\left(\mathrm{I}_n - \lambda \mathrm{W}_n\right)^{-1}$.

(c) $|\lambda| \leq k_\lambda < 1/\lambda_{\max}(\mathrm{W}_n)$, *où* $\lambda_{\max}(.)$ *dénote la valeur propre maximale en valeur absolue de* W_n.

L'hypothèse (2a) est une normalisation typique en économétrie spatiale. Les hypothèses (2b) et (c) sont satisfaites dans la plupart des applications empiriques et sont vérifiées si, par exemple, la matrice de poids W_n est standardisée en ligne et si $|\lambda| \leq k_\lambda < 1$ respectivement. Ces hypothèses sont typiquement imposées dans les modèles spatiaux (Kelejian et Prucha, 1999) et limitent l'étendue de l'autocorrélation spatiale entre les unités en coupe transversale. Elles sont satisfaites si la matrice de poids est creuse (i.e. chaque observation n'a qu'un nombre limité d'observations voisines). On note que de (2c), on déduit que la matrice $\left(\mathrm{I}_n - \lambda \mathrm{W}_n\right)^{-1}$ est inversible.

2.2. Erreurs de mesure

On considère maintenant la situation où la variable non-stochastique X_n est en fait non-observable mais mesurée avec erreur. La variable observée $\tilde{\mathrm{X}}_n$ est la somme de la variable X_n non observée et d'un terme d'erreur ξ_n :

$$\tilde{X}_n = X_n + \xi_n \tag{3}$$

On suppose également que les erreurs de mesure sont spatialement autocorrélées :

$$\xi_n = \rho M_n \xi_n + \upsilon_n \tag{4}$$

Nous faisons alors les hypothèses suivantes :

Hypothèse 3 - *sur* υ_n

La variable exogène X_n *est non-stochastique et composée d'éléments uniformément bornés en valeur absolue.*

Hypothèse 4 - *sur* ξ_n

(a) *Les innovations* υ_n *dans les erreurs de mesure sont d'espérance nulle et sont identiquement et indépendamment distribués avec des moments absolument finis d'ordre* $4+\delta_\upsilon$ *pour un* $\delta_\upsilon > 0$. *En outre, les éléments de* υ_n *et de* ε_n *sont indépendants et* $E\left(\upsilon_{i,n}^2\right) = \sigma_\upsilon^2$.

(b) *La matrice de poids* M_n *et le paramètre spatial décalé correspondant* ρ *satisfont l'hypothèse 2.*

(c) $\sigma_\xi^2 := \text{plim}_{n\to\infty} n^{-1}\xi_n'\xi_n$ *existe et est fini et* $\sigma_{\tilde{X}}^2 = p\lim_{n\to\infty} n^{-1}\tilde{X}_n'\tilde{X}_n$ *existe et est strictement positif et fini.*

Notons que l'existence et le fait que σ_ξ^2 est borné est une conséquence des hypothèses (4a) et (b) et du lemme de Chebyschev. En outre, dans la mesure où les éléments de X_n sont bornés, cela implique que $\sigma_{\tilde{X}}^2$ existe et est fini. Cependant, afin de garantir l'identification asymptotique du modèle avec erreurs de mesure, il est nécessaire de supposer en outre que $\sigma_{\tilde{X}}^2$ est inversible.

3. PROPRIÉTÉS ASYMPTOTIQUES DES ESTIMATEURS DES MCO ET DES MCG

Nous considérons dans cette section les propriétés en échantillon (3.1.) et les propriétés asymptotiques (3.2.) des estimateurs des MCO et des MCG en présence d'autocorrélation spatiale et d'erreurs de mesure sur la variable explicative.

3.1. Les estimateurs des MCO et des MCG

Dans la mesure où X_n n'est pas observé, le modèle estimé est :

$$y_n = \tilde{X}_n \beta + \tilde{u}_n \tag{5}$$

où $\tilde{u}_n = u_n + X_n\beta - \tilde{X}_n\beta = u_n - \xi_n\beta$. Selon qu'on considère l'autocorrélation dans les termes d'erreurs ou non, on peut estimer ce modèle par les MCO ou par les MCG. Les estimateurs des MCO et des MCG ont les formes suivantes :

$$\hat{\beta}_{MCO} = \left(\tilde{X}_n'\tilde{X}_n\right)^{-1}\tilde{X}_n'y_n \tag{6a}$$

$$\hat{\beta}_{MCG} = \left(\tilde{X}_n'\Omega_{u,n}^{-1}\tilde{X}_n\right)^{-1}\tilde{X}_n'\Omega_{u,n}^{-1}y_n \tag{6b}$$

avec $\Omega_{u,n} = E\left(u_n u_n'\right) = \sigma_\varepsilon^2\left(I_n - \lambda W_n\right)^{-1}\left(I_n - \lambda W_n'\right)^{-1}$.

Notons qu'il s'agit bien de l'estimateur des MCG purs et non réalisables car le paramètre λ est inconnu. En pratique, il faudrait également estimer ce paramètre. Cependant, nous considérons ici qu'il est connu afin d'étudier les propriétés asymptotiques de l'estimateur des MCG dans le meilleur des cas.

Ces deux estimateurs sont biaisés en présence d'erreurs de mesure puisque les conditions sur les moments sous-jacentes ne sont plus vérifiées. Dans le cas de l'estimation par les MCO en effet, la condition sur les moments basant l'estimation est : $E\left(\tilde{X}_n'\tilde{u}_n\right) = 0$. Cependant, compte tenu de la présence d'erreurs de mesure, nous avons :

$$\begin{aligned} E\left(\tilde{X}_n'\tilde{u}_n\right) &= E\left[\left(X_n + \xi_n\right)'\left(u_n - \xi_n\beta\right)\right] \\ &= E\left[X_n'u_n\right] - E\left[X_n'\xi_n\right]\beta + E\left[\xi_n'u_n\right] - E\left[\xi_n'\xi_n\right]\beta \\ &= -E\left[\xi_n'\xi_n\right]\beta = -n\sigma_{\xi,n}^2\beta \\ &\neq 0 \end{aligned} \tag{7}$$

où $\sigma_{\xi,n}^2 := n^{-1}E\left(\xi_n'\xi_n\right)$.

Un résultat analogue peut être prouvé pour l'estimateur des MCG.

3.2. Propriétés asymptotiques

Dans cette partie, nous dérivons les propriétés asymptotiques de l'estimateur des MCO et des MCG.

Tout d'abord, afin de simplifier les expressions pour les résultats asymptotiques de l'estimateur des MCO, basé sur la condition $E\left(\tilde{X}_n\tilde{u}_n\right) = 0$, nous supposons que la matrice des variances-covariances de cette condition converge et imposons l'hypothèse suivante :

Hypothèse 5

$$\sigma^2_{\tilde{X}'\tilde{u}} = p\lim_{n\to\infty} \frac{1}{n} \tilde{X}'_n \tilde{u}_n \tilde{u}'_n \tilde{X}_n \text{ } \textit{existe.}$$

Nous aurons besoin par la suite des éléments suivants :

$$m_1 := \lim_{n\to\infty} \frac{1}{n} tr\left[\left(I_n - \rho M'_n\right)^{-1}\left(I_n - \rho M_n\right)^{-1}\right] \quad (8a)$$

$$m_2 = \lim_{n\to\infty} \frac{1}{n} X'_n \left(I_n - \rho M'_n\right)^{-1} . diag\left[\left(I_n - \rho M'_n\right)^{-1}\left(I_n - \rho M_n\right)^{-1}\right] \quad (8b)$$

Ces quantités sont des fonctions des données et ne dépendent que du seul paramètre ρ qui mesure l'autocorrélation spatiale dans les erreurs de mesure. Si $\rho = 0$, alors $m_1 = 1$ et $m_2 = \overline{x} = \lim_{n\to\infty}(1/n)\sum_{i=1}^{n} x_i$.

Ensuite, afin de garantir l'existence et l'identification asymptotiques de l'estimateur des MCG, nous ajoutons l'hypothèse suivante :

Hypothèse 6

$$\sigma^2_{\xi^*} = p\lim_{n\to\infty} \frac{1}{n} \xi'_n \Omega^{-1}_{u,n} \xi_n \text{ } \textit{existe et est fini et}$$

$$\sigma^2_{\tilde{X}^*} = p\lim_{n\to\infty} \frac{1}{n} \tilde{X}'_n \Omega^{-1}_{u,n} \tilde{X}_n \text{ } \textit{existe, est fini et est inversible.}$$

En outre la quantité

$$m_3 = p\lim_{n\to\infty} \frac{1}{n} \tilde{X}'_n \left(I_n - \lambda W_n\right)^{-1}\left(I_n - \rho M_n\right)^{-1}\left(I_n - \rho M'_n\right)^{-1}\left(I_n - \lambda W'_n\right)^{-1} \tilde{X}_n$$

existe et est finie.

Nous observons que :

$$p\lim_{n\to\infty} \frac{1}{n} \tilde{X}'_n \Omega^{-1}_{u,n} \tilde{X}_n = p\lim_{n\to\infty} \frac{1}{n} X'_n \Omega^{-1}_{u,n} X_n + p\lim_{n\to\infty} \frac{1}{n} \xi'_n \Omega^{-1}_{u,n} \xi_n \quad (9)$$

En conséquence, l'hypothèse 6 implique que $\sigma^2_{X^*} := p\lim_{n\to\infty}(1/n) X'_n \Omega^{-1}_{u,n} X_n$ existe et est fini. La dernière partie de l'hypothèse 6 est nécessaire pour permettre l'écriture de la matrice des variances-covariances de l'estimateur des MCG.

Enfin, compte tenu de ces propriétés, nous pouvons démontrer les théorèmes suivants[1] :

Théorème 1 – *Distribution asymptotique de l'estimateur des MCO*

Sous les hypothèses 1 à 6, on a :

$$\sqrt{n}\left(\hat{\beta}_{MCO}-\beta\right)\xrightarrow{d}N\left(\Delta_{MCO},\Omega_{MCO}\right) \tag{10a}$$

Le biais asymptotique est donné par :

$$\Delta_{MCO}=-\frac{\sigma_{\xi}^{2}}{\sigma_{\tilde{X}}^{2}}\beta \tag{10b}$$

La matrice de variance-covariance asymptotique est donnée par :

$$\Omega_{MCO}=\sigma_{\tilde{X}}^{-4}\sigma_{\tilde{X}'\tilde{u}}^{2} \tag{10c}$$

où σ_{ε}^{2}, $\sigma_{\tilde{X}}^{2}$ *ont été définis auparavant et* $\sigma_{\tilde{X}'\tilde{u}}^{2}=\sigma_{X}^{2}\left(\sigma_{\varepsilon}^{2}+\sigma_{\upsilon}^{2}\beta^{2}\right)+\sigma_{\upsilon}^{2}\beta^{2}-2\sigma_{\upsilon}^{3}\beta^{2}\overline{x}$ *avec* $\sigma_{X}^{2}:=\lim_{n\to\infty}(1/n)X_{n}'X_{n}$.

Nous donnons également un théorème similaire pour l'estimateur des MCG :

Théorème 2 – *Distribution asymptotique de l'estimateur des MCG*

Sous les hypothèses 1 à 6, on a :

$$\sqrt{n}\left(\hat{\beta}_{MCG}-\beta\right)\xrightarrow{d}N\left(\Delta_{MCG},\Omega_{MCG}\right) \tag{11a}$$

Le biais asymptotique est donné par :

$$\Delta_{MCG}=-\frac{\sigma_{\xi^{*}}^{2}}{\sigma_{\tilde{X}^{*}}^{2}}\beta \tag{11b}$$

La matrice de variance-covariance asymptotique est donnée par :

$$\Omega_{MCG}=\sigma_{\tilde{X}^{*}}^{-4}\sigma_{\tilde{X}^{*}'\tilde{u}^{*}}^{2} \tag{11c}$$

où $\sigma_{\xi^{*}}^{2}$ *et* $\sigma_{\tilde{X}^{*}}^{2}$ *ont été définis précédemment et* $\sigma_{\tilde{X}^{*}'\tilde{u}^{*}}^{2}=\sigma_{X}^{2}+\sigma_{\xi}^{2}+\sigma_{\varepsilon}^{-2}\beta^{2}\sigma_{\nu}^{2}m_{3}$.

Nous retrouvons le fait qu'en présence d'erreurs de mesure sur une variable explicative, le coefficient associé est affecté d'un biais d'atténuation. Ces diffé-

[1] Pour des raisons de place, les démonstrations des théorèmes 1 et 2 ne sont pas reportées ici. Elles sont disponibles sur demande auprès des auteurs.

rentes formules nous permettent de comparer les biais et RMSE asymptotiques des estimateurs des MCO et MCG.

4. COMPARAISON DES BIAIS ET EFFICIENCES ASYMPTOTIQUES

4.1. Formulations analytiques

A l'aide des résultats établis dans la section précédente, nous pouvons dériver la forme du biais asymptotique relatif entre l'estimateur des MCO et celui des MCG à des fins de comparaison. Ce biais relatif s'écrit :

$$\frac{biais_{MCG}}{biais_{MCO}} = \frac{\sigma^2_{\tilde{X}}}{\sigma^2_{\tilde{X}^*}} \cdot \frac{\sigma^2_{\xi^*}}{\sigma^2_{\xi}} \tag{12}$$

La première partie de cette expression s'interprète comme la variance relative de la variable observée avant et après la transformation liée à la procédure des MCG. La seconde partie de cette expression s'interprète comme la variance relative de l'erreur de mesure avant et après la transformation liée à la procédure des MCG. Compte tenu de la structure du modèle, nous pouvons donner des formulations analytiques à chacun des éléments de l'expression (12).

On pose $s^2_X = \lim_{n\to\infty} n^{-1}X'X$ (l'existence de cette quantité est impliquée par l'hypothèse 4). On a alors :

$$\begin{aligned}
\sigma^2_{\tilde{X}} &= p\lim_{n\to\infty}\frac{1}{n}\left(X+\xi\right)'\left(X+\xi\right) \\
&= p\lim_{n\to\infty}\frac{1}{n}X'X + p\lim_{n\to\infty}\frac{1}{n}\xi'\xi \\
&= s^2_X + p\lim_{n\to\infty}\frac{1}{n}v'\left(I_n-\rho M'_n\right)^{-1}\left(I_n-\rho M_n\right)^{-1}v \\
&= s^2_X + \sigma^2_v \underbrace{\lim_{n\to\infty}\frac{1}{n}tr\left[\left(I_n-\rho M'_n\right)^{-1}\left(I_n-\rho M_n\right)^{-1}\right]}_{:=s_{MM}}
\end{aligned} \tag{13}$$

Les calculs précédents impliquent que :

$$\sigma^2_{\xi} = \sigma^2_v \cdot \lim_{n\to\infty}\frac{1}{n}tr\left[\left(I_n-\rho M'_n\right)^{-1}\left(I_n-\rho M_n\right)^{-1}\right] = \sigma^2_v \cdot s_{MM} \tag{14}$$

De façon analogue, pour les variables transformées :

$$\begin{aligned}
\sigma^2_{\tilde{X}^*} &= p\lim_{n\to\infty}\frac{1}{n}(X+\xi)'(I_n-\lambda W_n')(I_n-\lambda W_n)(X+\xi) \\
&= p\lim_{n\to\infty}\frac{1}{n}X'(I_n-\lambda W_n')(I_n-\lambda W_n)X + p\lim_{n\to\infty}\frac{1}{n}\xi'(I_n-\lambda W_n')(I_n-\lambda W_n)\xi \\
&= p\lim_{n\to\infty}\frac{1}{n}X'(I_n-\lambda W_n')(I_n-\lambda W_n)X \\
&\quad + p\lim_{n\to\infty}\frac{1}{n}v'(I_n-\rho M_n')^{-1}(I_n-\lambda W_n')(I_n-\lambda W_n)(I_n-\rho M_n)^{-1}v \\
&= s^2_{X^*}+\sigma^2_v\cdot\underbrace{\lim_{n\to\infty}\frac{1}{n}tr\left[(I_n-\rho M_n')^{-1}(I_n-\lambda W_n')(I_n-\lambda W_n)(I_n-\rho M_n)^{-1}\right]}_{:=s_{MW}}
\end{aligned} \tag{15}$$

et $\sigma^2_{\xi^*}=\sigma^2_v\cdot\lim_{n\to\infty}\frac{1}{n}tr\left[(I_n-\rho M_n')^{-1}(I_n-\lambda W_n')(I_n-\lambda W_n)(I_n-\rho M_n)^{-1}\right]=s_{MW}$ (16)

Au final, le biais asymptotique relatif n'est déterminé que par les forces relatives de l'autocorrélation spatiale dans les erreurs de mesure et l'autocorrélation spatiale dans l'équation initiale.

La quantité $s^2_{\tilde{X}^*}=p\lim_{n\to\infty}n^{-1}X'(I_n-\lambda W_n')(I_n-\lambda W_n)X$ est uniquement une fonction de la variance explicative et du paramètre de décalage spatial λ, tous deux étant connus. Il est possible de calculer l'équivalent de cette expression en échantillon fini. Supposons par exemple que les variables explicatives sont indépendantes entre observations, i.e. $E(X_nX_n')=\sigma^2_{X,n}I_n$, alors :

$$\begin{aligned}
s^2_{\tilde{X}^*} &= p\lim_{n\to\infty}\frac{1}{n}X'(I_n-\lambda W_n')(I_n-\lambda W_n)X \\
&= p\lim_{n\to\infty}\frac{1}{n}tr\left[XX'(I_n-\lambda W_n')(I_n-\lambda W_n)\right] \\
&= \lim_{n\to\infty}\frac{1}{n}tr\left[E(XX')(I_n-\lambda W_n')(I_n-\lambda W_n)\right]
\end{aligned} \tag{17}$$

si les espérances et les $p$lim existent. Dans ce cas :

$$\begin{aligned}
s^2_{\tilde{X}^*} &= \lim_{n\to\infty}\frac{\sigma^2_{X,n}}{n}\cdot tr\left[(I_n-\lambda W_n')(I_n-\lambda W_n)\right] \\
&= \lim_{n\to\infty}\sigma^2_{X,n}\cdot\lim_{n\to\infty}\frac{1}{n}tr\left[(I_n-\lambda W_n')(I_n-\lambda W_n)\right] \\
&= s^2_X\cdot\underbrace{\lim_{n\to\infty}\frac{1}{n}tr\left[(I_n-\lambda W_n')(I_n-\lambda W_n)\right]}_{:=s_{WW}}
\end{aligned} \tag{17}$$

Au final, le biais asymptotique relatif s'écrit :

$$\frac{biais_{MCG}}{biais_{MCO}} = \frac{s_X^2 + \sigma_v^2 . s_{MM}}{s_X^2 . s_{WW} + \sigma_v^2 s_{MW}} \cdot \frac{s_{MW}}{s_{MM}} \tag{18}$$

On est alors en mesure de calculer ce ratio pour différentes valeurs de λ, ρ et du rapport signal-sur-bruit $ssb = s_X^2 / \sigma_v^2$.

Des calculs similaires nous permettent de calculer l'efficience relative des deux estimateurs [2] :

$$\frac{\Omega_{MCG}}{\Omega_{MCO}} = \frac{ssb + 1 + 2s_{MW} + \frac{2}{ssb}\left(s_{MWMMWM} / s_{MM}\right)}{\left(ssb+2\right)\left(s_{W^{-1}W^{-1}} / s_{MM}\right) + 1} \tag{19}$$

où ssb, s_{MW} et s_{MM} ont été définis précédemment et :

$$s_{MWMMWM} := \lim_{n\to\infty} \frac{1}{n} tr\left[\left(I_n - \rho M_n'\right)^{-1}\left(I_n - \lambda W_n\right)\left(I_n - \rho M_n\right)^{-1} \left(I_n - \rho M_n'\right)^{-1}\left(I_n - \lambda W_n\right)\left(I_n - \rho M_n\right)^{-1}\right] \tag{20a}$$

$$s_{W^{-1}W^{-1}} := \lim_{n\to\infty} \frac{1}{n} tr\left[\left(I_n - \lambda W_n\right)^{-1}\left(I_n - \lambda W_n'\right)^{-1}\right] \tag{20a}$$

4.2. Représentations graphiques

Afin d'analyser le biais asymptotique relatif entre les deux estimateurs et l'efficience asymptotique relative entre les deux estimateurs, nous avons calculé les expressions (18) et (19) pour différentes valeurs des paramètres.

Plus précisément, nous avons généré n = 400 points dans un carré de côté unitaire, points dont les coordonnées suivent une loi uniforme. Sur la base de ces 400 points, nous avons ensuite construit une matrice de poids où les poids sont égaux à l'inverse de la distance au carré entre les points. Par souci de simplification, cette matrice de poids correspond à la fois à W_n et à M_n. Les expressions (18) et (19) ont ensuite été générées pour des valeurs de λ et ρ allant de 0,1 à 0,9 par incrément de 0,1 et pour deux valeurs du signal-sur-bruit (*ssb*) : 10 et 50. Le premier cas correspond à une situation où la part de la variance provenant de la variable non observée est relativement peu importante par rapport à la variance provenant de l'erreur de mesure. Dans le second cas, la va-

[2] Pour des raisons de place, ces calculs ne sont pas reportés ici. Ils sont disponibles sur demande auprès des auteurs.

riance provenant de l'erreur de mesure est très faible par rapport à la variance provenant de la variable non observée.

La Figure 1 représente toutes les courbes de niveau du biais relatif pour $n = 400$, $sbb = 50$ et pour toutes les valeurs possibles de λ, l'autocorrélation spatiale des erreurs de l'équation initiale, en abscisse et de ρ, l'autocorrélation spatiale de l'erreur de mesure, en ordonnée. La courbe A représente toutes les valeurs de λ et de ρ pour lesquelles le biais relatif est égal à 1, en d'autres termes il s'agit de toutes les situations pour lesquelles le biais de l'estimateur des MCO et celui des MCG sont égaux. Lorsque le signal-sur-bruit est important, il existe peu de combinaisons de valeurs de λ et de ρ pour lesquelles le biais relatif est unitaire. Pour toutes les autres valeurs (autres courbes que A), le biais de l'estimateur des MCG est inférieur à celui des MCO mais la différence est faible dans la mesure où les autres courbes de niveau représentent des valeurs de 98%, 96%, 94%, 92% et 90%. Ainsi, dans un modèle avec autocorrélation spatiale des erreurs et erreurs de mesure, ne corriger que l'autocorrélation spatiale *via* une estimation par les MCG n'est en mesure que de réduire légèrement le biais de l'estimateur. Rappelons en outre qu'il s'agit de l'estimateur des MCG, pour lequel on suppose λ connu, alors qu'en pratique, il faudrait également estimer ce paramètre.

La Figure 2 représente le biais relatif pour un signal-sur-bruit plus faible, $sbb = 10$, correspondant au cas où l'erreur de mesure sur la variable expliquée est importante. Dans ce cas, les combinaisons de paramètres de λ et de ρ pour lesquelles le biais de l'estimateur des MCG est moins important que celui des MCO sont plus nombreuses.

Cette situation est inverse dès lors qu'on considère l'efficience relative entre les deux estimateurs (Figures 3 et 4). Lorsque le signal-sur-bruit est important (Figure 3), il existe des combinaisons de paramètres pour lesquelles l'estimateur des MCG est moins efficient que l'estimateur des MCO (courbes B et C pour des niveaux de 1,05 et 1,1). Il s'agit de cas où il existe une forte autocorrélation spatiale dans l'erreur de mesure. Lorsque le signal-sur-bruit diminue (Figure 4), l'estimateur des MCG voit les cas dans lesquels il est plus efficient que l'estimateur des MCO se réduire fortement. La courbe de niveau unitaire, centrale dans la Figure 3, se décale en effet vers la droite dans la Figure 4.

En d'autres termes, nombreuses sont les combinaisons de paramètres entre λ et de ρ pour lesquelles l'estimateur des MCO est plus efficient que celui des MCG. Au final, ces représentations graphiques illustrent un arbitrage entre le biais et la variance : on peut essayer de réduire le biais en corrigeant par l'autocorrélation spatiale au prix d'une réduction de l'efficience de l'estimateur.

Figure 1

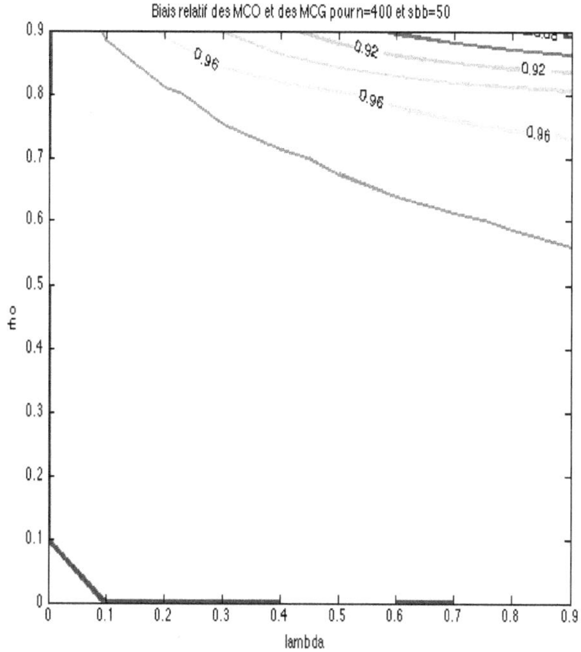

A

Figure 2

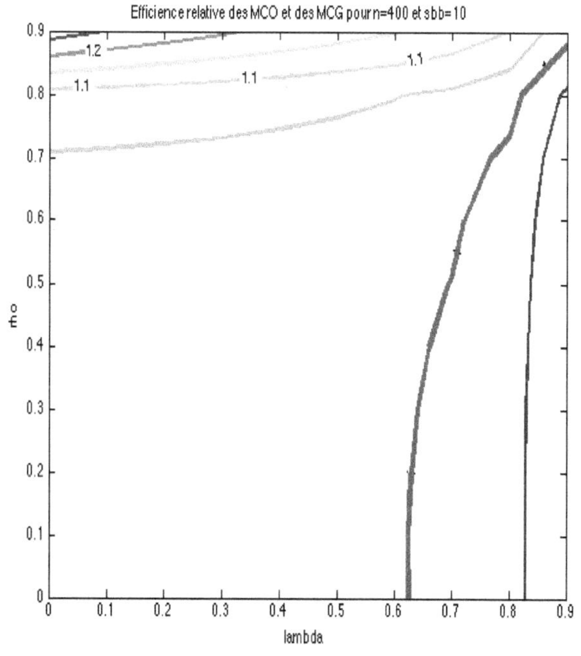

Figure 3

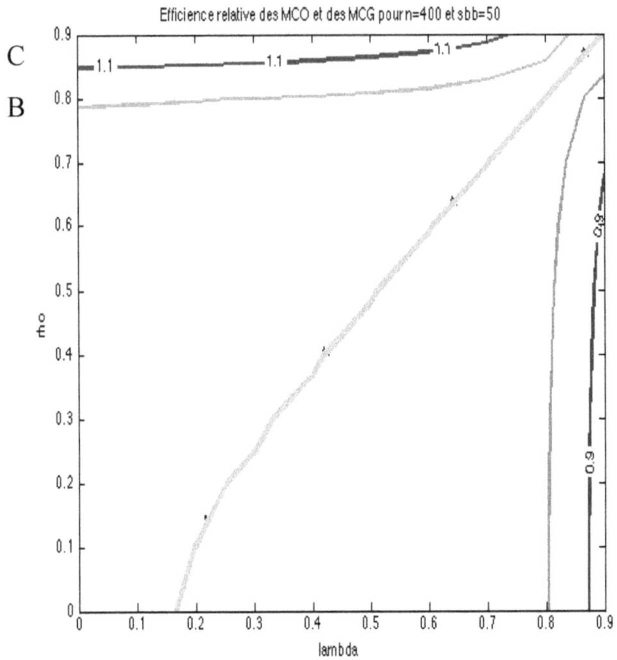

Figure 4

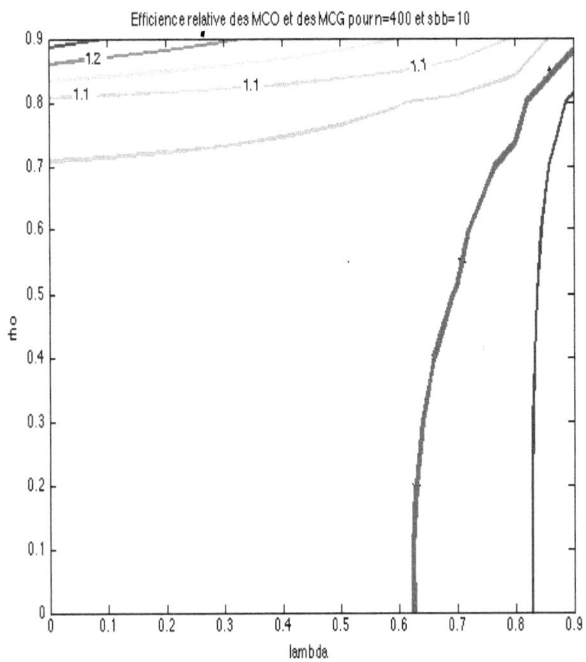

4. CONCLUSION

Dans cet article, nous avons dérivé les distributions asymptotiques de l'estimateur des MCO et de l'estimateur des MCG purs dans un modèle comportant une autocorrélation spatiale des erreurs et une erreur de mesure affectant la variable explicative. Nous avons également dérivé la forme du biais asymptotique relatif et de l'efficience asymptotique relative compte tenu de la structure du modèle. Ceci nous a permis de montrer que la présence simultanée de l'autocorrélation spatiale et d'une erreur de mesure sur la variable explicative conduit à un arbitrage entre le biais et la variance. Une estimation par les MCG permet de réduire le biais mais de façon très limitée. Cependant, il existe de nombreuses combinaisons de paramètres pour lesquelles cette réduction du biais se fait au détriment d'une perte d'efficience.

Les interactions entre autocorrélation spatiale et erreurs de mesure sont ainsi complexes et méritent des recherches supplémentaires. Il serait ainsi intéressant de mener le même type d'analyse lorsque l'autocorrélation spatiale prend la forme d'une variable endogène décalée pour analyser les propriétés d'une estimation par les variables instrumentales. Plus généralement, il est nécessaire de se poser la question d'une méthode d'estimation convergente en présence d'autocorrélation spatiale et d'une erreur de mesure. Une voie possible serait de se baser sur les moments de second ordre d'une autre variable explicative dans le cadre de systèmes triangulaires, comme suggéré par Lewbel (2012) dans un cadre a-spatial.

REFERENCES

Arbia G., 2014, *A Primer for Spatial Econometrics with Applications in R*, Palgrave Mac Millan.

Anselin L., 1988, *Spatial Econometrics: Methods and Models*, Dordrecht : Kluwer Academic Publishers.

Dagenais M., 1994, "Parameter estimation in regression models with errors in the variables and autocorrelated disturbances", *Journal of Econometrics*, 64, pp. 145-163.

Drukker D.M., Egger P., Prucha I.R., 2013, "On two-step estimation of a spatial autoregressive model with autoregressive disturbances and endogenous regressors", *Econometric Reviews*, 32, pp. 686-733.

Dubé J., Legros D., 2014, *Econométrie spatiale appliquée des microdonnées*, ISTE editions.

Elhorst J.P., 2014, *Spatial Econometrics: From Cross-sectional Data to Spatial Panels*, Berlin: Springer-Verlag.

Fingleton B., Le Gallo J., 2007, "Finite sample properties of estimators of spatial models with autoregressive, or moving average, disturbances and system feedback", *Annales d'Economie et de Statistique*, 87-88, pp. 39-62.

Fingleton B., Le Gallo J., 2008, "Estimating spatial models with endogenous variables, a spatial lag and spatially dependent disturbances : finite sample properties", *Papers in Regional Science*, 87, pp. 319-339.

Fischer M.M, Nijkamp P. (Eds.), 2014, *Handbook of Regional Science*, Berlin: Springer-Verlag.

Greene W.H., 2011, *Econometric Analysis*, 7th Edition, Pearson.

Jin F., Lee L.-F., 2013, "Generalized spatial two stage least squares estimation of spatial autoregressive models with autoregressive disturbances in the presence of endogenous regressors and many instruments", *Econometrics*, 1, pp. 71-114.

Kelejian H.H., Prucha I.-R., 1999, "A generalized moments estimator for the autoregressive parameter in a spatial model", *International Economic Review*, 40, pp. 509-533.

Le Gallo J., 2002, "Econométrie spatiale : l'autocorrélation spatiale dans les modèles de régression linéaire", *Economie et Prévision*, 155, pp. 139-158.

Le Gallo J., 2014, "Cross-section spatial regression models", in Fischer M.M., Nijkamp P. (Eds.), *Handbook of Regional Science*, Springer-Verlag, pp. 1511-1533.

Le Gallo J., Fingleton B., 2012, "Measurement errors in a spatial context", *Regional Science and Urban Economics*, 42, pp. 114-125.

LeSage J., Pace K.P., 2009, *Introduction to Spatial Econometrics*, CRC Press.

Lewbel A., 2012, "Using heteroscedasticity to identify and estimate mis-measured and endogenous regressor models", *Journal of Business and Economic Statistics*, 30, pp. 67-80.

Liu X., Lee L.-F., 2013, "Two-stage least squares estimation of spatial autoregressive models with endogenous regressors and many instruments", *Econometric Reviews*, 32, pp. 734-753.

SPATIAL ERROR AUTOCORRELATION AND MEASUREMENT ERRORS: HOW DO THEY INTERACT?

Abstract *- In this paper, we derive the asymptotic distributions of the Ordinary Least Squares and the (unfeasible) Generalized Least Squares estimators in a spatial error model with measurement error on an explanatory variable. We specify analytically the forms of the relative asymptotic bias and the relative asymptotic efficiency between the two estimators given the structure of the model. This allows showing that the joint presence of spatial autocorrelation and measurement error leads a bias-efficiency trade-off. Estimation with GLS allows decreasing the bias but in a limited way. However, there exists a high number of parameter combinations for which this reduction of the bias comes at the cost of an efficiency loss.*

Key-words - SPATIAL AUTOCORRELATION, MEASUREMENT ERRORS, LARGE SAMPLE RESULTS

HOW RELIABLE ARE THE GEOGRAPHICAL SPATIAL WEIGHTS MATRICES?

Davide FIASCHI[a], Angela PARENTI[b]

Abstract - *This paper shows how it is possible to estimate the interconnections between regions by a connectedness matrix recently proposed by Diebold and Yilmaz (2014), and discusses how the connectedness matrix is strictly related to the spatial weights matrix used in spatial econometrics. An empirical application using growth rate volatility of per capita GDP of 199 European NUTS2 regions (EU15) over the period 1981-2008 illustrates how our estimated connectedness matrix is not compatible with the most popular geographical weights matrices used in literature.*

Keywords - FIRST-ORDER CONTIGUITY, DISTANCE-BASED MATRIX, CONNECTEDNESS MATRIX, EUROPEAN REGIONS, NETWORK

JEL Classification - C23; R11; R12; O52

[a] Dipartimento di Economia e Management, Pisa, Italy.
E-mail: davide.fiaschi@ec.unipi.it
[b] IMT Institute for Advanced Studies Lucca, e-mail: angela.parenti@imtlucca.it

1. INTRODUCTION

In spatial econometric literature, "the matrix is the fundamental tool used to model the spatial interdependence between regions. More precisely, each region is connected to a set of neighboring regions by means of a *spatial pattern* introduced *exogenously* as a spatial weight matrix W " (Le Gallo et al., 2003, p.110).

The traditional specification of the spatial weights matrix relies on the geographical relation between observations, implying that areal units are neighbors when they share a common border (first-order contiguity), or the distance between their centroids is within a distance cut-off value (distance-based contiguity). As pointed out by Anselin and Bera (1998), other specifications of the spatial weights matrix are possible as, for example, weights reflecting whether or not two individuals belong to the same social network, or based on some "economic" distance. Although these specifications are desired, the resulting spatial process must satisfy necessary regularity conditions. "For example, this requires constraints on the extent on the range of interaction and/or the degree of heterogeneity implied by the weights matrices" (Anselin and Bera, 1998, p. 244).

Moreover, "in the standard estimation and testing approaches, the weights matrix is taken to be *exogenous*" (Anselin and Bera, 1998, p. 244). Therefore, the W matrix represents the *a priori* assumption about interaction strength between regions. However, in many cases considerable attention should be given to specifying the matrix W to represent as far as possible economic links (see Corrado and Fingleton, 2012).

In a companion paper (see Fiaschi and Parenti, 2013) we show how is possible to estimate the interdependence between European regions by a *connectedness matrix*, which is the result of a general variance decomposition analysis on the residuals of a VAR model. The connectedness matrix has the advantage to be immediately interpretable as a network, allowing for the use of network connectedness measures to understand the interdependence among regions (see Diebold and Yilmaz, 2014).

The aim of the paper is to discuss how our (contemporaneous) connectedness matrix is strictly related to the spatial matrix W, and to compare the network deriving from connectedness matrix with that deriving from a spatial model that can display mixed dynamics in both space and time. An empirical application using growth rate volatility of per capita GDP of 199 European NUTS2 regions (EU15) over the period 1981-2008 is used to illustrate our analysis.

The paper it is organized as it follows: Section 2 explains the methodology to estimate the connectedness matrix. Section 3 traces a comparison between our connectedness matrix and the spatial weights matrix. Section 4 contains the empirical application to EU regions. Section 5 concludes.

2. THE METHODOLOGY

The estimate of connectedness matrix follows the methodology described in Fiaschi and Parenti (2013). To sum up: firstly, a panel of growth rate volatilities (GRV) of per capita GDP for a sample of regions is estimated; then, the panel is used to perform a general variance decomposition analysis (GVD hereafter) on the residuals from a VAR in order to estimated the so-called *connectedness matrix*. The procedure is largely inspired by Diebold and Yilmaz (2014), with the additional difficulty arising in the estimate of VAR, that the number of observations for each region is generally lower than the number of regions, i.e. we face a typically high-dimensional problem (see Hastle et al. 2008). To overcome this problem a Bayesian Model Averaging is used.

2.1. The Connectedness Matrix

Following McConnell and Perez-Quiros (2000) and Fiaschi and Lavezzi (2011) the basic idea to build a panel of GRV is that the dynamics of growth rate of per capita GDP can be well-approximated by an autoregressive process of order p (denoted by $\mathrm{AR}(p)$):

$$\gamma_{jt} = \mu_j + \phi_1 \gamma_{j,t-1} + \ldots + \phi_p \gamma_{j,t-p} + \varepsilon_{jt} \tag{1}$$

where ε_{jt} is assumed to be normally distributed. Given that ε_{jt} follows a normal distribution, an unbiased estimator of the standard deviation of ε_{jt}, $\sigma^{\varepsilon}_{jt}$, is given by:

$$\hat{\sigma}^{\varepsilon}_{jt} = \sqrt{\frac{\pi}{2}} \mid \hat{\varepsilon}_{jt} \mid \tag{2}$$

From Eq. (2) we derive the unbiased estimator of the standard deviation of the growth rate of per capita GDP, σ^{γ}_{jt}. For example, if the growth rate follows an AR(1) process (see Hamilton 1994, p. 53), the standard deviation of the growth rate is given by:

$$\hat{\sigma}^{\gamma}_{jt} = \frac{\hat{\sigma}^{\varepsilon}_{jt}}{\sqrt{1-\phi_1^2}} = \frac{\sqrt{\frac{\pi}{2}} \mid \hat{\varepsilon}_{jt} \mid}{\sqrt{1-\phi_1^2}} \tag{3}$$

This method is easily extended to higher-order AR models (see Hamilton 1994, pp. 58-59).

Once the panel of GRV has been estimated, we follow Diebold and Yilmaz (2014) in the use of a vector-autoregressive (VAR) model to represent the process governing the GRV of regions, and estimate the GVD which allows to measure the population *connectedness*, i.e. assessing the share of forecast error variance in a region due to shocks arising *elsewhere*.

The use of VAR implicitly implies that relationships across units of observations are essentially linear, and that the contemporaneous relationships are well represented by pairwise correlations (i.e., the variance-covariance matrix). Moreover, the use of GVD is subject to some restrictive assumptions, the most notable is the Gaussian distribution of shocks.[1]

Assume that a VAR of order p is a good approximating model of the process governing the GRV of regions:[2]

$$\mathbf{x}_t = \mathbf{c} + \sum_{i=1}^{p} \mathbf{\Phi}_i \mathbf{x}_{t-i} + \varepsilon_t,\ t = 1,...,T, \tag{4}$$

where $\mathbf{c}$ is a $N \times 1$ vector of constants, $\mathbf{x}_t = (x_{1t},...,x_{Nt})'$ is a $N \times 1$ vector of jointly determined dependent variables, $\mathbf{\Phi}_i, i = 1,...,N$ is the $N \times N$ coefficients matrix and ε_t is an error term such that $E(\varepsilon_t) = \mathbf{0}$, $E(\varepsilon_t \varepsilon_{t'}) = \Sigma\ \forall t$, where $\mathbf{\Sigma} = \{\sigma_{ij}, j = 1,...,N\}$ is an $N \times N$ positive definite matrix, and $E(\varepsilon_t \varepsilon_{t'}') = \mathbf{0}$ for all $t \neq t'$.

Assuming also that all roots of $|\mathbf{I}_N - \sum_{i=1}^{p} \mathbf{\Phi}_i z^i| = 0$ fall inside the unit circle, that is $\mathbf{x}_t$ is covariance-stationary (see Pesaran and Shin, 1998), Eq. (4) can be rewritten as the infinite moving average representation:

$$\mathbf{x}_t = \mu + \sum_{i=0}^{\infty} \mathbf{\Theta}_i \varepsilon_{t-i},\ t = 1,...,T, \tag{5}$$

where $\mu = (\mathbf{I}_N - \mathbf{\Phi}_1 - \cdots - \mathbf{\Phi}_p)^{-1}\mathbf{c}$ is the mean of the process, and the $N \times N$ coefficient matrices $\mathbf{\Theta}_i$ can be obtained as
$\mathbf{\Theta}_i = \mathbf{\Phi}_1 \mathbf{\Theta}_{i-1} + ... + \mathbf{\Phi}_p \mathbf{\Theta}_{i-p},\ i = 1,2,...$ with $\mathbf{\Theta}_0 = \mathbf{I}_N$ and $\mathbf{\Theta}_i = 0$ for $i < 0$.

To measure the effect of shocks at a given point in time on the expected future values of variables in a dynamical system, Koop et al. (1996), advance the *generalized impulse response function*. In particular the *scaled* generalized impulse response function of x_t at horizon H is given by:

[1] Alternatively, the use of Cholesky-factor identification is sensitive to ordering of the units of observations.
[2] Notation refers to Pesaran and Shin (1998).

$$\psi_j^g(H) = \sigma_{jj}^{-\frac{1}{2}} \mathbf{\Theta}_H \mathbf{\Sigma} \mathbf{e}_j, \tag{6}$$

where $\mathbf{e}_j$ is the selection vector (a vector of all zeros with 1 in the j-th element), which measures the effect of one standard error shock to the j-th unit of observations at time t on expected values of $\mathbf{x}$ at time $t+H$.

From the above generalized impulses, Pesaran and Shin (1998) derive the generalized (i.e., order-invariant) forecast error variance decomposition, defined as the proportion of the H-step ahead forecast error variance of variable i which is accounted for by innovations in variable j. Then, for $H=1,2,...$, H-step GVD matrix $\mathbf{D}^{gH} = [d_{ij}^{gH}]$ has entries:[3]

$$d_{ij}^{gH} = \frac{\sigma_{jj}^{-1} \sum_{h=0}^{H-1} (e_i' \mathbf{\Theta}_h \mathbf{\Sigma} e_j)^2}{\sum_{h=0}^{H-1} (e_i' \mathbf{\Theta}_h \mathbf{\Sigma} \mathbf{\Theta}_h' e_i)} \tag{7}$$

where $\mathbf{\Theta}_h$ is the coefficient matrix of the h-lagged shock vector in the MA representation of the *non-orthogonalized* VAR, $\mathbf{\Sigma}$ is the covariance matrix of the shock in the *non-orthogonalized* VAR, and σ_{ii} its diagonal.

As in Diebold and Yilmaz (2014) we normalize the GVD matrix by row in order to have unity sums of forecast error variance contribution (remember that the shocks are not necessarily orthogonal in GVD, therefore their sum is not equal to 1 in the standard decomposition). Therefore, the *connectedness matrix* has entries as:

$$\tilde{d}_{ij}^{gH} = \frac{d_{ij}^{gH}}{\sum_{j=1}^{N} d_{ij}^{gH}}. \tag{8}$$

In particular, $\tilde{d}_{ij}^{gH}$ is the fraction of region's i H-step forecast error variance due to shocks in region j. The *cross*-variance decomposition, that is the off-diagonal elements (i.e., $i \neq j$), measure the *pairwise directional connectedness*; in general, $\tilde{d}_{ij}^{gH} \neq \tilde{d}_{ji}^{gH}$), i.e. GVD matrix is not symmetric. On the other hand, the diagonal elements (*own connectedness*) measure the fraction of region's i H-step forecast error variance due to shocks arising in the same region (i.e. idiosyncratic shocks).

[3] Notice that $H=1$ actually corresponds to the contemporaneous connectedness.

Table 1. Connectedness Matrix derived from the GVD Matrix

	x_1	...	x_N	From Others
x_1	$\tilde{d}_{11}^{gH}$	...	$\tilde{d}_{1N}^{gH}$	$\sum_{j=1}^{N} \tilde{d}_{1j}^{gH}$, $j \neq 1$
$\vdots$	$\vdots$		$\vdots$	$\vdots$
x_N	$\tilde{d}_{N1}^{gH}$	...	$\tilde{d}_{NN}^{gH}$	$\sum_{j=1}^{N} \tilde{d}_{Nj}^{gH}$, $j \neq N$
To Others	$\sum_{i=1}^{N} d_{i1}^{H}$, $i \neq 1$	...	$\sum_{i=1}^{N} \tilde{d}_{iN}^{gH}$, $i \neq 1$	$\frac{1}{N}\sum i, j = 1^N \tilde{d}_{ij}^{gH}$, $i \neq j$

The connectedness matrix is conditioned to the predictive horizon H, which is in turn related to the concept of *dynamic* connectedness. In particular, GVD 1-step ahead represents the *contemporaneous* connectedness. As the predictive horizon H increases there is more possibility for connectedness to appear. In this sense, we can distinguish between short-run and long-run connectedness.

The typical dimensions of datasets used in cross-country and cross-region analysis are such that the number of countries/regions N is much higher than the length of time series T, i.e. we generally face a high-dimensional problem with $N >> T$. Firstly, this suggests to maintain the order of VAR at the minimum level equal to 1, i.e. GRV of each region at time t will depend on a constant, on its lagged GRV at time $t-1$, and on the GRV of all other regions at time $t-1$. Secondly, since the total number of parameters to be estimated equal to $K = N+1$, i.e. all lagged GRV of regions plus constant, is higher than the number of observations T, the VAR(1) cannot be estimated by standard OLS. We overcome this problem by using a Bayesian Model Averaging approach (see Fiaschi and Parenti (2013), for technical details).

2.2. A Network Interpretation of Connectedness Matrix

The proposed methodology has a straightforward interpretation in terms of network and of percolation of shocks through it. As stated by Diebold and Yilmaz, (2014, p.123) "[...] *variance decompositions are networks*. More precisely, the variance decomposition matrix D, which defines our connectedness table, and all associated connectedness measure, is a network adjacency matrix A. Hence network connectedness measures can be used in conjunction with variance decompositions to understand connectedness among components". Specifically, GVD defines a weighted, directed network.

For the sake of simplicity consider the case with three regions and a representation by VAR(1), whose variance-covariance matrix $\mathbf{\Sigma}$ is given by:

$$\mathbf{\Sigma} = \begin{bmatrix} \sigma_{11} & \sigma_{12} & 0 \\ \sigma_{21} & \sigma_{22} & \sigma_{23} \\ 0 & \sigma_{32} & \sigma_{33} \end{bmatrix} \tag{9}$$

from which the GVD matrix at $H=1$:

$$\mathbf{D}^{g1}=\begin{bmatrix} 1 & \dfrac{\sigma_{12}}{\sigma_{22}} & 0 \\ \dfrac{\sigma_{21}}{\sigma_{11}} & 1 & \dfrac{\sigma_{23}}{\sigma_{33}} \\ 0 & \dfrac{\sigma_{32}}{\sigma_{22}} & 1 \end{bmatrix} \tag{10}$$

In case of VAR(1) $\mathbf{\Theta}_0=\mathbf{I}_N$, $\mathbf{\Theta}_1=\mathbf{\Phi}$, $\mathbf{\Theta}_2=\mathbf{\Phi}^2$, ..., where $\mathbf{\Phi}$ is the coefficient matrix of VAR.

The network representation related to $\mathbf{D}^{g1}$ in Eq. (10) is reported in Fig. (1). The structure of *contemporaneous* network fully reflects the shape of $\mathbf{\Sigma}$ both in terms of existence of links and in terms of their strength. However, differently from $\mathbf{\Sigma}$, $\mathbf{D}^{g1}$ is not symmetric, i.e. the contemporaneous network is both *weighted* and *directional*. The row standardization has not an impact on the analysis in the case we are interested in only the existence of links between two regions. In a more complete analysis of percolation of shocks trough network this normalization is however not neutral and the use of the original values of GVD matrix is the best option.

Assuming that the coefficient matrix $\mathbf{\Theta}_1$ of the *1*-lagged shock vector in the MA representation of the VAR(1) is given by:

$$\mathbf{\Theta}_1=\mathbf{\Phi}=\begin{bmatrix} \phi_{11} & 0 & \phi_{13} \\ 0 & 0 & 0 \\ \phi_{31} & 0 & \phi_{33} \end{bmatrix} \tag{11}$$

GVD matrix at $H=2$ is given by:

$$\mathbf{D}^{g2}=\begin{bmatrix} \dfrac{\sigma_{11}+\phi_{11}^2\sigma_{11}}{\sigma_{11}+\phi_{11}^2\sigma_{11}+\phi_{13}^2\sigma_{33}} & \dfrac{\sigma_{12}}{\sigma_{22}}\left[1+\left(\phi_{11}+\phi_{13}\dfrac{\sigma_{32}}{\sigma_{12}}\right)^2\right] & \dfrac{\phi_{13}^2\sigma_{33}}{\phi_{33}\phi_{13}\sigma_{33}+\phi_{31}\phi_{11}\sigma_{11}} \\ \dfrac{\sigma_{21}}{\sigma_{11}} & 1 & \dfrac{\sigma_{23}}{\sigma_{33}} \\ \dfrac{\phi_{31}^2\sigma_{11}}{\phi_{11}\phi_{31}\sigma_{11}+\phi_{13}\phi_{33}\sigma_{33}} & \dfrac{\sigma_{32}}{\sigma_{22}}\left[1+\left(\phi_{33}+\phi_{31}\dfrac{\sigma_{12}}{\sigma_{32}}\right)^2\right] & \dfrac{\sigma_{33}+\phi_{33}^2\sigma_{33}}{\sigma_{33}+\phi_{33}^2\sigma_{33}+\phi_{31}^2\sigma_{11}} \end{bmatrix} \tag{12}$$

The network representation related to $\mathbf{D}^{g2}$ in Eq. (12) is reported in Fig. (2). The structure of network appears crucially affected by $\mathbf{\Phi}$ both in terms of the emergence of new links and in terms of their strength.

In particular, new links appear connecting Regions 1 and 3 through the VAR coefficients ϕ_{13} and ϕ_{31}.

Figure 1. Network representation of GVD matrix at horizon $H = 1$

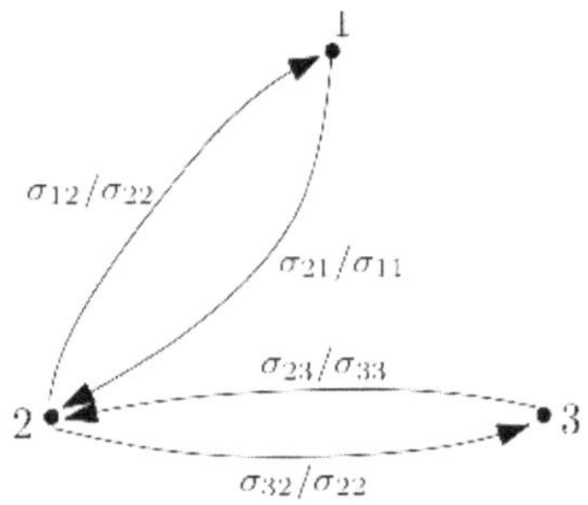

Figure 2. Network representation of GVD matrix at horizon $H = 2$

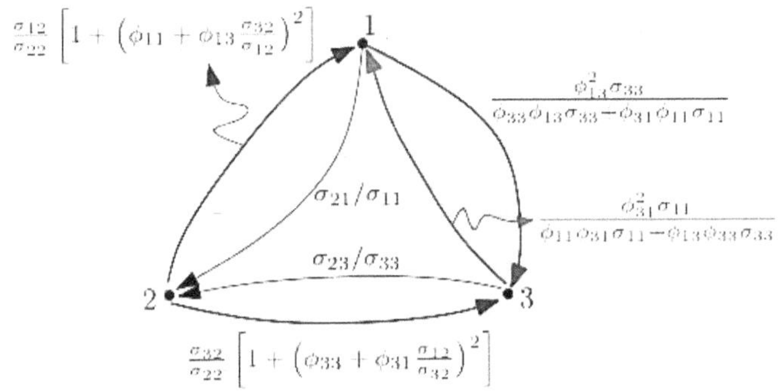

VAR coefficients also drive the extent of persistence of shocks over time; for example, d_{11}^{g2} depends on ϕ_{11} (the effect of autoregressive component of Region 1) and ϕ_{13} (the shocks received from Region 3); coefficients appear to have a power proportional to time horizon (i.e. for $H = 2$), that is shocks have an exponential decay. It is straightforward to show that a longer time horizon increases the strength of links with an exponential decay (for example d_{11}^{g3} includes terms like ϕ_{11}^4 and ϕ_{13}^2).

Region 2, missing any lag with itself and with the other regions in the VAR, displays a network partially independent of the time horizon considered. In particular, the connectedness from Region 2 to other regions are affected through the contemporaneous covariances σ_{12}, σ_{22}, and σ_{32}, while the connectedness from other regions to Region 2 are not affected by H.

Relaxing the assumption of VAR(1), for example in favor of VAR(2), increases both the percolation of shocks through network and their persistence, but the qualitative results remain the same.

3. CONNECTEDNESS MATRIX VERSUS SPATIAL WEIGTHS MATRIX

As discussed in the introduction the main goal of the paper is to get some insights on the shape of spatial weights matrix $\mathbf{W}$, which in spatial literature measures the spatial dependence across different regions.

$\mathbf{W}$ is generally taken as exogenous in spatial literature, and it is specified or in term of geographic contiguity or in terms of geographical distance (see Anselin, 2001). Corrado and Fingleton (2012) formulate three main critiques to current literature: i) the values in the cells of $\mathbf{W}$ comprise an explicit hypothesis about the strength of interlocation connection", in particular, "*a priori* assumption about interaction strength"; ii) "Typically, isotropy is assumed, so that only distance between j and h is relevant, not the direction j to h"; iii) "The potential for dynamic $\mathbf{W}$ matrices poses some problems for estimation, given the assertion that $\mathbf{W}$ is necessarily a fixed entity. While this may not be such an issue for cross-section approaches, [...], with the extension of spatial econometrics to include panel data modelling it may be the case that $\mathbf{W}$ is evolving."

To discuss how our contemporaneous connectedness matrix $\mathbf{D}^{g1}$ is strictly related to $\mathbf{W}$ assume that the data generating process of GRV of N regions y follows:

$$\mathbf{y}_t = (\mathbf{I}_N - \rho\mathbf{W})^{-1}[\mu_N + \mathbf{X}_t\beta + \mathbf{u}_t] = (\mathbf{I}_N - \rho\mathbf{W})^{-1}[\mu_N + \mathbf{X}_t\beta] + \mathbf{v}_t \qquad (13)$$

where $\boldsymbol{\mu}_N$ is the vector of fixed effects of length N, $\mathbf{y}_t$ is a vector of length N, $\mathbf{X}_t$ is a matrix of dimensions $(N \times k)$, $\boldsymbol{\beta}$ is a vector of coefficients of length k, and $\mathbf{u}_t$ is the vector of error component of length N, and $\mathbf{v}_t$ is the vector of spatially filtered error component of length N.[4] The error component $\mathbf{u}_t$ is specified as:

$$\mathbf{u}_t = \lambda\mathbf{W}\mathbf{u}_t + \psi\mathbf{W}\mathbf{u}_{t-1} + \delta\mathbf{u}_{t-1} + \varepsilon_t, \qquad (14)$$

where ε_t is the vector of innovations, with $E[\varepsilon_{t'}] = 0$, $E[\varepsilon_t\varepsilon'_{t}] = \sigma_\varepsilon^2 I_N$, and $E[\varepsilon_t\varepsilon'_{t'}] = 0$ for each $t' \neq t$. Eq. (14) reflect the possibility that $\mathbf{u}_t$ can display mixed dynamics in both space and time. We follow the literature

[4] See Elhorst (2014) for a general introduction to spatial panel models.

assuming that $\mathbf{W}$ is the same for the spatially lagged dependent variable and the errors.

From Eq. (14) we derive:[5]

$$\mathbf{u}_t = (\mathbf{I}_N - \lambda\mathbf{W})^{-1}\left\{\sum_{i=0}^{\infty}\delta^i\left[\left(\mathbf{I}_N + \left(\frac{\psi}{\delta}\right)\mathbf{W}\right)(\mathbf{I}_N - \lambda\mathbf{W})^{-1}\right]^i \varepsilon_{t-i}\right\}$$

from which we get the variance-covariance matrix of $\mathbf{u}_t$, $\mathbf{U}$, for all t, i.e.:

$$\mathbf{U} = E[\mathbf{u}_t\mathbf{u}'_t] = \sigma_\varepsilon^2(\mathbf{I}_N - \lambda\mathbf{W})^{-1}\times$$

$$\times\left[\mathbf{I}_N - \delta^2(\mathbf{I}_N - \lambda\mathbf{W}')^{-1}\left(\mathbf{I}_N + \left(\frac{\psi}{\delta}\right)\mathbf{W}'\right)\left(\mathbf{I}_N + \left(\frac{\psi}{\delta}\right)\mathbf{W}\right)(\mathbf{I}_N - \lambda\mathbf{W})^{-1}\right]^{-1}\times$$

$$\times(\mathbf{I}_N - \lambda\mathbf{W}')^{-1} \tag{15}$$

Therefore, the variance-covariance matrix of $\mathbf{v}_t$, $\mathbf{V}$, for all t is given by:

$$\mathbf{V} = E[\mathbf{v}_t\mathbf{v}'_t] = (\mathbf{I}_N - \rho\mathbf{W})^{-1}\mathbf{U}(\mathbf{I}_N - \rho\mathbf{W}')^{-1}. \tag{16}$$

Assuming that the VAR representation well approximates the dynamics of $\mathbf{y}_t$, a possible estimation of $\mathbf{V}$ is given by the variance-covariance matrix of the VAR(1) model, i.e. $\hat{\mathbf{\Sigma}}$.

The approximation of stochastic process of $\mathbf{y}_t$ through a VAR representation allows to overcome the *incidental parameters* problem discussed in Anselin (2002). In our model the total number of parameters to be estimate is equal to $N^2 - N + 5$ (all no-zero elements of $\mathbf{W}$ plus λ, δ, ψ, ρ, and σ_ε^2) and the number of observations are equal to N^2 (the elements of $\mathbf{V}$); under the assumption $N > 5$ it is therefore possible to estimate the elements of $\mathbf{W}$ as well as the other parameters of Eq. (16). But the estimate of $\mathbf{W}$ from $\hat{\mathbf{\Sigma}}$ becomes very unreliable already for small N: for our sample of $N = 199$ observations, the total number of parameters o estimate is equal to 39407 against a number of observations equal to 39601.

However, a comparison between Eqq. (7) and (16) makes clear that $\mathbf{D}^{g1}$ and $\mathbf{W}$ are calculated on the same information set, i.e. $\hat{\mathbf{\Sigma}}$.

5 We are assuming that the first-order spatial autoregressive process is ergodic.

Moreover, the comparison highlights how spatial panels whose observations refer to variable with different timing (e.g. panel of annual observations versus panel with five-year average observations) should include different spatial matrix reflecting the different degrees of interconnectedness (five-year average observations are likely to have a higher level of interconnectedness). A similar argument is made in network literature (see, e.g., Newman, 2009).

4. EMPIRICAL APPLICATION

Our sample consists of a panel of GRV of per capita GDP of 199 European NUTS2 regions belong to EU15 over the period 1981-2008.[6]

In order to compare our connectedness matrix with the spatial weights matrices mostly used in the spatial econometric literature, we construct a network derived from the contemporaneous connectedness matrix $\mathbf{D}^{g1}$ (that is the GVD at time horizon H=1)[7] and two networks derived from the GVD of the variance-covariance matrix of a spatial model as the one in Eq. (16) of Section 3. In particular, we assume two different spatial weights matrices, i.e. a first-order contiguity matrix, $\mathbf{W}_{cont}$, and a distance based matrix with cut-off, $\mathbf{W}_{invDistQ1}$, (both row-standardized) whose weights are given by:

$$w_{cont}(i,j) = \begin{cases} 1 & \text{if i and j share a border} \\ 0 & \text{otherwise} \end{cases}$$

and

$$w_{invDistQ1}(i,j) = \begin{cases} dist_{ij}^{-2} & \text{if } dist_{ij} < 370 \text{ miles} \\ 0 & \text{otherwise} \end{cases};$$

We have calibrated the parameters of the model as ρ=0.32, λ=0.42, ϕ=0.32, ψ=0 and σ_{ε}^{2}=1 to get networks which are similar to our contemporaneous network in terms of mean degrees (see Table 2).[8]

[6] See Fiaschi and Parenti (2013) for details on the sample, sources of data and estimation of the GRV. All the calculations are made using R (R Core Team, 2014). Codes and data are available on author's web page http://dse.ec.unipi.it/ fiaschi/.

[7] In Fiaschi and Parenti (2013) we extensively discuss the connectedness matrix estimated at different time horizons (contemporaneous H1, 5-year ahead H5, 10-year ahead H10 and 20-year ahead H20).

[8] Table 2 reports some basic statistics of the networks. We follow the notation in Newman (2009) labelling by n the number of vertices (the number of regions), m the number of edges (the number of no-zero links), c the mean degree (i.e. m/n), S the fraction of vertices in the largest (weakly connected) component, l the mean geodesic distance (any two no-connected links are excluded by calculation), d the diameter of network (the length of the longest finite geodesic path), C the average clustering coefficient (based on transitivity in weak form), and r the assortative coefficient.

To analyze our connectedness matrix as an unweighed and direct network links, i.e. pairwise directional connectedness, with a strength greater than 2.12% will be set equal to 1, while all the others equal to 0. In other words, we have assigned a value of 1 to the *ij* element of adjacent matrix if the fraction of region's i 1-year ahead forecast error variance due to shocks in region j, d_{ij}^{1}, is higher than 2.12%, which corresponds to a significance level equal to 2.5% under the null hypothesis of no percolation of shocks from region j to region i (see Fiaschi and Parenti, 2013 for details).[9]

Table 2. Characteristics of the networks derived from the GVD matrix

	n	m	c	S	l	d	C	r
$\mathbf{D}^{g1}$	199	1188	**5.97**	1	3.3	6	0.15	0.83
$\mathbf{W}_{cont}$	199	1082	**5.44**	18	2.47	16	0.56	0.94
$\mathbf{W}_{invDistQ1}$	199	1237	**6.22**	5	4.05	21	0.63	0.97

with H=1, $\mathbf{D}^{g1}$, $\mathbf{W}_{cont}$ *and* $\mathbf{W}_{invDistQ1}$. n *is the number of vertices (the number of regions),* m *the number of edges (the number of no-zero links),* c *the mean degree (i.e.* m/n*),* S *the fraction of vertices in the largest (weakly connected) component,* l *the mean geodesic distance (any two no-connected links are excluded by calculation),* d *the diameter of network (the length of the longest finite geodesic path),* C *the average clustering coefficient (based on transitivity in weak form), and* r *the assortative coefficient (see Newman, 2009).*

Figures (3)-(5) report the Kamadakawai network for the adjacent matrix derived from D^{g1}, W_{cont} and $W_{invDistQ1}$ respectively. In all the figures the colours of the vertices are the same for regions belonging to the same country.

The network for the adjacent matrix derived from the contemporaneous connectedness matrix $\mathbf{D}^{g1}$, is very different from $\mathbf{W}_{cont}$ and $\mathbf{W}_{invDistQ1}$. In particular, although the number of mean degrees, i.e. the mean number of links, is very similar across the three networks (we choose the parameters in Eq. 16 to match this characteristic), the network derived from the GVD matrix with H=1 shows no evidence of specific geographical pattern.[10] The opposite holds for the networks derived from the GVD matrix with $\mathbf{W}_{cont}$ and $\mathbf{W}_{invDistQ1}$, which obviously impose a geographical structure through the exogenous definition of $\mathbf{W}$.

[9] In the estimation of the unweighed and direct networks derived from the two spatial matrices we have used the same level of significance on the pairwise directional connectedness equal to 2.12%.

[10] In Fiaschi and Parenti (2013) we show that a clear pattern of core-periphery exists but not defined in geographical terms, and that most of the regions belonging to Belgium, Finland and Sweden tend to be more connected to the rest of Europe than to regions belonging to their country, while for most of the regions of Denmark, Greece and Italy the opposite holds.

Figure 3. Kamadakawai network with threshold on the share of GVD equal to 2.12% for the adjacent matrix derived from $\mathbf{D}^{g1}$

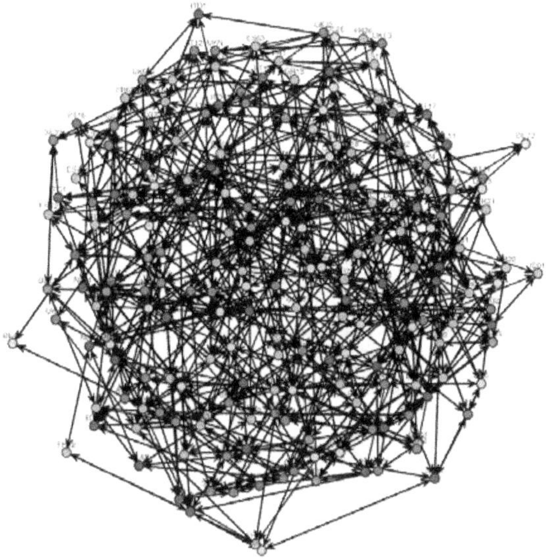

Figure 4. Kamadakawai network with threshold on the share of GVD equal to 2.12% for the adjacent matrix derived from the spatial model with $\mathbf{W}_{cont}$

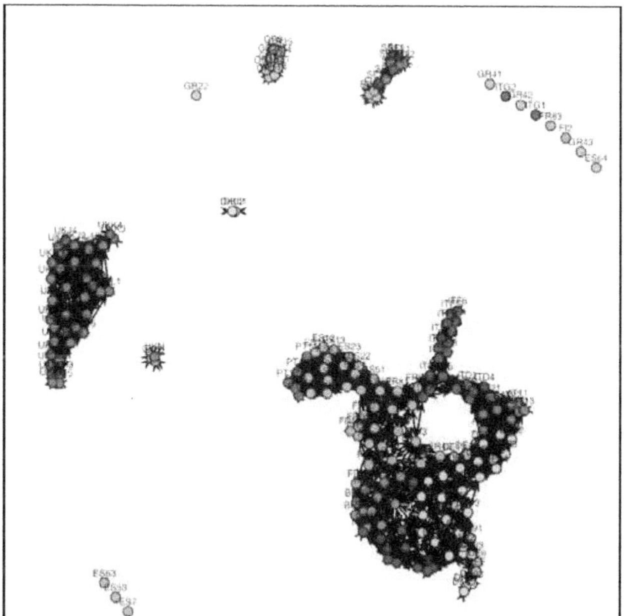

Figure 5. Kamadakawai network with threshold on the share of GVD equal to 2.12% for the adjacent matrix derived from the spatial model with $\mathbf{W}_{invDistQ1}$

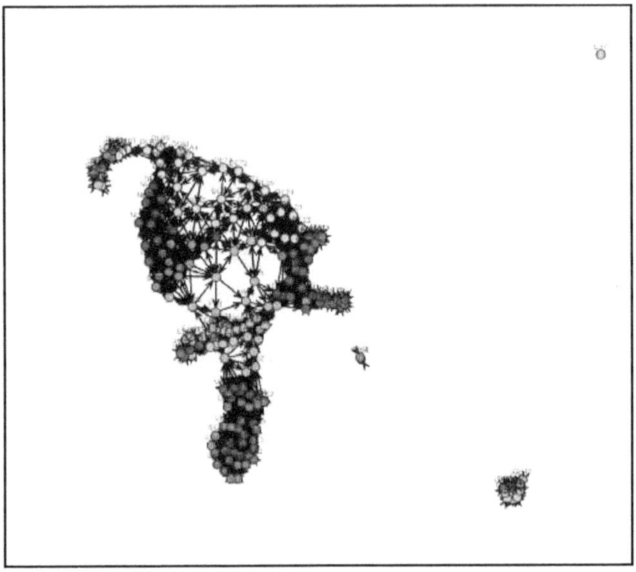

Hence, the assumption that spatial interaction between regions is represented by a geographical weights matrix can lead to a misspecification of the spatial interdependence structure. The effects of such a misspecification are studied by Florax and Rey (1995), who show that both over and under-specification of the geographical weights matrix increases the mean square errors for spatial econometric models. However, no systematic exploration has been conducted so far; the intuition is that misspecification of the spatial weights matrix could lead to a substantial bias in the estimate.

5. CONCLUDING REMARKS

The estimate of the connectedness matrix for EU regions proposed in the paper has allowed to highlight how the most popular spatial weights matrices used in literature are very far from the true spatial weights matrix (if any).

This paper would represent a first step in the development of a methodology to estimate a spatial weights matrix which explicitly takes into account the critiques advanced by Corrado and Flingleton (2013). The next step should be the definition of a methodology that, starting from the estimated connectedness matrix, allows to estimate the associated spatial weights matrix. The biggest obstacle appears the high number of matrix elements to estimate, which calls for some non-standard econometrics techniques and /or for imposing some regularity conditions on the shape of the spatial weights matrix.

REFERENCES

Anselin, L. (2001). Spatial econometrics. In B. Baltagi (Ed.), *A Companion to Theoretical Econometrics*, pp. 310–330. Oxford: Blackwell.

Anselin, L. (2002). Under the hood issues in the specification and interpretation of spatial regression models. *Agricultural economics* 27(3), 247–267.

Anselin, L. and A. Bera (1998). Spatial dependence in linear regression models with an introduction to spatial econometrics. *Statistics Textbooks and Monographs* 155, 237–290.

Corrado, L. and B. Fingleton (2012). Where is economics in spatial econometrics? *Journal of Regional Science* 52(2), 210–239.

Diebold, F. and K. Yılmaz (2014). On the network topology of variance decompositions: Measuring the connectedness of financial firms. *Journal of Econometrics* 182(1), 119–134.

Elhorst, J. (2014). Spatial panel models, in Fischer M.M., Nijkamp P. (Eds.) *Handbook of Regional Science*, Springer.

Fiaschi, D. and A. M. Lavezzi (2011). Economic Growth and Development (Frontiers of Economics and Globalization, Volume 11), Chapter Growth Volatility and the Structure of the Economy, pp. 203–245. Emerald Group Publishing Limited.

Fiaschi, D. and A. Parenti (2013). An estimate of the degree of interconnectedness between european regions: A lasso approach. Discussion Papers del Dipartimento di Economia e Management, University of Pisa, n. 171 (http://wwwdse.ec.unipi.it/ricerca/discussion-papers.htm).

Florax, R. J. and S. Rey (1995). The impacts of misspecified spatial interaction in linear regression models. In Anselin L., Florax R. (Eds.), *New directions in spatial econometrics*, pp. 111–135. Springer.

Hamilton, J. (1994). *Time Series Analysis*. Princeton: Princeton University Press.

Hastie, T., R. Tibshirani, and J. J. H. Friedman (2008). *The Elements of Statistical Learning*. New York: Springer.

Koop, G., M. H. Pesaran, and S. M. Potter (1996). Impulse response analysis in nonlinear multivariate models. *Journal of Econometrics* 74(1), 119–147.

Le Gallo, J., C. Ertur, and C. Baumont (2003). A Spatial Econometric Analysis of Geographic Spillovers and Growth for European Regions, 1980-1995, in Fingleton B. (Ed.), *European Regional Growth*, pp. 99–129. Springer.

McConnell, M. and G. Perez-Quiros (2000). Output fluctuations in the united states: What has changed since the early 1980's? *The American Economic Review* 90, 1464–1476.

Newman, M. (2009). *Networks: an Introduction*. Oxford University Press.

Pesaran, H. H. and Y. Shin (1998). Generalized impulse response analysis in linear multivariate models. *Economics letters* 58(1), 17–29.

R Core Team (2014). *R: A Language and Environment for Statistical Computing*. Vienna, Austria: R Foundation for Statistical Computing.

EST-CE QU'UNE DÉFINITION GÉOGRAPHIQUE DES MATRICES DE POIDS EST PERTINENTE ?

Résumé - *L'objectif de cet article est d'estimer la pertinence de l'utilisation de la matrice d'interconnection de Diebold et Yilmaz (2014) dans l'étude de l'autocorrélation spatiale entre des régions institutionnellement définies. L'article montre que l'utilisation d'une telle matrice d'interconnection fournit des résultats sensiblement différents de ceux obtenus par les matrices de poids spatial, généralement utilisées en économétrie spatiale. Nous illustrons ces deux approches par l'étude de la volatilité des taux de croissance annuels du PIB par habitant dans 199 régions européennes (NUTS2 durant la période 1981-2008 (UE15). L'article montre clairement que les résultats obtenus avec l'utilisation d'une matrice d'interconnection diffèrent de ceux obtenus lorsqu'on s'appuie sur les matrices de poids spatial, utilisées en économétrie spatiale.*

Mots-clés - CONTIGUITÉ DE PREMIER ORDRE, MATRICES DE DISTANCES, MATRICES DE CONNECTIVITÉ, RÉGIONS EUROPÉENNES, RÉSEAU

EMPOWERMENT ZONES AND THE HOUSING MARKET IN PARIS INNER CITY

Stéphane GREGOIR*, **Tristan-Pierre MAURY****

Abstract - *We test for the impact of local enterprise zones on house prices in inner Paris. In 1997, a new urban policy program was launched in France which created three kinds of Enterprise Zones (ZUS, ZRU and ZFU). Notably, 9 first tier EZs (ZUS) were created in Paris. We use this natural experiment and compare the evolution of flat prices in these areas to that in a control group of neighboring areas (that could also have been converted into ZUS). We develop a new semi-parametric spatial matching methodology. Each sale observed before the reform is matched with a similar post-reform counterfactual. This matching procedure is done for housing units within the EZ, as well as for units in the vicinity of the EZ. In contrast to what have been evidenced in other administrative districts of the Paris Region and for other kinds of EZs (i.e., ZFUs), we detect no significant effect of this expensive EZ program implementation on housing values.*

Key-words - ENTERPRISE ZONES ; HOUSE PRICES ; SEMI-PARAMETRIC SPATIAL MATCHING METHODOLOGY

JEL Classification - C21, R31, R38

---

* INSEE, France.
** EDHEC Business School, Lille, France; tristan.maury@edhec.edu

1. INTRODUCTION

Empowerment Zone programs consist of tax incentives in areas with a high unemployment level and a low density of locally-based firms. Tax deductions are granted to firms setting up in these areas and creating jobs locally. Following the first experiments in the US (in the 1980s) or in the UK and France (in the 1990s), an important body of empirical literature has tested whether these programs have reached their objectives in terms of jobs or businesses creations and provided low evidence of significant direct effects stemming from locally-targeted EZ programs. However, the purpose of these EZ programs was often not limited to the local labor market. In France, the policies were extended to subsidies for local home ownership and social housing landlords, as well as to the development of public amenities. In the US, the federal EZ program launched in 1994 also involved subsidies for social services and local amenities. These measures may thus have impacted the local housing market.

Our goal is to extend the literature on the magnitude of EZ effect on local home prices. In the US, the number of studies focussing on the real estate consequences of these locally-targeted programs is limited (see e.g., Engberg and Greenbaum, 1999, Busso and Kline, 2007, or Krupka and Noonan, 2009). Most of them provided evidence of a significantly positive, but moderate, effect on property values. To our knowledge, the only study in France is a companion paper (Gregoir and Maury, 2014) putting the emphasis on a very specific French administrative unit (the Seine-Saint-Denis *département*). We extend this analysis and focus on the inner Paris housing market. We use an integrated econometric setup, simultaneously assessing the possible effects of the local program within the boundaries of the EZ and beyond the limits of the EZ. We rely on a a street-by-street mapping of EZs. We estimate the spatial spillover effect with a semi-parametric distance-to-the-EZ-boundary gradient function. Consequently, we can test for the significance of the EZ impact on house price levels within targeted zones, as well as on house price gaps between units within EZs and units in the vicinity of EZs, controlling for the distance between these two units.

In France, the EZ programs were initiated at the end of 1996 (the Round I program hereafter). Three types of targeted zones were defined with a growing amount of tax exemptions: 750 ZUS (*Zones Urbaines Sensibles*), 416 ZRU (*Zones de Redynamisation Urbaines*), selected among the 750 ZUS) and 44 ZFU (*Zones Franches Urbaines*) were selected and geographically-delimited among the most distressed ZUS. The concentration of targeted zones is relatively high in inner Paris, with 9 newly created ZUS. We collect housing sales values, precise location and attributes in 1996 and 1997 (i.e., the year before and the year after the program implementation). We select all pre-reform (1996) sales observations within or in the vicinity of a ZUS. For each observation (the focal point), we construct a post-reform counterfactual (after the Round I implementation), by selecting a fixed number of sales at the same location or an immediate proximity. We then construct the pre- and post- reform differences of the logarithms of house prices for each focal point within and beyond ZUS borders. We proceed in the same manner for a selected control group of zones that did not become ZUSs in 1996, but could have become so, according to the public criteria based on some descriptive statistics. The log of price gaps (for treated ZUS or controls, within or beyond the considered zone) are pooled and a partially linear single-index model is estimated. Among the linear set of covariates, we include the difference of the main house attributes of the reference and counterfactual observations. The non-parametric component (i.e., the single index) includes all other factors that may potentially interact in a non-linear manner: in particular, the way the distance to the closest EZ (or control) boundary affects the log of house price differences is assessed with a non-linear link function $\eta(.)$ modeled with a penalized spline (P-spline) (Yu and Ruppert (2002)). This type of spline offers an interesting trade-off between the flexibility of the functional form and the computational costs.

We detect no significant effect of the EZ program on housing values in Paris, at least in the short run. This result is at odds with the companion contribution, Gregoir and Maury (2014), which detected a significantly negative effect of the EZ program in the Seine-Saint-Denis district. However, this study was based on a different period (Round II implementation in 2004) and another kind on EZ (i.e., second tier EZs converted into third tier EZs).

The rest of the paper is organized as follows. We provide a survey of the literature on empowerment zones in France in the second section. In Section 3, we present the French EZ program and detail its implementation in Paris. We describe our dataset in the fourth section. Section 5 provides our detailed econometric methodology: the spatial matching process, control group selection, the penalized spline estimation of the partially linear single index model. Section 6 presents the results. The last section concludes.

2. DESCRIPTION OF THE FRENCH PROGRAM

In the beginning of 1997, the French authorities initiated the first Empowerment Zone program following experiments in the UK and the US. As said above, three categories of EZ have been created with a growing amount of public aid: ZUS (first tier), ZRU (second tier) selected among the ZUS, and ZFU (third tier) selected among the most distressed ZUS. First tier EZs (i.e., ZUSs that are not ZRUs or ZFUs) may theoretically be exempt from local business and property taxes. It should be noted that such public grants are at the discretion of local authorities and are not compensated by the central government. Moreover, local authorities (municipalities) with a first tier EZ must establish a local housing program as well as promote urban regeneration projects. Households wishing to become homeowners in ZUSs benefit under certain conditions from substantial increases in the maximum amount of publicly funded zero-interest rate loans (*Prêt à Taux Zéro*, PTZ) they are entitled to. Hence, even though aid for ZUSs is mainly focused on business creation and local employment (which can indirectly affect the housing market), aid may also impact on local urban projects (housing programs, local amenities) through enlarged incentives to conduct such projects for local authorities which benefit from this support. Real estate values appear to be an ideal measure for assessing the effect of local ZUSs, since the wealth created by these programs should be capitalized in the local housing stock.

Many descriptive studies have been published on the evaluation of different rounds of the French EZ program with contrasting conclusions (see Thélot, 2004, Gilli, 2006, or Ernst, 2008). The two most significant statistical contributions are Gobillon, Magnac and Selod (2010) and Givord, Rathelot and Sillard (2011). Gobillon et al. (2010) propose an assessment of the effects of the first round of the French EZ program. They use a two-stage procedure to estimate the impact of EZs on individual unemployment durations. First, they estimate a stratified partial likelihood estimator with a panel dataset at the municipality level, from 1993 to 2003. They obtain average municipal effects and illustrate the changes in these effects over time. Comparing these results for treated municipalities (those including an EZ) and counterfactual municipalities with similar characteristics, they provide evidence of moderate but significant effects on the French program in the short run (i.e., for the semesters immediately following the policy implementation). No significant effect is detected over larger horizons. Givord et al. (2011) evaluate the consequences of the Round II French EZ program on economic activity: business creations and employment. They use establishment level data from 2002 to 2007 with a geographic mapping methodology, in order to establish the exact street address. They investigate the impact of the program on treated areas (firms located with EZs boundaries) with a two stage method (propensity score to control the probability for an area becoming a ZFU, plus a kernel matching method). They find significant effects of the program on both business creation and employment. It should be noted that they also find evidence of negative spatial spillover effects on areas in the vicinity of EZs.

3. DATA

Data on sales prices come from the Paris Chamber of Notaries. We restrict our sample to transactions in existing apartments. New properties and house sales both represent only a small share of the total sales for the Paris Region and their price and physical attributes strongly differ from those of the existing apartments. We collect individual information on the sale price, the floor area of the apartment, the floor level, the construction period of the building, the presence of an elevator in the building, the number of rooms, of bathrooms, of garages, etc. We also have the precise location (street address) of each housing unit. This is of crucial importance for the geographic mapping procedure of the data (i.e., the distinction of dwellings inside or beyond the EZ's boundaries and distance to the closest EZ boundary). Data are available for the 1996-2007 time period, on a monthly basis.

We focus on sales occurring in the inner Paris *département*, one of the eight administrative units of the Paris Region. Nine ZUS have been created in inner Paris in January 1997 (see Figure 1). Table 1 summarizes some descriptive statistics of the main characteristics of people living in each of these nine zones. We compare these results to those obtained with a set of 8 control zones located in the same area of inner Paris than the 9 treated ZUS (i.e., the North East of Paris). These control zones have been spatially delimited by another urban program (CUCS, *Contrat Urbains de Cohésion Sociale*) that has been launched much later (in 2007) to implement joint actions (contract between the state and local governments) to improve the daily lives of residents in neighborhoods experiencing difficulties (unemployment, violence, etc.). Since they were created according to a different program, these control zones did not receive the same public grants as ZUS in 1997. However, Table 1 shows that treated and control zones are not so different when considering the share of low income households, the share of households getting unemployment benefits or the activity rate. Nevertheless, it should be noted that the share of tenants in the social housing sector is much higher in some ZUS than in control zones (98.1% in the *HBM Aubervilliers* EZ and 99.1% in the *Porte de Montmartre* EZ). In theory, the modelling should be developed to take into account for the possible bias implied by the endogeneity of the Round I selection process. In a similar framework, such a modelling did not allow the econometricians to exhibit the impact of a particular variable on the dependent one in the selection process (see Gregoir and Maury, 2014).

Figure 1. Map of Inner Paris

Grey areas are Round I ZUSs (treated zones).
Black areas are zones of the control group (CUCS).

Table 1. Descriptive statistics on treated and control zones in Paris

Name	low income	social housing	unemp. benefits	activity rate	employees/ workers
HBM Aubervilliers (T)	25.0	98.1	19.7	70.0	78.2
HBM Ménilmontant (T)	14.5	46.1	17.6	75.4	46.1
La Goutte d'Or (T)	25.5	18.6	22.1	74.8	61.5
Porte Saint-Denis (T)	11.2	6.4	18.2	82.1	38.2
Fontaine au Roi (T)	17.5	14.9	19.7	79.8	47.5
Porte de Saint-Ouen (T)	15.6	61.5	17.5	77.7	64.0
Porte de Montmartre (T)	23.0	99.1	19.4	69.2	78.8
Curial (T)	16.8	59.1	20.4	77.0	63.1
Belleville (T)	22.6	34.4	22.0	77.6	54.7
Buisson Saint-Louis (C)	15.4	22.5	20.1	80.0	50.8
La Chapelle hors ZUS (C)	19.3	20.9	19.3	75.7	61.5
Amiraux Simplon (C)	15.1	14.1	18.7	78.0	55.6
Curial hors ZUS (C)	21.2	47.3	19.5	75.6	60.9
Amandiers hors ZUS (C)	15.5	37.9	21.0	78.8	48.8
Porte de Saint-Denis hors ZUS (C)	11.7	7.1	18.5	82.5	40.5
Porte de Montmartre hors ZUS (C)	20.0	80.4	19.7	71.5	69.9
Porte de Saint-Ouen hors ZUS (C)	15.6	63.0	17.9	77.6	64.5
Paris Metropolitan Area	8.8	21.6	15.2	81.1	49.3

9 treated (T) and 8 control (C) are considered. 'Low Income' is the share of low income households in 2009. 'Social Housing' is the share of tenants in a social dwelling in 2009. 'Unemp. benefits' is the share of households where at least one member get unemployment benefits. 'Activity rate' is the activity rate among 25-64y in 2009. 'Emp/workers' is the share of employees or workers in 2007. Source: INSEE.

4. METHODOLOGY

Let $p_{i,c,t}$ be the log price of individual housing unit i, within (or in the vicinity of) EZ c, at time t. We suppose that this outcome is generated by a semi-parametric model of the form:

$$p_{i,c,t} = X'_{i,c,t}\beta + \mu(T_c, I_{i,c}, D_{i,c}, Z_{i,c,t}) + \theta_{c,i} + \varepsilon_{i,c,t} \quad \text{(D.1)}$$

where T_c is a treatment dummy variable (indicating whether or not the EZ c was treated in the Round I program in 1997). Hence, $T_c = 1$ is for the observations in the treated group and $T_c = 0$ in the control group. $I_{i,c}$ is a dummy variable indicating if housing unit i is located within (treated or the control) EZ c, and $D_{i,c}$ is the distance (as the crow flies) between housing unit i and the closest EZ border ($D_{i,c} = 0$ if $I_{i,c} = 1$). $X_{i,c,t}$ and $Z_{i,c,t}$ both are vectors containing information on the housing unit's characteristics, the EZ's characteristics and house market trends. We further discuss which variables should be included in the linear part of the model (i.e., included in vector X as done in traditional house price hedonic models) and which ones should be included as arguments of the unspecified function $\mu(.)$. β is the hedonic parameter vector. $\theta_{c,i}$ is a spatial location fixed effect. It captures unobserved local neighborhood characteristics that may potentially be correlated with the treatment variable T_c or the variables summarizing the distance to the nearest EZ ($I_{i,c}$ and $D_{i,c}$).

The model is a partially linear semi-parametric model that encompasses the standard linear hedonic setup $X'_{i,c,t}\beta$. The link function $\mu(.)$ is not specified *ex ante*. This semi-parametric specification allows for a non-linear impact on house prices of some house attributes $Z_{i,c,t}$, or the distance to the nearest EZ $\lfloor I_{i,c}, D_{i,c} \rfloor$, as well as their interaction with the treatment variable T_c. For instance, we expect home prices to be positively related to $D_{i,c}$, but dependent on some of the apartment's attributes, its size for example: the immediate proximity of an EZ may influence the price differently for large family dwellings (households with children) than for small apartments. We then include the dwelling's floor area variable among $Z_{i,c,t}$ instead of $X_{i,c,t}$. Furthermore, we do not know how the distance gradient may evolve after the new policy implementation. Consequently, the interaction between T_c and $D_{i,c}$ should not be specified ex ante (both are arguments of $\mu(.)$).

The estimation procedure is as follows. We first collect all pre-reform housing sales $p_{i,c,t}$ ($t < 1997$). Let n denote the total number of such observations. To control for individual and local unobserved heterogeneity, each reference sale *i* is spatially matched with a fixed number ($\bar{n}$) of post-reform housing sales $\bar{p}_{j,i,c,t'}$ ($t' \geq 1997$, $j = 1,...,\bar{n}$). Different values for the number of nearest neighbors are tested. The matching procedure is done according to the sole spatial criterion (i.e. we gather the $\bar{n}$ post-reform sales nearest to the pre-reform reference point i). We then compute the housing price differential between transaction i and the counterfactual transactions *j*, i.e. $\Delta p_{i,j,c,t,t'} = \bar{p}_{j,c,t'} - p_{i,c,t}$. All these $n \times \bar{n}$ observations are pooled and weighted according to the distance between the focal and counterfactual sales. Let $w_{i,j}$ denote the weight between sales *i* and *j*. $\bar{n}^{-1} \sum_{j=1,...,\bar{n}} w_{i,j} = 1$ for each *i*. In our framework, each pair (i, j) shares the same fixed unobserved effect $\theta_{c,i}$. This is reasonable if the distance between *i* and *j* remains low. Accordingly, the housing price differential becomes

$$\begin{aligned}\Delta p_{i,j,c,t,t'} &= \left(X'_{j,c,t'} - X'_{i,c,t}\right)\beta \\ &+ \left[\mu\left(T_c, I_{j,c}, D_{j,c}, Z_{j,c,t'}\right) - \mu\left(T_c, I_{i,c}, D_{i,c}, Z_{i,c,t}\right)\right] \\ &+ \left(\varepsilon_{j,c,t'} - \varepsilon_{i,c,t}\right)\end{aligned} \qquad \text{(D.2)}$$

where we take advantage of the fact that $I_{j,c} = I_{i,c}$ (if the focal point is within an EZ's boundaries, the spatial matching procedure is done inside the EZ, no counterfactual sale is selected beyond the EZ boundaries and similarly if the focal point is outside the EZ) and $D_{j,c} - D_{i,c} \approx 0$ to reformulate the nonparametric part of the model (second term in bracket in the RHS of preceding equation)

$$\begin{aligned}\overline{\mu}\left(T_c, I_{i,c}, D_{i,c}, Z_{i,c,t}, Z_{j,c,t'}\right) \equiv \mu&\left(T_c, I_{j,c}, D_{j,c}, Z_{j,c,t'}\right) \\ - \mu&\left(T_c, I_{i,c}, D_{i,c}, Z_{i,c,t}\right)\end{aligned} \qquad \text{(D.3)}$$

Such a general setup is subject to the curse of dimensionality due to the large number of covariates (arguments of function $\overline{\mu}$). We limit our approach to a partially linear single-index. The non-linear link function is then defined as $\eta\left(\gamma Y_{i,j,c,t,t'}\right) \equiv \overline{\mu}\left(T_c, I_{i,c}, D_{i,c}, Z_{i,c,t}, Z_{j,c,t'}\right)$ where $Y_{i,j,c,t,t'} = \left(T_c, I_{i,c}, D_{i,c}, Z_{i,c,t}, Z_{j,c,t'}\right)$ and γ is a parameter vector. This single-index assumption implies a lesser degree of generality, since all interactions of elements of Y are captured by the eventual non-linearity in the univariate function $\eta(.)$, but it may still capture important features of our high-dimensional problem and will greatly facilitate the numerical estimation procedure. Applications of the partially linear single-index model may be found in various fields, including housing economics (see for example, Wang et al. (2007) who propose an application of this model to the case of Boston House prices, using a different setup). We implicitly assume that conditionally on the covariates, the growth in housing prices is not related to the treatment variable, $\Delta p_{i,j,c,t,t'}$? $T_c \mid (X, Z, \eta, I, D)$.

Following Yu and Ruppert (2002), we model $\eta(.)$ with a penalized spline (P-spline hereafter). As detailed by Ruppert and Carroll (1997) or Ruppert (2002), P-splines are a generalization of smoothing splines allowing more flexibility in the choice of knots and penalty parameters. Moreover, according to other methods with different link function specifications, P-splines allow for easier and faster regression procedures. For example, we have also estimated our setup with local linear approximations and the minimum average variance estimation (MAVE, see Xia and Härdle, 2006), but convergence was much less rapid. The P-spline function for η is:

$$\eta(a) = \delta_0 + \delta_1 a + \ldots + \delta_p a^p + \sum_{k=1}^{K} \delta_{p+k}\left(a - \kappa_k\right)_+^p \qquad \text{(D.4)}$$

where $\{\kappa_k\}_{k=1}^{K}$ are the spline knots. They capture the jumps in the pth degree of the polynomial. $\delta = \{\delta_0, \delta_1, ..., \delta_{p+K}\}$. Following Yu and Ruppert (2002), the estimation is carried out with several numbers of knots K, ($K = 3$, $5, 10$, more than 10 knots is above the usual practice in applications). The knots are equally spaced along the quantiles of the index, $\gamma Y_{i,j,c,t,t'}$. We adopt the standard penalized and weighted least squares estimators of β, γ and δ which minimize:

$$P_{n,\bar{n},w,\lambda}(\beta,\gamma,\zeta,\delta) = \left(n\bar{n}\right)^{-1} \times$$

$$\sum_{i=1}^{n}\sum_{j=1}^{\bar{n}}\left\{w_{i,j}\left[\left(\bar{p}_{j,c,t'} - p_{i,c,t}\right) - \left(X'_{j,c,t'} - X'_{i,c,t}\right)\beta - \eta\left(\gamma Y_{i,j,c,t,t'}\right)\right]\right\}^2 \quad \text{(D.5)}$$

$$+ \lambda\delta' D\delta$$

where D is a positive semidefinite symmetric matrix. We select D equal to a diagonal matrix with its last K diagonal elements equal to 1 and the rest is zero (Ruppert and Carroll (1997)). We penalize the jumps in the P-spline. $\lambda \geq 0$ is the penalty parameter. Its value is chosen by a standard generalized cross-validation (GCV) selection process which is simultaneously run with the non-linear least squares estimation algorithm. The complete procedure (estimation + GCV) follows closely Yu and Ruppert (2002) approach. After selecting the size of the nearest-neighbors kernel ($\bar{n}$), the polynomial degree (p), the number of knots (K), we obtain initial estimates for β, ζ and γ with OLS on a linear (fully parametric) version of the model. A grid of values for the penalty parameter (λ) is created and $P_{n,\bar{n},w,\lambda}(.)$ is first minimized over δ (with OLS estimates of β, ζ and γ) and then over $(\beta, \zeta, \delta, \gamma)$ for each value of λ. A GCV score is computed for the selection of λ (see equation 21 in Yu and Ruppert, 2002) and the estimation outcome with this value is finally chosen.

5. RESULTS

We present here the results of our P-spline partially linear single-index model. The chosen sample period is [1996; 1997]: i.e., we consider apartment sales one year before the EZ implementation (1996), and one year after (1997). We select the control group as explained in the data presentation section: 8 zones (CUCS) than have not been converted into ZUSs in 1997, but could have been according to their characteristics. We pool all pre-reform sales observations within or close to treated areas (i.e., ZUSs) and within or close to control group zones: close to is defined here as being within a 300 meter radius of the nearest EZ.

Table 2. Estimation. Inner Paris for the 1996 to 1997 period

Hedonic Terms: $X\beta + \eta$	Estimates	s.e.
Level 1 (ref = ground level)	0.0919**	0.0113
Level 2	0.1308**	0.0112
Level 3	0.1306**	0.0111
Level 4 with elev.	0.2006**	0.0108
Level 4 no elev	0.1403**	0.0113
2 rooms (ref = studio)	0.0239**	0.0082
3 rooms	0.0524**	0.0119
4 rooms	0.0564**	0.0160
5+ rooms	0.0636**	0.0209
Parking space (ref = no)	0.0779**	0.0112
Bathroom (ref = no)	0.1486**	0.0057
constr. $\in [1948,1969]$ (ref<1948)	–0.0255	0.0171
constr. $\in [1970,1980]$	0.0622**	0.0178
constr. > 1981	0.1720**	0.0253
2nd quarter (ref = 1st)	–0.0030	0.0071
3rd quarter	–0.0029	0.0072
4th quarter	0.0037	0.0067
Index parameters: γ	Estimates	s.e.
T_c	0.0081	0.0357
$I_{i,c}$	-0.7201**	0.3139
$D_{i,c}$	0.0015	0.0023
$T_c \times I_{i,c}$	0.6404	0.4070
$T_c \times D_{i,c}$	–0.0030	0.0024
$Z_{i,c,t}$ (log floor area reference)	0.2541**	0.0107
$Z_{j,c,t'}$ (log floor area counterfactual)	–0.0822	0.00901
P-spline parameters: δ	Estimates	s.e.
δ_0	-0.1025**	0.0123
δ_1	0.0564**	0.0087
δ_2 (jump)	0.0890**	0.0085
δ_3 (jump)	0.0123	0.0095
δ_4 (jump)	0.0233**	0.0092
δ_5 (jump)	-0.0382**	0.0096
δ_6 (jump)	-0.0885**	0.0095

λ=0.0025, N=7,659. ** = 5% signif, * = 10% signif.
Standard errors are calculated with block-bootstrap procedures

We set $p = 1$ (first degree P-spline polynomial part), as usually done in the literature. We set $n = 3$ (results are qualitatively similar for other values of n). Each pre-reform sale is then spatially matched with 3 post-reform counterfactual sales. The whole sample size is 30,141, which includes all differences in the log of house prices, Δp, between the pre-and post-reform periods. The benchmark control group chosen is also included.

Vector $X_{i,c,t}$ includes a large set of structural attributes for each dwelling: the floor level and presence of an elevator, the number of rooms, the presence of a parking space, a bathroom, the period of construction of the building, the year and quarter of transaction. The only covariate included in $Z_{i,c,t}$ is the log of floor area (in square meters). This continuous variable allows us to capture interactions between the size of dwellings and the treatment effect. Finally, the list of variables used to constitute the index are: T_c, the treatment dummy; $I_{i,c}$ the within-EZ dummy; $D_{i,c}$ the distance (in hundreds of meters) to the nearest EZ boundary; $Z_{i,c,t}$ the log of floor area of the pre-reform reference housing sale i; and $Z_{j,c,t'}$ the log of floor area of post-reform counterfactual housing sale j.

We first conduct some preliminary estimates (obtained with standard parametric methods), in order to assess the relationship between the endogenous variable – the difference in the log of house prices $\Delta p_{i,c,t,t'}$ – and the univariate index $\delta Y_{i,j,c,t,t'}$. We then select the number of knots $K = 5$. As suggested by Ruppert and Carroll (1997), the total number of knots should not exceed 10. In our case, additional knots do not appear to capture significant new locally-linear trends, in the relationship between the endogenous variable (controlling for the linear hedonic term) and the index.

Table 2 gives estimates of model (differential). Results are reported for the three different sets of parameters: β, δ, ζ and γ. We emphasize that the estimates of the index parameter vector γ should not be directly quantitatively interpreted, since they depend on the link function $\eta(.)$ and its parameter estimates. The parameter estimates for the standard hedonic part of the model: i.e., $X\beta$, have the expected sign and magnitude. We put the emphasis on the results for the index $\mu(T_c, I_{i,c}, D_{i,c}, Z_{i,c,t})$. We detect no significant impact of the treatment dummy variable T_c on the dynamics of housing prices between 1996 and 1997. Second, the impact of covariate $(T_c \times I_{i,c})$ on the price growth rate between the pre- and post-reform years is positive, though not significant. The magnitude of the impact of this covariate on home values cannot be directly assessed from the parameters estimates (since it depends on the parameters of the p-spline) and we obtain the ATT (Average Treatment Effect for the Treated) with simulation methods (see Gregoir and Maury, 2014, for a detailed explanation): we find that growth in home prices between 1996 and 1997 has been slightly more than 3 percentage points higher within treated areas, though once again this effect is non significant. Hence, we do not provide evidence of a positive incidence of the French Round I program on targeted EZ in inner Paris. Looking at the data, it seems that this outcome stems from the heterogeneity in home price dynamics between ZUS in Paris: some of them experienced price growth rates above the average of control zones between 1996 and 1997, while other treated zones did not. These differences in price evolution may be the consequence of uncontrolled factors in the benchmark model, but could also be linked to the voluntary nature of aids in first tier EZs (the local authorities can decide in each case to grant aid or not, and these aids will not be compensated by the state). Maybe we would have obtained different results with second or third tier zones (notice that there are only first tier zones in Paris), since tax abatements are mandatory for them. In a companion paper, Gregoir and Maury (2014), working with another administrative unit (the Seine-Saint-Denis département), conclude that the implementation of the Round II local development program in 2004 seems to have contributed negatively to the local value of the housing market, suggesting there has been a stigmatizing effect on areas that became ZFUs (i.e., third tier EZs).

Finally, we detect no significant gap in home prices dynamics between housing units located inside a treated EZ ($I_{i,c}=1$, $T_c=1$) and housing units located in their immediate vicinity ($I_{i,c}=0$, $T_c=1$, $D_{i,c}\approx 0$). The positive impact of the $(T_c \times I_{i,c})$ covariate is dampened by the negative impact of the $I_{i,c}$ covariate. On the contrary, price have grown less inside a non-treated (control) zone ($I_{i,c}=1$, $T_c=0$) than in their immediate vicinity ($I_{i,c}=0$, $T_c=0$, $D_{i,c}\approx 0$). We find no significant relationship between the distance to the closest EZ border ($D_{i,c}$) and the growth rate of property values.

CONCLUSION

In a flexible semi-parametric framework, we analyze the impact of a particular EZ policy implemented in 1997 on real estate values within and in the vicinity of nine areas in Paris inner city. Whereas such policies are designed to regenerate urban environment through incentives to conduct local amenities projects and financial aid to new homeowners, we do not detect any significant impact of this program on housing prices at any level in comparison with what has been observed in areas, similar from a social and economic descriptive point of view but not included in the program. This is at odd with the objectives of such policies and with the results obtained in a companion study on their impacts on suburb areas in which a significant negative impact was detected. This may be due to the heterogeneity of the selected areas, some may have been positively impacted by the policy and some negatively, or to the fact the policy was undersized.

REFERENCES

Busso P. and P. Kline, 2007, Do Local Economic Development Programs Work? Evidence from the Federal Empowerment Zone Program, Yale Economics Department Working Paper 36.

Engberg J. and R. Greenbaum, 1999, State Enterprise Zones and Local Housing Markets, *Journal of Housing Research*, 10(2), 163-187.

Ernst E., 2008, L'activité économique dans les ZFU, *INSEE Première*, 1187.

Fack G. and J. Grenet, 2010, When do Better Schools Raise Housing Prices? Evidence from Paris Public and Private Schools, *Journal of Public Economics*, 94, 59-77.

Gilli F., 2006, Entreprises et Développement Urbain: les Zones Franches ont-elle rempli leur mission ?, in *Les Entreprises Françaises en 2006*, De Boissieu and Deneuve (eds), Economica, Chapter 10, 163-187.

Givord P., Rathelot R. and P. Sillard, 2011, Place-Based Tax Exemptions and Displacement Effects: An Evaluation of the Zones Franches Urbaines Program, *CREST* WP n° 2011-19.

Gobillon L., Magnac T. and H. Selod, 2010, Do Unemployed Workers Benefit from Enterprises Zones? The French Experience, *IDEI* WP n ° 645.

Gregoir S. and T.-P. Maury, 2014, Empowerment Zones and the Housing Market: The French Case, *mimeo*.

Krupka D. and D. Noonan, 2009, Empowerment Zones, Neighborhood Changes and Owner-Occupied Housing, *Regional Science and Urban Economics*, 39(4), 386-396.

Neumark D. and J. Kolko, 2010, Do Enterprise Zones Create Jobs? Evidence from California's Enterprise Zone Program, *Journal of Urban Economics*, 68, 1-19.

Ruppert D., 2002, Selecting the Number of Knots for Penalized Splines, *Journal of Computational and Graphical Statistics*, 11(4), 735-757.

Ruppert D. and R. Carroll, 1997, Penalized Regression Splines, Cornell University, School of Operations Research and Industrial Engineering, *mimeo*.

Thélot H., 2004, Les embauches en Zone Franche Urbaine en 2002, *Premières Informations, Premières Synthèses*, 35-1.

Wang J.-L., Xue L., Zhu L. and Y.S. Chong, 2010, Estimation for a Partial-Linear Single-Index Model, University of California at Irvine, *mimeo*.

Xia Y. and W. Härdle, 2006, Semi-Parametric Estimation of Partially Linear Single-Index Models, *Journal of Multivariate Analysis*, 97, 1162-1184.

Yu Y. and D. Ruppert, 2002, Penalized Spline Estimation for Partially Linear Single-Index Models, *Journal of the American Statistical Association*, 97, 1042-1054.

LE MARCHÉ DU LOGEMENT PARISIEN ET LES ZONES URBAINES SENSIBLES

Résumé - *Nous estimons l'impact des zones franches sur le marché du logement parisien. En 1997, trois types de zones franches ont été mis en place (ZUS, ZRU and ZFU). En particulier, 9 zones urbaines sensibles (ZUS) ont été créées dans Paris intra-muros. Nous comparons l'évolution des prix des appartements dans ces zones à celle observée dans des zones voisines comparables. Nous proposons une nouvelle méthode semi-paramétrique avec appariement géographique. Chaque vente observée avant la réforme est couplée à un ensemble de ventes observées après la mise en place de la réforme. Cette procédure d'appariement est effectuée pour des logements situés dans ou à proximité d'une ZUS. Nous ne détectons pas d'effet significatif de ce programme de zones franches sur les valeurs immobilières.*

Mots-clés - ZONES URBAINES SENSIBLES, PRIX DE L'IMMOBILIER, APPARIEMENT GÉOGRAPHIQUE

TESTING AREAL INTERPOLATION METHODS WITH US CENSUS 2010 DATA

Huyen DO VAN[1], Christine THOMAS-AGNAN[2], Anne VANHEMS[3]

Abstract - *The areal interpolation problem is that of projecting a characteristic of interest on a partition of space called target partition from the knowledge of the same characteristic on a different partition, so called source partition, using some auxiliary information. The objective of this paper is to use a demographic database available in the R package 'US census 2010' (Almquist, 2010) in order to test several areal interpolation methods based on regression in the case of count related data. The fact that data is available at many different spatial scales in this database make this comparison study unique. Another innovative point of view is that we compare the extensive approach versus the intensive approach for a variable which is a ratio of counts. We also include the comparison with the scaled regression for the extensive case introduced in Do et al. (2015) and with a scaled regression for the intensive case proposed here. Finally we give some empirical guidelines for the choice of auxiliary information.*

Keywords - AREAL INTERPOLATION, SPATIAL DISAGGREGATION, PYCNOPHYLACTIC PROPERTY

Classification JEL - C83; C15; R15

We would like to thank A. Ruiz-Gazen and C. Vignes for fruitful discussions. This work was supported by the French Agence Nationale de la Recherche through the ModU-Land project (ANR-11-BSH1-005).

[1] Toulouse School of Economics (GREMAQ) ; huyendvmath@gmail
[2] Toulouse School of Economics (GREMAQ) ; Christine.Thomas@tse-fr.eu
[3] Toulouse Business School and Toulouse School of Economics ; a.vanhems@tbs-education.fr

1. INTRODUCTION

The areal interpolation problem often arises in the analysis of socio-economic data involving the combination of several databases originating from different administrative sources. It is the problem of transferring a given variable called target variable known on an initial partition of space into source zones to another partition of the same space into target zones. Do et al. (2014) review these statistical spatial allocation rules concentrating on the simplest ones. Do et al. (2015) analyze the accuracy of these methods in the case of count data. For a set of random points in a region of space, a count variable is defined by the numbers of these points in given subdivisions of this region. Demographic data are of this nature since they are counts of different types of people in different subdivisions of space. A related type of variable is a density variable: number of points per areal unit associated to a set of random points in space. A count variable is said extensive when its value on a region is obtained by summing up its values on any partition into subregions. A density variable is said intensive in the sense that its value on a region is obtained from values on any partition into subregions by a weighted sum (see Do et al. 2014 for more details). In the case of population density, the weights are given by the areas of the subregions of the partition. A more general case of count related variable that we will consider is a ratio of two count variables which turns out to be intensive.

The aim of this paper is to derive some empirical guidelines of application for several areal interpolation methods and confront the empirical evidence with some theoretical results of Do et al. (2015) using the demographic database 'US census 2010' (Almquist, 2010) available in an R package. We concentrate on count related data and focus particularly on the following points. The data is presented in section 2. We recall the main methods in section 3. In section 4.1 we give some directives for the selection of a good auxiliary variable when there is a choice. In section 4.2 we compare the accuracy of the regression methods. The regression methods developed for the extensive case are different from the ones adapted to the intensive case. Since it is easy to transform an extensive variable into a corresponding intensive one and reversely, we explore in section 4.3 the question of whether it is best to use the extensive-type or intensive-type regression method. Finally we investigate in section 4.4 the effect of the spatial scale.

2. DATA

The UScensus2000 database contains data from the US decennial census at several different geographic levels (in particular: states, counties, tracts, block groups and blocks). The package contains functions for aggregating the demographic information at any of these levels. It is therefore highly adapted to test areal interpolation techniques. Since all considered variables are available at all geographical levels, we will be able to assess the accuracy of the considered interpolation methods based on the true target values on the selected target zones.

Following Almquist (2010), we choose to work with the target variable corresponding to the number of house owners in a given zone for the extensive case. We also select a corresponding intensive variable which is the percentage of house owners, the weights being given by the number of households in the given zone. As potential auxiliary information, we use the covariates presented in Almquist (2010) which are the number (resp: percentage) of non hispanic white, of non hispanic black, of non hispanic asian, of hispanic, of married households with children in the population. The first four percentages are with respect to the population whereas the last one is with respect to the number of households. As far as spatial scale is concerned, we decide to use three different scenarios in the state of Ohio. The first scenario is the disaggregation of the target variable from county level (source) to tract level (target) for the whole of the state of Ohio. Ohio has 88 counties and 2941 tracts so that on average one county contains 33 tracts. The second and third scenario use the county of Franklin as the whole region. Franklin counts 284 tracts, 887 block groups and 22826 blocks. The second scenario is the disaggregation of the target variable from tracts (source) to block groups (targets) in the county of Franklin. In this case, one track contains on average 3 block groups. The third scenario is the disaggregation of the target variable from tracts (source) to blocks (targets) and in that case one tract contains on average 80 blocks. A particular feature of these scenarios is that in all cases the target zones are nested within the source zones.

We first perform some exploratory analysis of the variables at source and at target levels. At the county level (source) for the whole Ohio, all extensive variables are strongly positively correlated whereas the corresponding intensive variables are much less correlated and display some negative correlations. For example the percentage of white is negatively strongly correlated with the percentage of black (-0.97) but the percentage of hispanic has no clear linear relationship with other intensive variables. At the tract level (source) on Franklin county, the correlations are smaller. More precisely, the number of house owners is still strongly positively correlated with population, number of households, number of whites and married households with children, but not clearly correlated with number of blacks, number of asians and hispanic. For corresponding intensive variables, correlations are smaller than 0.4 except for percentage of white and percentage of blacks which are strongly negatively correlated (-0.97). On Franklin, correlations at tract level are very similar to correlations at block group level (target).

3. METHODS

Let us first briefly summarize the methods we will compare. For more details about these methods, we refer the reader to Do et al. (2014). We focus on the family of simple regression methods which include as a special case the dasymetric methods (see Do et al., 2015).

The value of the target variable Y on a given subzone A is denoted by Y_A and similarly for other variables. For the source zones S_s ; $s = 1,..., S$ as well as for the target zones T_t ; $t = 1,..., T$ the notations S_s and T_t will be used instead to designate a generic source and a generic target. Because of the nested nature of our case here, the intersections between sources and targets coincide with targets.

As shown in Do et al. (2014), the correspondence between intensive and extensive is as follows. It is possible to associate an intensive variable to a given extensive variable by the following scheme. If Y is extensive, and if w_A is a weighting scheme of the form

$$w_{\Omega_k} = \frac{Z_{\Omega_k}}{Z_\Omega}, \tag{1}$$

where $w_k, k=1,2,...$ form a partition of a region Ω, and where Z is another count variable, the variable

$$\tilde{Y}_\Omega = \frac{Y_A}{Z_A} \tag{2}$$

is intensive since

$$\tilde{Y}_\Omega = \frac{\sum_k Y_{\Omega_k}}{Z_\Omega} = \sum_k \frac{Z_{\Omega_k}}{Z_\Omega}\frac{Y_{\Omega_k}}{Z_{\Omega_k}} = \sum_k w_{\Omega_k}\tilde{Y}_{\Omega_k}.$$

Reversely, if one starts from an intensive variable Y with weighting scheme w_A of the form (1), it can be transformed into an extensive variable by inverting equation (2). In our case, Y_A is the number of house owners in subregion A and $\tilde{Y}_A$ is the percentage of house owners in subregion A while Z_A is the number of households of subregion A.

Given one auxiliary information X, the general dasymetric method predicts the value of Y_t for $t \subset s$ as

$$\hat{Y}_t^D = \frac{X_t}{X_s} Y_s. \tag{3}$$

The formula is the same for intensive and extensive variables but one uses an auxiliary information of the same nature (intensive/extensive) as the target variable. Note that when the auxiliary information is simply the area of the zone, the method is called areal weighting interpolation and it is rather meant for an extensive variable. Note also that areal weighting interpolation applied to an intensive variable is actually equivalent to the dasymetric method applied to the corresponding extensive variable with auxiliary variable being given by its weights.

For regression methods, the type of regression will differ according to the intensive/extensive nature of the variable. For an intensive variable, a gaussian linear regression is used (Flowerdew and Green, 1992) whereas for an extensive variable, one uses rather a Poisson regression (Flowerdew and Green, 1989). As for dasymetric, one uses auxiliary information of the same nature (intensive/extensive) as the target variable.

Let us briefly recall the steps of Poisson regression for an extensive target variable. The distributional assumption is that the mean of Y depends linearly on a set of auxiliary variables X^i , $i=1,2,\ldots,p$ known at target level:

$$Y_A \sim \mathrm{P}\left(\sum_{i=1}^{p} \alpha_i X_A^i\right) \tag{4}$$

A regression of the set of source values based on model (4) is performed at source level yielding estimates $\hat{\alpha}_i$ and used at target level to predict the target values by

$$\hat{Y}_t^{REG} = \sum_{i=1}^{p} \hat{\alpha}_i X_t^i \tag{5}$$

For the intensive target variable case, the distributional assumption, as presented in Flowerdew and Green (1992), is that

$$Y_A \sim \mathrm{N}\left(\sum_{i=1}^{p} \alpha_i X_A^i , \sigma^2 / n_A\right) \tag{6}$$

where n_A are known and represent the number of underlying points in A. It is thus an intensive variable for which the weights at target level are given by $w_{t:t\subset s} = \dfrac{n_t}{n_s}$. Based on model (6) and on these aggregation weights for Y, one gets the following regression equation at source level

$$(Y_1,\ldots,Y_n)' = WX(\alpha_1,\ldots,\alpha_p)' + \varepsilon \tag{7}$$

where W is the $S\times T$ matrix with elements $w_{t:t\subset s}$ and X is the matrix with elements x_{tj} being the values of auxiliary variable j on target t. The estimation of this model yields estimates $\hat{\alpha}_i$ used to predict the target values by

$$(\hat{Y}_{t_1}^{REG},\ldots,\hat{Y}_{t_T}^{REG})' = X(\hat{\alpha}_1,\ldots,\hat{\alpha}_p)' \tag{8}$$

Do et al. (2015) introduce a so called scaled regression by constraining the Poisson regression to enforce the often quoted pycnophylactic property. It is the property of preservation of the initial data in the following sense: the predicted value on source S_s obtained by aggregating the predicted values on intersections with S_s coincides with the observed value on S_s:

$$\sum_{t:t\subset s} \hat{Y}_t = Y_s$$

For the Poisson regression, we get the following correction of the regression predictor, for $t \subset s$:

$$\hat{Y}_t^{SCL} = \frac{\hat{Y}_t^{REG}}{\hat{Y}_s^{REG}} Y_s \,, \tag{9}$$

where $\hat{Y}_s^{REG}$ is simply given by the aggregation rule $\hat{Y}_s^{REG} = \sum_{t \subset s} \hat{Y}_t^{REG}$. We propose here to do the same for gaussian regression of intensive variables by using the empirical conditional expectation of Y_t given the source values, i.e. for $t \subset s$

$$\hat{Y}_t^{SCL} = \hat{\mathrm{E}}(Y_t \mid Y_1, Y_2, \ldots, Y_s) = \hat{Y}_t^{REG} - \hat{Y}_s^{REG} + Y_s \,, \tag{10}$$

where $\hat{Y}_t^{REG}$ and $\hat{Y}_s^{REG}$ are the fitted values for Y_t and Y_s respectively and where $\hat{Y}_s^{REG}$ is simply given by the aggregation rule $\hat{Y}_s^{REG} = \sum_{t \subset s} w_t \hat{Y}_t^{REG}$.

A very important point for the sequel, which is shown in Do et al. (2015), is that the dasymetric method with a given auxiliary information is equivalent to the scaled Poisson regression with this auxiliary variable as unique regressor without a constant .

Another approach for this problem is to use an EM-algorithm strategy as done in Flowerdew and Green (1991) for the Poisson case and in Flowerdew and Green (1992) for the Gaussian case. Indeed the areal interpolation can be considered as a missing data problem with target values as missing data. We can summarize the steps as follows: the expectation step (E-step) is either (9) or (10) and yield values for the targets and the maximization step is the regression at target level based on models (4) or (6).

4. RESULTS

Table 1 summarizes the notations used for presenting the results. To illustrate the meaning of this table, let us take two examples. The indices have two or three positions: for example "Dhh" or "I.Dhh". When necessary, an additional index in position one will indicate either the intensive/extensive nature or the spatial support depending upon background.

In positions 2 and 3 (potentially after the dot), an index "Dhh" means that we are using the *dasymetric* method (D) with the auxiliary information *percentage of households* (hh). An index "I.Dhh" specifies moreover that it is for the *intensive* target variable (percentage of house owner).

In positions 2 and 3, an index "Ebe" means that we are using the regression method with the *EM* algorithm (E) for the *best* model choice (be) (independent variables are chosen by AIC criteria). An index "B.Ebe" specifies moreover that it is for the with *blocks* as target zones.

Table 1. Notations

Meaning		Notation	Index Position
Dependent Variables	Intensive	I.	1
	Extensive	E.	
Spatial support	Block	B.	1
	Block group	Bg.	
Methods	Dasymetric	D	2
	Regression	R	
	Scaled regression	S	
	EM	E	
Independent variables	number/percentage of white	w	3
	number/percentage of black	b	
	number/percentage of asian	a	
	number/percentage of hispanic	h	
	number/percentage of married with children	m	
	Population	p	
	Households	hh	
	Area	aa	
	full (all variables)	f	
	best variable choice	be	

At source level, the criterion for evaluating the quality of methods is the relative error of prediction

$$e_s = \frac{\sqrt{\sum_{t \subset s} (\hat{Y}_t - Y_t)^2}}{Y_s}.$$

4.1. Auxiliary information selection

The choice of a good auxiliary information is an important question for areal interpolation in practice. First of all, it is unclear whether a choice of variables which is good for the regression step will be the best for predicting target values. On the other hand, it it difficult to devise a prediction-targeted criterion adapted to this situation: indeed, one does not observe any target value hence it is not straightforward to extend cross-validation to this case. By lack of a better alternative, we have chosen to use a variable choice strategy based on the AIC criterion. Note this selection has been performed using the R package *MASS* for gaussian regression and the R package *glmulti* for Poisson regression.

Table 2. Performance of the dasymetric method for each auxiliary information

Methods	Dw	Dm	Dp	Dhh	Dh	Daa	Da	Db
error	2.76	3.10	3.14	3.75	14.97	21.95	22.87	31.31
correlation	0.99	0.99	1	1	0.88	0.02	0.93	0.95

We compare several dasymetric methods obtained by using the different auxiliary information at our disposal using scenario 1 (Ohio) for the extensive case. Table 2 displays the corresponding median error criterions showing that it is very important to select the best auxiliary information since the relative error can vary from around 3 percent to 30 percent. The second row displays the correlations and the non monotonicity of these numbers shows that one should not trust correlation to select an auxiliary information. Figure 1 presents the boxplots of the source errors for the best dasymetric (here: based on the number of whites), the worst dasymetric (here: the number of blacks) and an intermediate case corresponding to areal weighting interpolation. We see that not only the best choice outperforms the other ones by far but also that the variability accross sources is quite high for these choices.

Figure 1. Dasymetric methods for Ohio - extensive approach

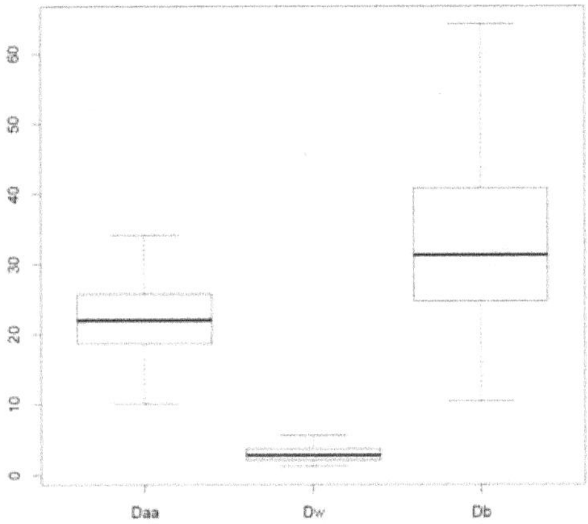

4.2. Comparison between different regression methods

In this section, we focus on comparing the different methods using scenario 1 (Ohio) for the extensive case. The implementation of the Poisson regression approach presents some peculiarities. The first one is about the choice of link function. The usual choice for Poisson regression is the logarithm link leading to $\mathrm{E}(Y)=\exp(\sum_{i=1}^{p}\beta_i X_i)$ and it is the so called natural link in this generalized linear model. However we argue in Do et al. (2015) that the identity link is more adapted when relating such extensive variables to auxiliary extensive variables. For example, it seems more natural that the *number of house owners* is proportional to the *population* rather than to be exponentially related to the population. Moreover, empirically, the AIC criterion is 1000 times bigger for the log link specification.

The second one is about the constant term. With the identity link, it does not make sense to include a constant in such a model because a constant is not an extensive variable.

Figure 2 presents the boxplots of the counties error criterions for the state of Ohio and for the Poisson regression performed on the *number of house owners*. Table 3 presents the corresponding median error criterions.

Figure 2. Poisson regression methods for Ohio - extensive approach

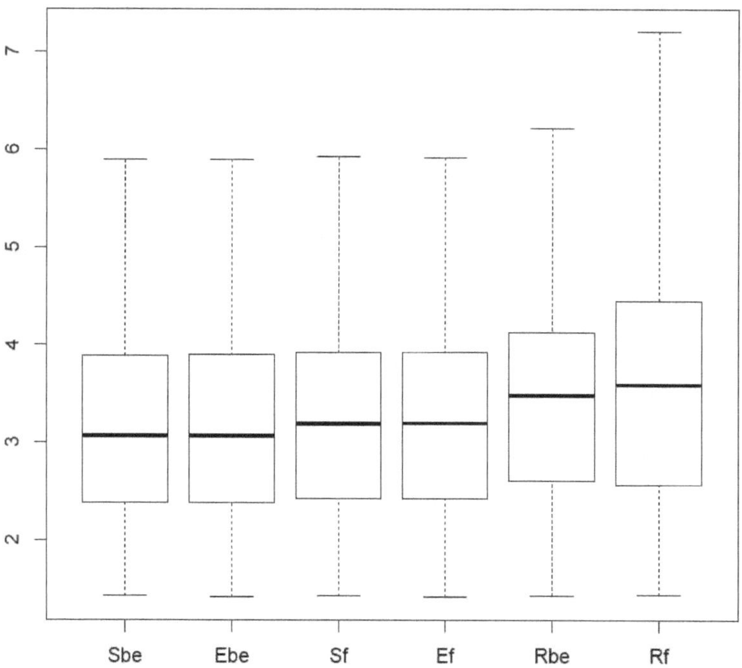

Table 3. Median error criterions - Poisson regressions for Ohio

Sbe	Ebe	Sf	Ef	Rbe	Rf
3.069	3.069	3.193	3.196	3.482	3.594

The order of magnitude of the errors is around 3 percent and they are very comparable. The selection of variables strategy selects the model without the variables *married household with children and area* but it seems that keeping a full model does not make a big difference. We see that the scaled regression tends to perform better in general, and even better than the EM approach. However, it turns out that the best of the regression methods gets a 3.069 error criterion and does not outperform the best dasymetric obtained in the previous section with a 2.764 error criterion.

4.3. Intensive versus extensive approach

For the purpose of interpolating the target variable *number of house owners*, we have the choice between two strategies. The first one is to work on the raw variable which is extensive and use a Poisson regression approach. The second one is to work on the *percentage of house owners*, use a gaussian regression approach and transform back the predicted percentages into counts using the knowledge of population on targets if known. In a different situation when this knowledge is not guaranteed, a more complex method is available which disaggregates separately numerator and denominator of this percentage using extensive variables methods. In this section we compare the first two approaches only, the last one giving results very similar to the second one in our case. We use scenarios 1 and 2. For Ohio in scenario 1, Figure 3 shows that the best method is the dasymetric method with auxiliary information given by the *number of whites* applied to the count target variable *number of house owners*. For Franklin in scenario 2, the right panel of Figure 6 shows again that the best result is obtained when working with the count variable rather than the percentage and it is obtained by the regression on the best subset of auxiliary variables. We also see that scaled gaussian regression that we introduced in section 3 is the second best.

Figure 3. Best methods for Ohio - intensive and extensive approaches

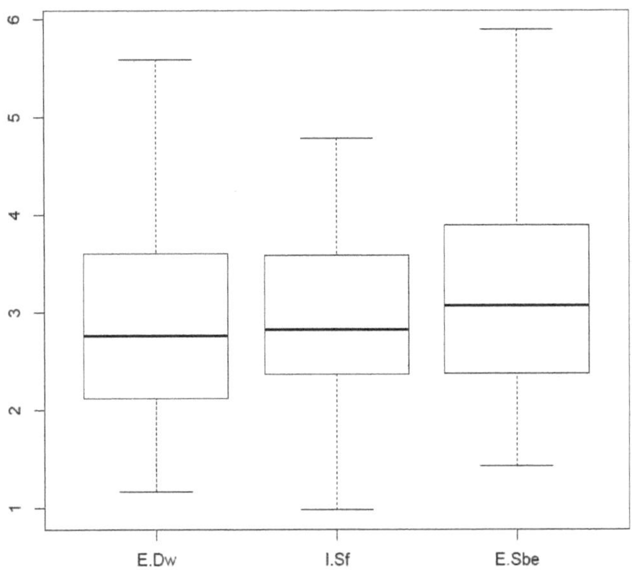

4.4. Spatial scale

In this section, we examine the effect of spatial scale on the areal interpolation problem. For this we compare scenarios 2 and 3 on the county of Franklin. Figure 4 (respectively Figure 5) presents the distributions across sources of the error criterion in the case of disaggregation of the extensive variable *number of house owners* (respectively of the intensive variable *percentage of house owners*) at block level and at block group level. Tables 4 and 5 display the corresponding median error criterions.

Figure 4. Methods for the extensive case for Franklin

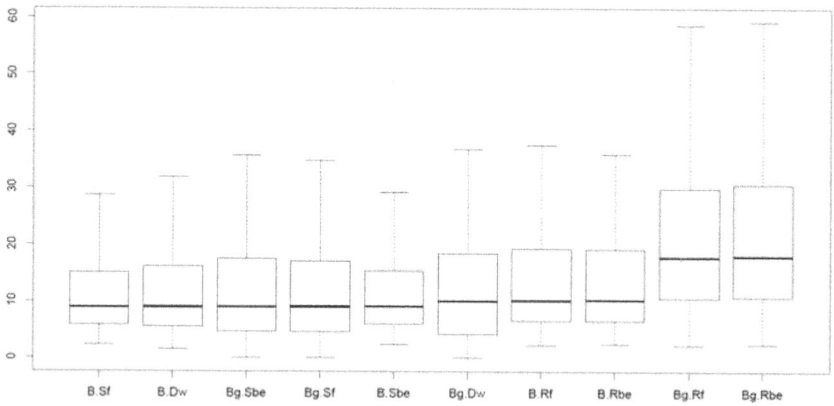

Table 4. Performance of the methods in the extensive case

B.Sf	B.Dw	Bg.Sb	Bg.Sf	B.Sb	Bg.Dw	B.Rf	B.Rb	Bg.Rf	Bg.Sb
8.884	8.962	8.964	9.041	9.097	10.041	10.178	10.246	17.808	17.969

For the extensive case, the best model strategy selects the model without the variables *number of blacks* and *area.* For the intensive case, the best model is the full model.

We note that the best accuracy for Franklin is around 10% whereas it is around 3% for Ohio. The two situations are difficult to compare because even though the number of targets per source is 33 for Ohio and is between 3 for scenario 2 on Franklin and 80 for scenario 3 on Franklin, on the other hand, there are larger numbers of house owners on the sources of Ohio than the sources of Franklin and the sizes of sources and targets are different.

When we compare scenarios 2 and 3 on Figure 6, we see that disaggregation to blocks is more accurate than to blockgroups. Even though the second problem seems easier because the blockgroups are coarser than blocks, one should not forget that the auxiliary information is used at target level resulting in a larger amount of information used for blocks. The medians of source error criterions at block level are thus slightly smaller and the variances are much smaller.

Figure 5. Methods for the intensive case for Franklin

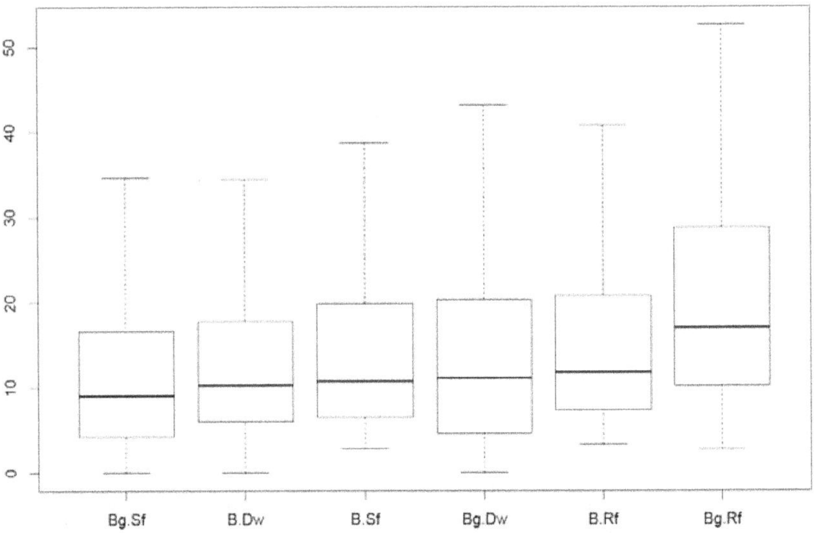

Table 5. Performance of the methods in the intensive case

Bg.Sf	B.Dw	B.Sf	Bg.Dw	B.Rf	Bg.Rf
8.993	10.24	10.684	11.102	11.761	17.013

Figure 6. Comparison of block (left) and blockgroup (right) levels for Franklin intensive and extensive variables

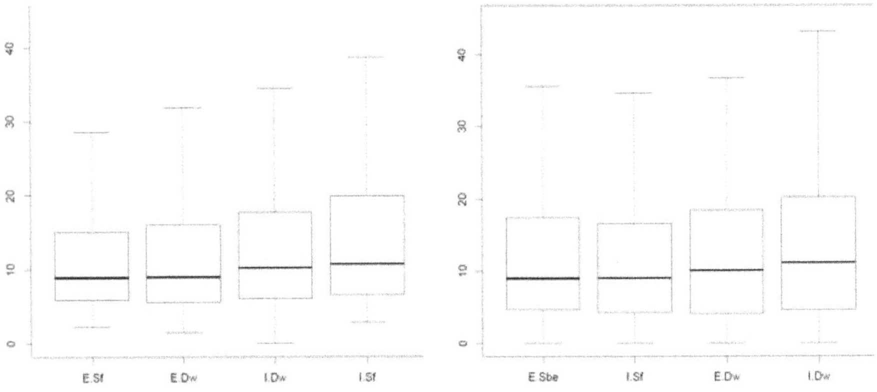

Finally, it turns out that the scaled regression methods always outperform the unscaled ones and that the improvement is stronger at block group level than at block level because the information is poorer at block group level. Indeed before scaling the regression methods at block group level were much worse than at block level and the scaling almost wipes off this difference.

5. CONCLUSION

We should keep in mind that this study has a particular geometry due to the nesting of targets into sources. In a more general case, some border effects will interplay but we believe that, as long as the size of targets is much smaller than the size of sources (disaggregation), the results should not be very different.

We would like to emphasize the three main conclusions of this study. About the choice of auxiliary variable for the dasymetric method we have seen that the performance can vary wildly from one choice to another so this choice is crucial. The second one is that sometimes dasymetric can be better than scaled regression which means that it might be more important to select one good auxiliary information rather than throwing a lot of weakly related variables in the regression. The last one is that scaled regression is very close to the EM algorithm (and much simpler) and often even better.

REFERENCES

Almquist Z. W. (2010). US Census spatial and demographic data in R: the UScensus2000 suite of packages. *Journal of Statistical Software*, 37, 1-31.

Calcagno V., de Mazancourt C. (2010). glmulti: An R Package for Easy Automated Model Selection with (Generalized) Linear Models. *Journal of Statistical Software*, 34, 12.

Do Van H., Thomas-Agnan C., Vanhems A. (2014). Accuracy of areal interpolation methods: Count data, preprint.

Do Van H., Thomas-Agnan C., Vanhems A. (2015). Spatial reallocation of areal data: a review, *Revue d'Economie Régionale et Urbaine*, Forthcoming.

Flowerdew R., Green M. (1992). Developments in areal interpolation methods and GIS, *The Annals of Regional Science*, 26, 67-78.

Flowerdew R., Green M., Kehris E. (1991). Using areal interpolation methods in geographic information systems. *Papers in Regional Science*, Vol. 70, Issue 3, 303-315

Hastie T., Tibshirani R., Friedman J. (2009). The Elements of Statistical Learning: Data Mining, Inference, and Prediction, Second Edition. *Springer Series in Statistics*. 2nd ed.

Ripley B., Venables B., Bates D.M., Hornik K., Gebhardt A., Firth D. http://cran.r-project.org/web/packages/MASS/MASS.pdf

COMPARAISON DES MÉTHODES DE RÉAFFECTATION SPATIALE DE DONNÉES SURFACIQUES SUR LA BASE DES DONNÉES DU RECENSEMENT DE POPULATION DE 2010 AUX ETATS-UNIS

Résumé - *Le problème d'interpolation spatiale de données surfaciques est celui de la réaffectation d'une caractéristique sur une partition cible de l'espace à partir de la connaissance de cette même caractéristique sur une autre partition appelée source en utilisant de l'information auxiliaire. L'objectif de ce travail est d'utiliser une base de données démographiques 'US census 2010' disponible dans le* package *de R (Almquist, 2010) dans le but de tester plusieurs méthodes basées sur la régression dans le cas de données liées à des comptages. Le fait que les données de cette base soient disponibles à différentes échelles spatiales fait l'originalité et l'intérêt de cette comparaison. Un autre apport original de notre démarche est la comparaison entre l'approche extensive et l'approche intensive pour une variable qui est un rapport de deux variables de comptage. Nous incluons également dans la comparaison la version normalisée de la régression dans le cas extensif introduit dans Do et al. (2015) et avec la version normalisée de la régression dans le cas intensif proposée ici. Finalement nous formulons quelques conseils pour choisir des variables auxiliaires.*

Mots-clés - INTERPOLATION DE DONNÉES SURFACIQUES, PROPRIÉTÉ PYCNOPHYLACTIQUE, DÉSAGRÉGATION SPATIALE

LOCAL DIRECTIONAL MORAN SCATTER PLOT - LDMS

Davide FIASCHI[a], Lisa GIANMOENA[b], Angela PARENTI[c]

Abstract - *This paper propose a novel methodology to estimate the distribution dynamics of income in presence of spatial dependence by representing spatial dynamics as a random vector field in Moran space. Inference on the local spatial dynamics is discussed, including a test on the presence of local spatial dependence. The methodology also allows to compute a forecast of future income distribution which includes also the effects of spatial dependence. An application to US States is used to illustrate the effective capacities of the methodology.*

Keywords - EXPLORATORY DATA ANALYSIS, POLARIZATION, RANDOM VECTOR FIELD, DISTRIBUTION DYNAMICS, SPATIAL DYNAMICS, SPATIAL DEPENDENCE, US STATES

Classification JEL - C14; O51; R11

[a] Dipartimento di Economia e Management, Via Ridolfi 10, 56124, Pisa, Italy. E-mail: dfiaschi@ec.unipi.it
[b] IMT Institute for Advanced Studies Lucca, e-mail: lisa.gianmoena@imtlucca.it
[c] IMT Institute for Advanced Studies Lucca, e-mail: angela.parenti@imtlucca.it

1. INTRODUCTION

This paper proposes a new methodology to study the distribution dynamics of income in presence of spatial dependence. Our proposal is the result of two converging strands of literature denoted ETSDA (Exploratory Time-Space Data Analysis) and ESTDA (Exploratory Space-Time Data Analysis) by Rey (2014).

From one hand, literature on ETSDA extends the methods used in the temporal studies on income dynamics in order to incorporate spatial dimension. Quah (1993) can be considered the pioneering contribution to ETSDA for his attempt to measure the impact of spatial dependence mapping unconditioned income levels of countries into *normalized* income levels, where normalization is respect to the incomes of neighbouring countries. Gerolimetto and Magrini (2014) represents one of more recent and most significant contribution in this line of research.

On the other hand, literature on ESTDA extends the spatial methods generally used for detecting spatial dependence in cross-sectional analysis, as the Moran's I and LISA statistics, to incorporate temporal dimension. Recently within this line of research Rey et al. (2011) have proposed the *Directional Moran Scatter Plot* to study the spatial dynamics of US states. The latter consists in analysing in the Moran space (the space defined by countries' income and its spatially lagged value) the directions of the movement vectors standardized by their beginning points, i.e. the transitions that each state has experimented between the first and the last year centered in the orgin of axes.[4]

In this paper we propose a *local* version of the Directional Moran Scatter Plot, labelled *Local Directional Moran Scatter Plot* (LDMS), which consists in the estimate of a random vector field in the Moran space exploiting the information from the observed movement vectors. With respect to Directional Moran Scatter Plot our methodology allows to conduct inference on the local spatial dynamics, and to provide a forecast of the future income distribution which takes into account also spatial dependence.

The next section gives an heuristic introduction to the Local Directional Moran Scatter Plot; Section 3 discusses the nonparametric methodology used in its estimate, and how to make some inference at local level; Section 4 illustrates the use of LDMS to forecast the distribution dynamics of income in presence of spatial dependence. Section 5 concludes.

2. THE LOCAL DIRECTIONAL MORAN SCATTER PLOT

To gain the intuition of our proposed methodology consider Fig. 1, which reports the Moran Scatterplot (i.e. the levels of relative per capita GDP y

[4] The movement vectors can also be standardized by their ending point. In any case, the standardized movement vectors are placed at a common origin, but they preserve their length and direction.

versus its spatially lagged values Wy) for a sample of 49 US states in 1987 (red points) and 2013 (black points).[5]

Figure 1. Moran Scatterplot of relative GDP per capita of a sample of 49 US states for 1987 (red points) and 2013 (black points)

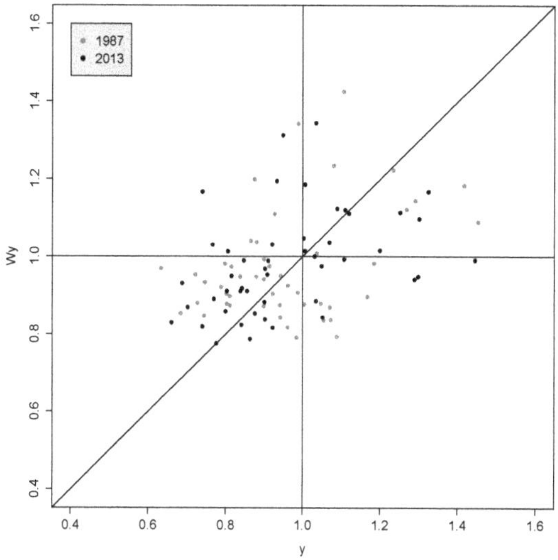

Spatial matrix W is defined by rook contiguity.

For both years Moran's I is positive (equal to 0.10 in 1987 and 0.13 in 2013) and statistically significant at 10%, suggesting that some spatial dependence should be at work; however, from Moran Scatter Plot no information can be extracted on the *impact* of this spatial dependence on the distribution of GDP per capita in terms of its strength and direction.[6]

A possibility to fill this gap is to assume that, in the same spirit of the distribution dynamics approach (see Quah 1997), the dynamics of GDP per capita of an economy can be expressed as a (random) function of only its position in the Moran space, i.e. the dynamics of GDP per capita follows a Markovian process, where the states are defined in terms both of the (relative) level of GDP per capita y and its spatially lagged values Wy (instead of only y). This corresponds to the estimate of a *random vector field* in Moran space, which we label *Local Directional Moran Scatter Plot* (LDMS).[7]

---

[5] The spatial matrix Wy is defined by rook contiguity; given this definition of spatial dependence, we exclude from the sample the two US states without any link (Alaska and Hawaii).

[6] Using a six-nearest neighbor spatial weight matrix, Gerolimetto and Magrini (2014) finds statistically significant spatial dependence across US States. Morevoer, their estimated Moran's I is generally higher.

[7] A vector field in a plane can be visualized as a collection of arrows with a given

Figure 2. Movement vectors in the Moran space (y, Wy) for a sample of 49 US states over the period 1987-2013

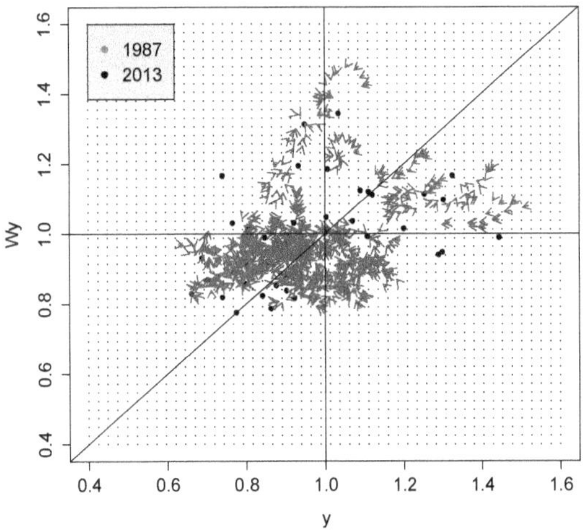

The *movement vectors* reported in Fig. 2, representing all the observed transitions calculated with a time lag of 10 years and expressed in annual scale (1-year ahead) in the Moran space (y, Wy), provides the basic information set to estimate a LDMS.[8] In particular, Fig. 2 contains 49 x (2013-1987-10+1) = 833 movement vectors. For comparison, Rey et al. (2011) in the upper panel of their Fig. 2 reports only 49 movement vectors, representing the transitions from the first to the last year (1969 and 2008 respectively) of each state in the sample. Nonetheless the different time period considered, the overall picture of spatial dynamics looks very similar in the most of Moran space (the south-west quadrant contains the most of observations with a spatial dynamics converging toward bisector), but with some important differences (the spatial dynamics in the north-east and south-east quadrants).

Figure 2 suggests an overall pattern of convergence to bisector and, in particular, towards the region around point (1,1), although such convergence is absent or very weak for other regions of the Moran space, as for example that around (1.3,1.1). In general, the presence of a strong random component in US states' movements makes difficult to identify any spatial pattern by only a graphical inspection, especially when the number of movement vectors is very large as in our case.

In the next section we discuss how to properly estimate a LDMS by the set of observed movement vectors.

magnitude and direction (our movement vectors) each attached to a point in the plane (Polyanin and Manzhirov 2006). A *random* vector field consider for each point in the plane not just a movement vector, but a set of movement vectors with an associate probability distribution (Polyanin and Manzhirov 2006).

[8] All the calculations are made using R (R Core Team, 2014). Codes and data are available on author's web page http://dse.ec.unipi.it/ fiaschi/.

3. ESTIMATION OF A LOCAL DIRECTIONAL MORAN SCATTERPLOT

Consider a sample of N economies observed for T periods; economy j is characterized by its level of relative (to the sample average) income in each point in time y_{jt}, and by the average income of its neighbours Wy_{jt}, where W is the the j-the row of the spatial weight matrix expressing which economies are neighbours of j ($j = 1,...,N$ and $t = 1,...,T$), and y_t is the vector of relative income of all economies.

We assume that the spatial dynamics of economy j at period t, i.e. the dynamics of economy j in the space (y, Wy), only depends on (y_{jt}, Wy_{jt}), i.e. y_{jt} follows a *time invariant* and *Markovian* stochastic process.

The spatial dynamics of the sample in the Moran space can be therefore represented by a random vector field (RVF). In particular, given a subset L of the possible realization of (y, Wy) (i.e. a lattice in Moran space, see small black points in Figure 2), a RVF is represented by a random variable $\Delta_\tau z_i$, where $\Delta_\tau z_i \equiv (\Delta_\tau y_i, \Delta_\tau Wy_i) \equiv (y_{it+\tau} - y_{it}, Wy_{it+\tau} - Wy_{it})$, indicating the spatial dynamics (i.e. the dynamics from period t to period $t+\tau$ represented by a movement vector) at $z_i \equiv (y_i, Wy_i) \in L$.

For each point in the lattice z_i, with $i = 1,...,L$, we therefore estimate the distribution of probability $\Pr(\Delta_\tau z \mid z_i)$ on the $N(T-\tau)$ observed movement vectors $\Delta_\tau^{OBS} z$. In particular, $\Pr(\Delta_\tau^{OBS} z_{jt} \mid z_i)$ measures the probability that the dynamics at z_i follows $\Delta_\tau^{OBS} z_{jt}$; this suggests that $\Pr(\Delta_\tau^{OBS} z_{jt} \mid z_i)$ should decrease as function of the distance between z_i and z_{jt}^{OBS}.

Following this intuition Fig. 3 depicts a point of the lattice z_i and four observed movement vectors, which origin at different distance from z_i. Function $\omega(z_i, z_{jt}^{OBS})$ measures for each observed movement vector its probability to affect the movement at z_i; these probabilities decline with distance from z_i (i.e. $\omega(z_i, z_{1t}^{OBS}) < \omega(z_i, z_{2t}^{OBS}) < \omega(z_i, z_{3t}^{OBS})$), and very far observed movement vectors should have zero probability ($\omega(z_i, z_{4t}^{OBS}) = 0$). Blue vector is the *expected movement* from z_i, $\mu_{\Delta_\tau z_i}$, calculated on the base of the distribution of probabilities on the observed movement vectors.

Figure 3. Local mean estimation of the *expected movement* from z_i ($\mu_{\Delta_\tau z_i}$) from four observed movement vectors (z_{jt}^{OBS})

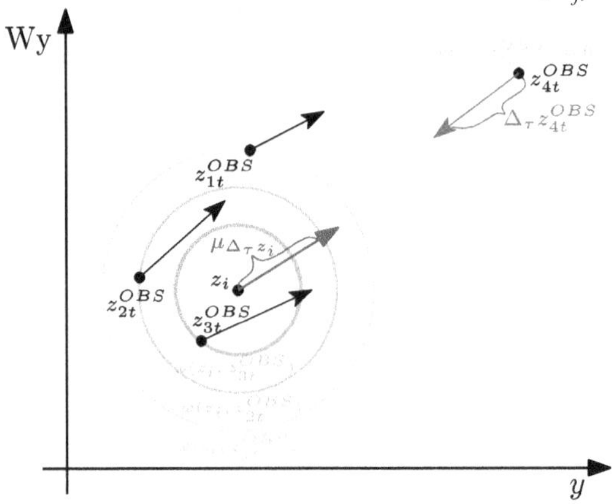

Probabilities attached to each observed movement vectors, given by $\omega(z_i, z_{jt}^{OBS})$, are a negative function of the distance between z_i and z_{jt}^{OBS}.

A convenient way to calculate these probabilities is to use a kernel function to measure the distance between z_i and z_{jt}^{OBS}. In particular:

$$\omega(z_i, z_{jt}^{OBS}) = \frac{K\left(\frac{(z_i - z_{jt}^{OBS})^T S^{-1}(z_i - z_{jt}^{OBS})}{h^2}\right)\frac{\det(S)^{-\frac{1}{2}}}{2h^2}}{\sum_{t=1}^{T-\tau}\sum_{j=1}^{N} K\left(\frac{(z_i - z_{jt}^{OBS})^T S^{-1}(z_i - z_{jt}^{OBS})}{h^2}\right)\frac{\det(S)^{-\frac{1}{2}}}{2h^2}} \qquad (1)$$

is assumed to be an estimate of the probability that at z_i spatial dynamics follows observed movement vectors $\Delta_\tau^{OBS} z_{jt}$, where $K(\cdot)$ is the kernel function, h is the smoothing parameter and S is the sample covariance matrix of z^{OBS}. The kernel function $K(\cdot)$ is generally a smooth positive function which peaks at 0 and decreases monotonically as the distance between the observation z_{jt} and the point of interest z_i increases (see Silverman, 1986 for technical details). The smoothing parameter h controls the width of the kernel function.[9] In the estimation we use a multivariate Epanechnikov kernel (see Silverman, 1986 pp. 76-78), i.e.:

[9] In all the estimation we use the optimal normal bandwidth; for a discuss on the choice of bandwidth see Silverman (1986).

$$K(u^T S^{-1} u) = \begin{cases} \frac{2}{\pi}(1 - u^T S^{-1} u) & \text{if} \quad u^T S^{-1} u < 1 \\ 0 & \text{if} \quad u^T S^{-1} u \geq 1, \end{cases} \tag{2}$$

where $u \equiv \left(z_i - z_{jt}^{OBS}\right)/h$. Multivariate Epanechnikov kernel is particularly adapted to our scope because it assigns zero probability to observed movement vectors very far from z_i.[10] The exact quantification of "very far" is provided by bandwidth h, i.e. higher bandwidth means higher number of observed movement vectors entering in the calculation of the movement at z_i.

Given Eq. (1) for each point in the lattice z_i we estimate the τ-period ahead *expected movement* $\mu_{\Delta_\tau z_i} \equiv E[\Delta_\tau z_i \mid z_i]$ using a *local mean estimator*, firstly proposed by Nadaraya (1964) and Waston (1964), where the observations are weighted by the probabilities derived from the kernel function, i.e.:[11]

$$\hat{\mu}_{\Delta_\tau z_i} = \sum_{t=1}^{T-\tau} \sum_{j=1}^{N} \omega\left(z_i, z_{jt}^{OBS}\right) \Delta_\tau z_{jt}^{OBS} = \widehat{\Pr}\left(\Delta_\tau z \mid z_i\right) \Delta_\tau z^{OBS}. \tag{3}$$

The estimation of Eq. (3) strongly depends on the choice of τ. This choice is the result of a trade-off: from one hand, a too short τ can increase the noise in the estimation due to the possible presence of business-cycle fluctuations; on the other hand, a too long τ could contrast with the local characteristics of the estimate, increasing the probability that observed movement vectors very far from z_i affects the estimate of $\mu_{\Delta_\tau z_i}$.[12]

Figure 4 reports the *annualized* 10-year ahead expected movements based on Eq. (3) for a lattice $50 \times 50 = 2500$ points in the range $(0.4 - 1.6) \times (0.4 - 1.6)$ in Moran space. For a wide area of Moran space we cannot calculate any expected movement due to lack of observed movement vectors sufficiently close to the points in the lattice (as discussed above such threshold in the distance is proportional to the bandwidth h).

The overall spatial dynamics pattern suggested by the estimated expected movements in Figure 4, is convergence toward a region around the bisector close but below point (1,1) for the most of trajectories starting from points in

[10] Other possible kernels, as the Gaussian, does not allow such possibility.
[11] See Bowman and Azzalini (1997) for details.
[12] For samples with a very short time span a further limit to the choice of a long τ is the relatively strong loss of observations.

the lattice below the horizontal line $Wy=1$; while for points above $Wy=1$ a convergence toward regions around points (1.3,1.1) and (1,1.3) is expected.

Figure 4. The Local Directional Moran Scatter Plot including all the annualized 10-years ahead expected movements for the points in the lattice where observed movement vectors are available

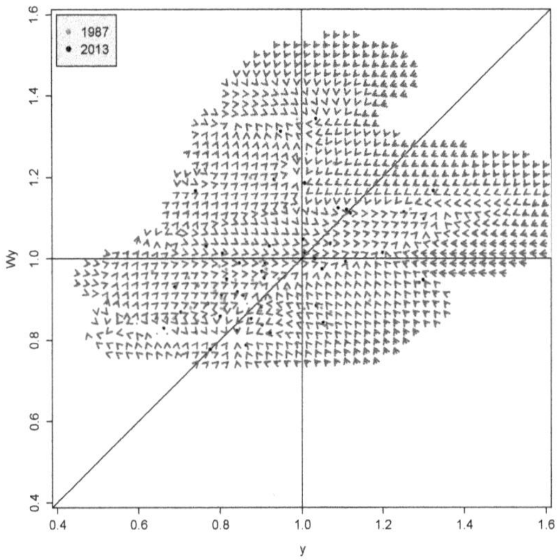

Figure 5. The Local Directional Moran Scatter Plot including all the annualized 10-years ahead expected movements for the points in the lattice where the estimated movements are statistically significant at 5% level

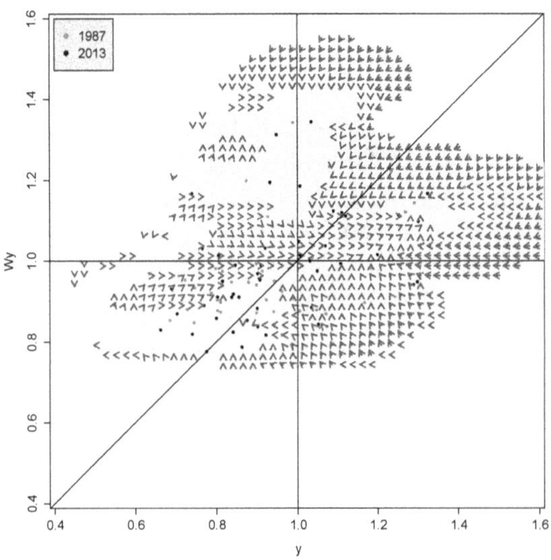

These findings are confirmed also after controlling for the statistical significance of the estimated expected movements, whose results are reported in Figure 5 (see the next section for the bootstrap procedure used for the inference). In particular, the overall convergent spatial dynamics is confirmed; in addition, within regions previously identified as loci of convergence no significant spatial dynamics is present, suggesting that they are indeed regions of steadiness.

With respect to Rey et al. (2011) our analysis confirms the presence of spatial dependence, i.e. y and Wy tends to have the same sign of variation over time (the movement vectors show an orientation from south-west to north-east or vice versa); however, the proposed *Standardized Directional Moran Scatter Plot* reported in the bottom panel of Fig. 2 in Rey et al. (2011) cannot identify the remarkable heterogeneity of spatial dynamics among different regions of Moran space emerging from Fig. 5, and its implications in term of the existence of regions of steadiness.

3.1. Inference on Local Directional Moran Scatter Plot

Below we discuss in details how we have conducted the inference on the estimated expected movements by a bootstrap procedure, whose results is reported in Fig. 5.

Given the observed sample of observations z_{jt}^{OBS}, with $j = 1,...,N$ and $t = 1,...,T$, the bootstrap procedure consists of four steps.

1. Estimate the expected value of the τ-period ahead movement $\mu_{\Delta_\tau z_i}$ by Eq. (3) for each point of the lattice ($i = 1,...,L$).
2. Draw B samples $z^b = \left(z_1^b,...,z_{N(T-\tau)}^b\right)$ and the associated $\Delta_\tau^b z = \left(\Delta z_1^b,...,\Delta z_{N(T-\tau)}^b\right)$, with $b = 1,...,B$, by sampling with replacement from the observed z^{OBS} and the associated movement vectors $\Delta^{OBS} z$.
3. For every bootstrapped sample b and for each point of the lattice i estimate by Eq. (3) the expected value of the τ-period ahead movement $\mu_{\Delta_\tau z_i}^b$.
4. Calculate the two-side p-value of the estimated movement vector at point i in the lattice under the null hypothesis of no dynamics (note that null hypothesis of no dynamics is separately tested in the two directions y and Wy) as:
$$\widehat{ASL}_i = 2 \times \min\left(\sum_{b=1}^{B} \hat{\mu}_{\Delta_\tau z_i}^b \leq 0, \sum_{b=1}^{B} \hat{\mu}_{\Delta_\tau z_i}^b > 0\right) / B \quad (4)$$

In the analysis we have set $B = 300$, and used the usual significance level of 5% to decide which expected movements to report in Fig. 5.

3.2. Test on the Presence of Local Spatial Dependence

The local characteristics of LDMS allows also to test on the presence of *local* spatial dependence in the same spirit of LISA (see Anselin1995). In particular, the null hypothesis of no spatial dependence in the estimated movements in Moran space can be formulated as follows:

$$H_0 : \mu_{\Delta_\tau z_i} \equiv E[\Delta_\tau z_i \mid z_i] = E[\Delta_\tau z_i \mid y_i], \tag{5}$$

that is the null hypothesis is that the dynamics in point z_i only depends on the value of y_i.

Figure 6. Permutation test for the presence of local spatial dependence in RVF

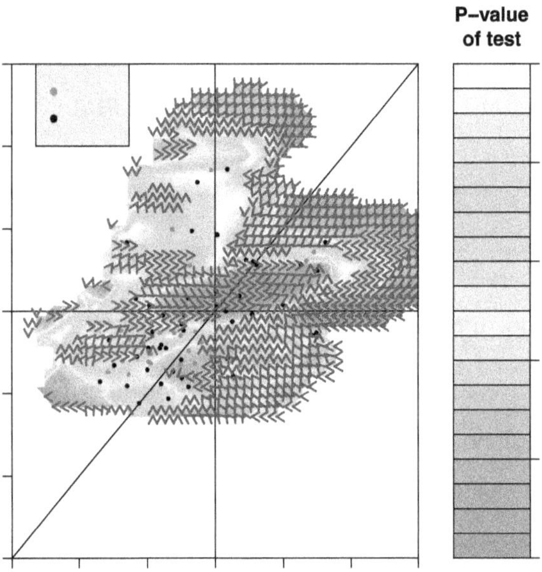

In the f pothesis in Eq. (5).

1. Generate P independent permutation samples $z^p = (y^p, Wy^p)$, with $p = 1,...,P$, by taking the entire time-series of an economy but randomly permuting its neighbours (therefore in every permutation sample y^p is equal to y^{OBS}, but Wy^p will be randomly different from Wy^{OBS}).
2. For every permutation sample p and for each point of the lattice i by Eq. (3) estimate the expected value of the τ-period ahead movement $\mu^p_{\Delta_\tau z_i}$.
3. For each point of the lattice i calculate the difference $\Delta_{\hat{\mu}_i} \equiv \hat{\mu}_{\Delta_\tau z_i} - \hat{\mu}^p_{\Delta_\tau z_i}$.

4. Calculate the two-side p-value of the estimated movement vector at point i in the lattice under the null hypothesis of no spatial dependence as

$$\widehat{ASL}_i^P = 2 \times \min\left(\sum_{p=1}^{P} \Delta_{\hat{\mu}_i} \leq 0, \sum_{p=1}^{P} \Delta_{\hat{\mu}_i} > 0\right) / P. \qquad (6)$$

Figure 6, which reports the results of the permutation test for $P = 300$ permutations, highlights how within the three regions previously indicated as of steadiness, spatial dependence is absent, while is particularly effective at the borders of the north-east quadrant. Spatial dependence appears to be a significant force also around (1,1).

The overall picture suggests that spatial dependence is a pervasive phenomenon, but its effects appears not so important at aggregate level because it is not significant in the regions of steadiness, where the most of US states are concentrated.[13]

4. FORECASTING BY A LOCAL DIRECTIONAL MORAN SCATTER PLOT

The estimated LDMS also allows to compute $F \times \tau$ -year ahead projections starting from the observed cross-economy income distribution. The proposed procedure is similar in the distribution approach to the use of the estimated stochastic kernel to project in the future the actual distribution; in the limit such projection leads to the ergodic (equilibrium) distribution. In particular, the randomness of the estimated LDMS suggests to replicate S time the procedure of computation of the F -period ahead projection and to calculate the average distribution (the replications allows also to calculate confidence bands for our $F \times \tau$ -year ahead projected distribution).

The procedure for the computation of the $F \times \tau$ -year ahead distribution starting from the distribution in the last year T z_T^{OBS} is as follows.

1. For each replication s, with $s = 1,...,S$:
   (a) For each economy $j = 1,...,N$ set $z_j^f = z_j^{f-1}$ ($z_j^1 = z_{jT}^{OBS}$).
   (b) For each economy j individuate the closest point in the lattice, and assign to the economy j the estimated probability distribution on the observed movement vectors for that point,

   i.e. $\widehat{\Pr\left(\Delta_\tau z | z_{i_j^*}\right)}$, where. $i_j^* = \text{argmin}_{\{i\}_{i=1}^{L}} \left\| z_j^f - z_i \right\|$

[13] From the point of view of distribution dynamics the regions of steadiness can be seen as also the loci in the plane where the US states should pass more time.

(c) For each economy j draw one transition, denoted by $\Delta_\tau z_j^f$, from the observed $\Delta_\tau^{OBS} z$ with probability $\widehat{\Pr\left(\Delta_\tau z | z_{i_j^*}\right)}$ and calculate $\tilde{z}_j^{f+1} = z_j^f + \Delta_\tau^f z_j^f$.

(d) For each economy j normalize $y_j^{f+1} = \frac{\tilde{y}_j^{f+1}}{\sum_{j=1}^N \tilde{y}_j^{f+1}}$ in order to maintain that the new calculated distribution y_j^{f+1} has mean one.

(e) For each economy j calculate the spatial lagged value Wy_j^{f+1} and set $z_j^{f+1} = \left(y_j^{f+1}, Wy_j^{f+1}\right)$.

(f) Repeat steps (a)-(e) for $f = 2,...,F$.

(g) Estimate the cross-economy income distribution for the last forecast period F $\hat{\phi}_{F\times\tau}^s = \hat{f}\left(y^F\right)$.

2. Take the average of the estimated income distributions on all replications $\bar{\hat{\phi}}_{F\times\tau} = \sum_{s=1}^S \hat{\phi}_{F\times\tau}^s / S$ as the expected $(F \times \tau)$ -year ahead forecast distribution.

Setting $F = 5$ and $S = 1000$, the distribution in Moran space of all computed 50-year ahead forecasts for a total of 49.000 points (49 US states times 1000 replications) reported in Fig. 7 highlights how no particular dispersion/polarization emerges from the computation of forecast distributions; the most of economies is expected to populate the regions of steadiness, and a region in the north-east quadrant just above horizontal line $Wy = 1$.

Fig. 8 shows how the computed 50-year ahead forecast distribution of y (green line) is not statistically different from the estimated income distribution in 2013 (black line). The actual income distribution across US states therefore should tend to persist at least for the next 50 years.

We also report the 50-year forecast distribution of y based on the use of a stochastic kernel (SK) (orange line), which appears centered around 1 and more or less symmetric. [14] The difference between the 50-year ahead forecast distribution calculated by LDMS and SK measures the magnitude of the bias in the estimate of distribution dynamics deriving from the omission of spatial dependence.

[14] We use a Gaussian kernel with adaptive bandwidth. See Quah (1997) for more details on the meaning of stochastic kernel and its use to forecast future distributions, and (Silverman, 1986, p. 100) for the procedure to estimate a stochastic kernel with adaptive bandwidth.

Figure 7. All computed 50-year ahead forecasts for a total of 49.000 points (49 US states times 1000 replications) (green points), the obser[...] ed LDMS

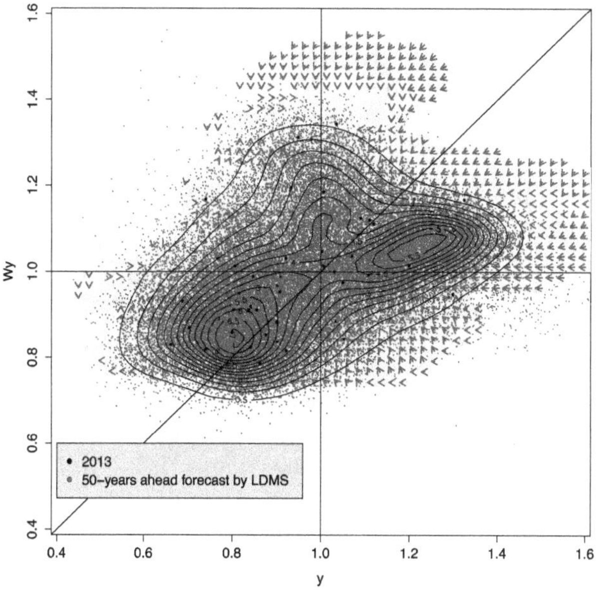

Figure 8. Expected 50-year ahead forecast cross-economy income distribution (ID), its 95% confidence bands (dotted lines), the observed distribution in 2013 (OD) and the 50-year ahead forecast distribution calculated by the estimated stochastic kernel (SK)

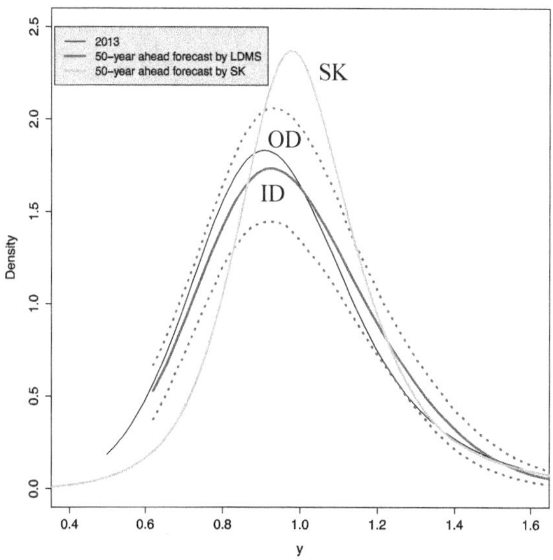

With a very different approach Gerolimetto and Magrini (2014) find a similar results. By using quarterly data for 48 conterminous US states over three decades running between 1981:Q1 and 2010:Q4, they show that neglecting spatial dependence substantially affect the estimate of distributional tendencies; in particular, in the second decade (1991:Q1 and 2000:Q4) the spatial estimator shows a stronger tendency towards divergence in the ergodic distribution with respect to the non spatial estimator.[15]

5. CONCLUDING REMARKS

This paper has proposed a novel methodology to analyse the distribution dynamics in presence of spatial dependence by estimating a random vector field in Moran space. The methodology has successfully identified local heterogeneity in spatial dynamics for US States from 1987 to 2013. Inference on such local heterogeneity has shown how spatial dependence is present only in some regions of Moran space, and that there exists a converging dynamics to three regions where local spatial dependence is instead very weak. The forecast of future income distribution suggests that the most of US States should persist within the three regions, and that no particular change is expected in the income distribution with respect to 2013. The comparison with the forecasted distribution calculated by stochastic kernel generally used in the distribution dynamics literature has shown how the former can be bias from the omission of spatial dependence.

The methodology could be refined by adopting an adaptive kernel in the estimation of LDMS, i.e. a kernel whose bandwidth changes accordingly to the density of observation around the point in the lattice (in particular, the bandwidth is larger where observations are less numerous, see Silverman, 1986). More important, the analysis can be extended to include other explanatory variables of the movement vectors (e.g. the typically Solovian variables such as investment rates and population growth); the limit is the so-called "curse of dimensionality" that generally plagues the use of kernel in multivariate analysis (see, again, Silverman, 1986).

[15] Their results are not exactly comparable with ours both for the data used in the analysis (we have a more limited time span), and for the estimation of the stochastic kernel made using a nearest-neighbor bandwidth in the first year, normal scale bandwidth in the last year, a Gaussian kernel and mean bias adjustment via a local linear estimate.

REFERENCES

Anselin L., 1995, Local indicators of spatial association - LISA. *Geographical Analysis*, 27 (2):93–115, ISSN 1538-4632.
doi: 10.1111/j.1538-4632.1995.tb00338.x.
URL http://dx.doi.org/10.1111/j.1538-4632.1995.tb00338.x.

Bowman A.W. and Azzalini A., 1997, *Applied Smoothing Techniques for Data Analysis: the Kernel Approach with S-Plus Illustrations*. Oxford University Press, Oxford.

Gerolimetto M. and Magrini S., 2014, *Spatial distribution dynamics*. mimeo, 2014.

Nadaraya E.A., 1964, On estimating regression. *Theory of Probability & Its Applications*, 9(1):141–142.

Polyanin A.D. and Manzhirov A.V., 2006, *Handbook of mathematics for engineers and scientists*. CRC Press.

Quah D., 1993, Empirical cross-section dynamics in economic growth. *European Economic Review*, 37 (2-3):426–434.

Quah D., 1997, Empirics for Growth and Distribution: Stratification, Polarization, and Convergence Clubs. *Journal of Economic Growth*, 2(1):27–59.

R Core Team, 2014, R: A Language and Environment for Statistical Computing. R Foundation for Statistical Computing, Vienna, Austria.
URL http://www.R-project.org/.

Rey S.J., 2014, Spatial dynamics and space-time data analysis. In *Handbook of Regional Science*, p. 1365–1383. Springer.

Rey S.J., Murray A.T., and Anselin L., 2011, Visualizing regional income distribution dynamics. *Letters in Spatial and Resource Sciences*, 4(1):81–90.

Silverman B.W., 1986, *Density Estimation for Statistics and Data Analysis*. Chapman and Hall, London.

Watson G.S., 1964, Smooth regression analysis. Sankhyā: *The Indian Journal of Statistics*, Series A, p. 359–372.

UN DIAGRAMME DE MORAN DIRECTIONNEL - LDMS

Résumé - *Cet article s'appuie sur une démarche méthodologique originale permettant d'estimer l'évolution de la distribution des revenus, en présence d'effets de dépendance spatiale. Dans ce travail, nous admettons l'hypothèse que les dynamiques spatiales peuvent être représentées comme un vecteur aléatoire dans le diagramme de Moran. Les effets de causalité des dynamiques spatiales sont analysés par le biais d'un test de dépendance spatiale. La méthodologie utilisée permet de prévoir la future distribution des revenus, en tenant compte des effets de dépendance spatiale, aux Etats-Unis.*

Mots-clés - ANALYSE DE DONNÉES EXPLORATOIRE, POLARISATION, VECTEUR ALÉATOIRE, DÉPENDANCE SPATIALE, DISTRIBUTION DES REVENUS

CONTAGION DES CRISES DE 1997 ET 2008 EN ASEAN+3 : UN MODÈLE VAR STRUCTUREL

Marine COUPAUD*

Résumé *- Les crises de 1997 et 2008 offrent un terrain riche en possibilités d'analyses afin d'étudier l'impact de chocs monétaires et réels sur les pays de l'Asean. Cette étude vise à analyser les réactions des pays membres de l'Asean+3 face à des perturbations de grande envergure et à étudier les phénomènes de contagion qui se sont manifestés lors de ces deux épisodes afin d'en tirer des recommandations de politiques macro-prudentielles dans une problématique de faisabilité d'une union monétaire à moyen terme. Nous parvenons au moyen d'un VAR Structurel à mettre en évidence des phénomènes de contagion pure ainsi qu'une tendance à l'homogénéité des réponses des pays d'Asie du sud-est notamment face à des perturbations de nature financière.*

Mots-clés - VAR STRUCTUREL, CONTAGION, CRISE DE LIQUIDITÉ, ASEAN, UNION MONÉTAIRE

Classification JEL - F21, F22, O3

Je tiens à remercier le referee anonyme de la revue, Céline Gimet pour ses précieux conseils ainsi que les membres du LAREFI pour leurs nombreuses remarques et suggestions.

*Université Montesquieu Bordeaux 4 – LAREFI ; marine.coupaud@u-bordeaux4.fr

1. INTRODUCTION

L'association des pays d'Asie du sud-est (Asean) a été créée en 1967 à Bangkok dans le contexte de la guerre froide : l'objectif fondamental était de contrer le développement du communisme en établissant une union favorisant la croissance et la stabilité économique des pays membres. Le projet s'est tout d'abord développé entre cinq pays : Thaïlande, Malaisie, Indonésie, Singapour et Philippines. L'Asean s'est ensuite élargie à 10 pays[1], puis, avec la dernière entrée en date, le Cambodge en 1999. Parallèlement, l'Asean+3 émerge en 1995, au sommet de Singapour, et rassemble les pays de l'ASEAN ainsi que la Chine, le Japon et la Corée du Sud. L'intégration économique de la zone s'est développée au fil des accords signés par les pays membres. L'AFTA, l'Asian Free Trade Area, signée au sommet de Singapour en 1992 pose les bases d'une union de libre-échange entre les pays de l'Asean+3 qui vise à éliminer les barrières tarifaires et non-tarifaires qui freinent les échanges entre les pays. Le 1er Janvier 2010, le CEPT (*Common Effective Preferential Tariff*), est entré en vigueur pour les membres originels de l'association, les membres ultérieurs ont quant à eux jusqu'à 2015 pour mettre en place la suppression totale des taxes sur les produits échangés intra-Asean.

Le processus d'intégration en marche en Asie du sud-est ne concerne pas uniquement le volet commercial, de nombreuses mesures ont été lancées concernant l'intégration financière et monétaire de la zone. La première de ces mesures est la *Chiang Mai Initiative* (CMI) en 2000. La CMI est destinée à éviter une nouvelle occurrence de la crise qui a touché ces pays en 1997. Elle consiste en la mise en place d'un système bilatéral de swaps de devises et la mise en commun de réserves de monnaies étrangères en vue d'éviter de nouvelles attaques spéculatives pouvant fragiliser la zone. Le projet a finalement été signé en décembre 2009 et officiellement lancé en mars 2010. Le fonds initial de 120 milliards de dollars du projet a été doublé en mai 2012 lors du 15ème sommet à Manille où se sont rassemblés non seulement les ministres des finances des pays membres mais également les gouverneurs des banques centrales, nouveau signe d'un approfondissement de l'intégration financière de la zone. L'Asean a lancé un autre chantier, celui de l'AEC (*Asean Economic Community)*, dont la finalisation est prévue pour 2015 afin de compléter l'intégration financière de la zone. Avec l'AEC, seule la mise en place d'un tarif extérieur commun reste à finaliser pour que l'Asean soit considérée comme une zone ayant atteint la 3ème étape de l'intégration économique prévue par la classification de Balassa (1961), c'est-à-dire une région sans barrières tarifaires et non-tarifaires sur les biens et services mais également une région au sein de laquelle les capitaux et les travailleurs sont libres de se déplacer. L'intégration financière de la zone se concrétise en août 2003, durant la rencontre des ministres des finances des pays membres de l'Asean+3, lorsque l'ABMI (*Asian Bond Market Initiative*) est créé. Cette mesure a pour objectif de développer les marchés obligataires des pays de l'Asie du sud-est dans une perspective d'intégration régionale. Cette initiative ouvre un espace d'échanges d'informations et de connaissances destiné aux

[1] Brunei (1984), Vietnam (1995), Myanmar (1997), Laos (1997), Cambodge (1999).

autorités nationales pour assurer le bon fonctionnement des marchés obligataires nationaux. Cet accord est une mesure phare de la lutte contre les causes de la crise de 1997 avant laquelle les capitaux disponibles étaient libellés en devises étrangères et dont la maturité ne correspondait à celle des investissements pour lesquels ils étaient utilisés, laissant les économies face à un risque important de *currency mismatch*. La même année, l'ABF (*Asian Bond Fund*) est lancé lors d'un meeting des banques centrales de l'Asie du sud-est et du Pacifique (EMEAP). Ce fonds permet aux pays membres d'investir dans des obligations émises par les économies d'Asie du sud-est. Son prolongement, l'ABF 2, lancé en 2005 permet l'émission d'obligations en monnaie nationale. Toutes ces mesures ont été prises dans le but de lutter contre le problème majeur que rencontraient les pays d'Asie du sud-est pour se financer : la disponibilité de capitaux uniquement étrangers et de court terme. Prises au cours des quinze dernières années, ces mesures ont permis dans un premier temps d'envoyer un signal positif (Ma et Remolona, 2005) mais elles ont été suivies d'actes et d'améliorations et augmentées de nouveaux objectifs, preuves de la réelle implication des pays membres de cette association dans l'objectif de poursuivre l'intégration de la zone.

La coopération monétaire des pays d'Asie du sud-est a commencé en 1956 avec la création de la SEANZA (*South East Asia, New-Zealand and Australia*), groupe de travail destiné à la formation du personnel des banques centrales et au règlement de problèmes rencontrés par les pays membres grâce à un réseau d'échange de connaissances (Guillaumin, 2008). Parallèlement, *The South East Asian Central Banks* (SEACEN), créé en 1966 à l'origine pour fournir un espace d'échange d'idées et d'informations économiques et financières aux pays d'Asean, est désormais doté depuis 1982 d'un centre de recherche et de formation spécialisé sur les questions financières, monétaires, bancaires et de développement économique. Il assure la fourniture de conseils et services techniques aux pays membres (ADB, 2013) et l'organisation de meetings annuels rassemblant les gouverneurs des banques centrales. La CMI dont les moyens et les objectifs ont été décrits plus haut, constitue la dernière avancée de la zone en matière d'intégration monétaire.

L'objet de cet article est de mesurer l'impact des crises de 1997 et de 2008 sur les économies émergentes d'Asean +3. L'étude porte sur les pays fondateurs de l'Asean : la Thaïlande, l'Indonésie, la Malaisie et les Philippines[2]. Le Japon, la Corée du Sud et la Chine font également partie de l'analyse.

D'une part, nous cherchons à analyser les effets des chocs financiers qui ont conduit aux deux crises qui ont touché ces pays en 1997 et en 2008. D'autre part, nous nous intéressons aux effets de chocs réels sur les mêmes périodes. Pour chaque période, nous déterminons un pays d'origine des chocs impulsés : la Thaïlande pour la période 1993-2003, les États-Unis pour la période 2001-2010. Nous choisissons la Thaïlande comme pays d'origine des chocs pour la première période car nous voulons modéliser un choc monétaire et un choc réel,

[2] Singapour a été exclu de l'étude en raison d'un manque de données concernant la variable de dette internationale du gouvernement que nous décrivons ensuite.

tous deux internes à la zone. En 1997, la Thaïlande a été le premier pays touché par une attaque spéculative. Afin de la contrer, les autorités ont dépensé près de cinq milliards de dollars avec l'aide de Singapour pour défendre le bath. En vain puisque la monnaie thaïlandaise s'est dépréciée de 25% en juillet 1997, date à laquelle le pays a adopté un régime de change flottant contrôlé. La crise se propage ensuite à la Malaisie, les Philippines et l'Indonésie mais aussi à Singapour et à la Corée du Sud en juillet 1997. Un rapport du Conseil d'Analyse Économique (Davane, 1998) désigne la Thaïlande comme point d'entrée de la crise financière en Asie à la suite de la mauvaise gestion de ses déséquilibres en matière de mode de financement des investissements et de rentabilité de ces derniers. Les pays sont contraints de faire appel aux grandes institutions internationales (FMI, Banque mondiale) afin d'obtenir des prêts pour soutenir leurs économies. Parallèlement, nous choisissons les États-Unis comme pays d'origine du choc sur la décennie 2001-2010. Dans la décennie 2000, la crise majeure qui a ébranlé l'économie mondiale est bien sûr celle de 2008. C'est d'abord la sphère bancaire américaine qui est touchée, largement exposée aux fluctuations du marché immobilier et aux crédits subprimes. Les économies américaine et mondiale subissent ensuite les effets de l'assèchement du canal du crédit et de l'exposition des institutions financières aux produits financiers risqués facilitée par la titrisation (Artus et al., 2008). La crise financière américaine devient alors une crise réelle d'envergure mondiale. L'objectif est de mesurer la réaction des pays d'Asean à deux chocs (financier et réel) émanant de l'intérieur de la zone et à deux chocs (financier et réel) émanant de l'extérieur.

Nous étudions la nature de la propagation de ces chocs entre les pays d'Asean considérés, nous analysons si les réactions et les mécanismes de contagion ont évolué entre les deux périodes. Nous effectuons ainsi une comparaison de la nature de la contagion non seulement entre les périodes mais également entre les types de chocs (réels ou financiers). Nous nous intéressons aussi à la gestion de ces crises par les pays, notamment à travers leurs relations de dépendance envers les autres pays au travers de la dette. Nous verrons comment les pays ont tiré les leçons de la crise de 1997 afin d'être mieux armés face à la survenue de perturbations internationales.

Cette étude s'inscrit dans une perspective plus large, celle d'une union monétaire en Asean. En effet, les avancées récentes en termes d'intégration économique effectuées par l'Asean constituent un sujet de recherche intéressant. La zone affiche sa volonté d'avancer dans le processus amorcé il y a plus de quatre décennies mais ralenti avec la crise de 1997. L'étude vise ainsi à souligner les évolutions en termes de politique économique et financière de la zone en général qui ont permis à cette région d'avancer en tant qu'union dans la classification telle que déterminée par Balassa (1961). Les crises successives de 1997 et 2008 offrent la possibilité d'identifier dans quelle mesure les pays membres ont retenu la leçon de la crise de 1997 et comment ceci leur a éventuellement permis d'approfondir leur intégration financière pour parvenir à une relative stabilité macroéconomique. L'étude des phénomènes de propagation des deux crises nous amène à la conclusion que la contagion pure est un phénomène important dans cette région du monde mais l'évolution des politiques macro-prudentielles de ces économies à la suite de 1997 entraîne des résultats encourageants quant à la maîtrise de leur stabilité économique en cas de crise financière.

Dans la section 2, nous effectuons une revue de la littérature concernant le déclenchement des deux crises et les phénomènes de contagion. La section 3 présente le modèle VAR Structurel. L'analyse des résultats et de la contagion s'effectue dans la section 4. Enfin, la section 5 conclut.

2. REVUE DE LA LITTÉRATURE

La littérature s'est largement penchée sur les phénomènes qui ont conduit à la crise asiatique de 1997 et à la crise des subprimes de 2008 aux Etats-Unis. Ces deux crises se caractérisent par l'impact qu'elles ont eu, non seulement dans les économies où elles se déclenchent mais également dans d'autres régions du monde. Autre caractéristique commune, ces deux crises économiques et financières trouvent leur origine dans une crise de liquidité bancaire.

Des auteurs ont fustigé les gouvernements asiatiques pour leurs actions en faveur d'une rapide libéralisation des systèmes financiers combinée à des problèmes d'aléa moral, de sur-investissement et de corruption qui auraient précipité la survenue de la crise asiatique (Sarno et Taylor, 1999). Esquivel et Larrain (1998) qui analysent les déterminants des crises de change sur une vingtaine d'années entre 1975 et 1996, soulignent également l'importance de plusieurs facteurs explicatifs de ce type de crises, dont un déséquilibre du compte courant, la distorsion au niveau du taux de change réel et une faible croissance.

Dans leur article de 2008, Reinhart et Rogoff déterminent cinq variétés de crises économiques : crise de défaut de paiement extérieur, crise de défaut domestique, crise de change, crise d'inflation et crise bancaire. Nous nous intéressons à la dernière classification de crise, la crise bancaire, pour illustrer le déclenchement des crises économiques de 1997 et 2008. Ces auteurs considèrent le déclenchement de crises bancaires à la lumière d'évènements propres à ces situations, notamment les fermetures, les fusions et nationalisations à grande échelle des institutions bancaires comme ce fut le cas en Thaïlande en 1997. Les auteurs soulignent la difficulté d'établir un indicateur unique pour anticiper le déclenchement des crises bancaires.

Plusieurs auteurs soulignent le problème d'illiquidité auquel a fait face le système bancaire thaïlandais à la veille de la crise de 1997 (Chang et Velasco, 1999, 2001; Radelet et Sachs, 1998). Le pays, comme la plupart des pays d'Asie du sud-est, a connu une période de boom bancaire alimentée par les capitaux étrangers au cours de laquelle les banques ont excessivement prêté au secteur immobilier et à l'industrie pour des projets à visée spéculative ou simplement non rentables (Turner, 1998 ; Guglietta et Sgard, 1998). Lorsque les banques des économies émergentes font face à un problème de liquidité, elles ont tendance à se tourner vers le marché des capitaux pour trouver des fonds supplémentaires. Ce système fonctionne tant que les banques nationales apparaissent solvables aux yeux des investisseurs étrangers. Lorsque ces derniers perdent leur confiance en ces institutions, elles se trouvent incapables de trouver de nouvelles liquidités (Chang et Velasco, 2000). Le reflux soudain des capitaux étrangers en Asie du sud-est, plus précisément en Thaïlande, après une longue période d'afflux importants, illustre parfaitement cette théorie. C'est dans cette perspective que nous caractérisons la crise de 1997 en Asie du sud-est comme une crise de liquidité bancaire.

De même concernant la crise de 2008, dite crise des subprimes, le consensus général fait état d'un problème de crédits excessifs au secteur immobilier qui s'est soldé par une crise bancaire entraînant l'assèchement du canal du crédit interbancaire et donc la raréfaction du crédit disponible pour l'économie dans son ensemble. Les articles d'Ackermann (2008) et de Brunnermeier (2009) offrent une vue d'ensemble sur les causes et conséquences de cette crise bancaire. À nouveau, nous retrouvons le problème de liquidité bancaire dans cette crise, dix années après celle survenue en Asie.

Concernant la contagion, il n'existe pas de consensus sur sa définition. La littérature oppose traditionnellement la contagion fondamentale et la contagion pure. Le premier type de contagion repose sur l'état des fondamentaux pour expliquer les phénomènes de propagation (Kaminsky et Reinhart, 2000). Le second type de contagion s'explique par un changement de comportement des acteurs du marché financier et ne s'appuie pas sur l'état des variables économiques des pays durant la période précédant la crise pour expliquer la propagation de la crise à d'autres économies (Radelet et Sachs, 1998 ; Masson, 1999), les canaux de transmission n'existent pas avant le déclenchement de la crise. Dans la contagion fondamentale, deux effets sont distingués. Tout d'abord, l'effet mousson (Masson et Mussa, 1995) met en cause des changements de politique macroéconomique dans des pays industrialisés qui impactent des pays émergents de manière plus ou moins importante selon leur degré d'exposition à ces changements de politique. La dette externe du gouvernement, la fragilité du système financier et la dépendance aux investisseurs étrangers sont des facteurs de vulnérabilité des pays émergents. Une deuxième explication est donnée par l'effet spillover : cette contagion résulte de l'interdépendance des pays émergents entre eux. Lorsque, par exemple une dévaluation touche un pays comme ce fut le cas en Asie, cette perturbation peut affecter les pays voisins dans la mesure où elle entraîne une perte de leur compétitivité et par conséquent une baisse de leurs exportations. L'effet spillover passe par les canaux commerciaux et financiers. La contagion par les relations commerciales établies entre les pays d'une zone a été développée avant la crise asiatique de 1998 (Gerlach et Smets, 1995 ; Eichengreen et al., 1996). Elle est souvent due à la modification des rapports de compétitivité entre les pays : quand un pays d'une zone expérimente une dévaluation de sa monnaie, ses exportations deviennent plus compétitives et les autres pays sont contraints de dévaluer à leur tour. Dans une étude de 1996, Eichengreen et al. ont mis en évidence l'importance des relations commerciales entre deux pays pour expliquer la vitesse de propagation des chocs entre les économies. La contagion par le canal financier s'explique par différents mécanismes repris par Kaminsky et al. dans leur article de 2003. Shleifer et Vishny (1997) soulignent le rôle des investisseurs spécialisés prenant de larges positions qui, lorsqu'ils prennent peur face à des retours sur investissement moins élevés à la suite d'un choc, liquident leurs positions, entraînant des perturbations sur les marchés financiers. De manière générale, la présence de prêteurs communs, qu'ils soient des banques commerciales, des fonds d'investissement ou des détenteurs particuliers d'actifs financiers, peut entraîner des perturbations massives sur les marchés lors de chocs financiers (Kaminsky et al., 2003). Le caractère liquide de certains actifs financiers entraîne les mêmes conséquences. Les investisseurs rencontrant la nécessité de vendre des actifs à la suite d'un appel de marge peuvent se retrouver confrontés à un problème type "marché des tacots" (Akerlof, 1970) dû à une asymétrie d'information au sein du marché. Cette asymétrie les conduit à devoir vendre leurs produits à bas prix. Par conséquent, ils se rabattent sur les actifs dont les prix n'ont pas été touchés, entrainant des ventes en masse et donc une baisse du prix de ces actifs, perturbant les marchés financiers dans leur ensemble (Calvo, 1998). Kodres et Pritsker (2002) posent le problème des effets de décisions prises à la suite de signaux privés reçus par les investisseurs dits « informés ». Ces derniers, après avoir reçu une information privée spécifique à un pays, réorganisent leur portefeuille pour limiter l'exposition aux autres pays partageant les mêmes risques macroéconomiques. Les investisseurs « non-informés » interprètent ces mouvements comme liés à l'état de leur propre pays et engendrent des mouvements perturbateurs sans fondement macroéconomique. Là encore, les pays avec des marchés financiers très liquides seront d'autant plus touchés par ces comportements moutonniers (Calvo et Mendoza, 2000). Enfin, les banques commerciales jouent un rôle important dans la contagion des crises par le canal financier. Elles peuvent amplifier le problème originel en rappelant les prêts et limitant le crédit dans le pays de la crise mais également dans d'autres pays afin d'équilibrer leur portefeuille face au risque général.

Depuis plus d'une dizaine d'années, la littérature s'est amplement développée autour du phénomène de la crise asiatique de 1997. Le modèle VAR structurel (SVAR) est un outil économétrique très utilisé pour analyser l'effet de différents types de chocs sur une économie (Gimet, 2007) et plus précisément dans l'analyse de la crise de 1997. Les SVAR constituent un outil plus précis par rapport aux VAR classiques car ils permettent d'identifier les chocs structurels grâce à des éléments issus de la théorie économique, non plus simplement par l'utilisation de la décomposition de Cholesky (Lütkepohl et Krätzig, 2004 ; Couharde et Guillaumin, 2011). L'étude de l'impact des chocs internes (Kim, 2007) et externes (Chang et Velasco, 2000) sur les économies asiatiques a conduit à des conclusions sur l'inaptitude de cette zone à mettre en place une union monétaire et sur l'importance des facteurs extérieurs sur la stabilité de ces économies (Mackowiak, 2007). Gimet (2009) souligne néanmoins l'existence d'un bloc de pays émergents au sein de l'Asean+3[3] dont les réponses à un choc financier international sont homogènes, laissant présager la possibilité d'une union monétaire à condition de lutter contre les disparités régionales. Dans un article de 2006, après avoir analysé la synchronisation des cycles économiques des pays d'Asie du sud-est, Sato et Zhang parviennent à la conclusion que certaines paires de pays sont particulièrement synchronisées, notamment Singapour, la Thaïlande et l'Indonésie. Ce résultat va dans le sens de la faisabilité d'une union monétaire dont la perte d'autonomie en matière de politique moné-

[3] Philippines, Thaïlande, Malaisie, Indonésie et Corée du Sud.

taire constitue le coût principal, coût minimisé par la synchronisation des réponses aux chocs intervenant dans les économies.

3. LE MODÈLE

3.1. Spécification du modèle VAR Structurel

Soit VAR(q) la représentation du modèle sous forme réduite :

$$\Delta Y_t = \sum_{i=1}^{q} A_i \, \Delta Y_{t-i} + e_t \qquad (1)$$

où q est le nombre de retards, Y_t est le vecteur des variables observables de dimension $n \times 1$, avec n le nombre de variables du modèle, A est la matrice des paramètres du modèle et e_t est un bruit blanc : $E(e_t e_t^T) = \Omega$ et $E(e_t) = 0$. À chaque date t les innovations e_t sont exprimées comme la combinaison linéaire des chocs structurels ε_t associés à chaque variable : $e_t = P\varepsilon_t$ et donc $\varepsilon_t = P^{-1}e_t$.

P est une matrice de passage qu'il faut estimer afin d'identifier les chocs structurels. C'est une matrice de dimension $n \times n$. La caractéristique du VAR structurel est d'imposer des restrictions issues de la théorie économique, ces restrictions se traduisent par la nullité de certains coefficients de la matrice de passage P.

Soit le vecteur des chocs structurels associés à chaque variable :

$$\varepsilon_t = \begin{pmatrix} \varepsilon_{ext} \\ \varepsilon_{er} \\ \varepsilon_{ir} \\ \varepsilon_{int\_DebtFin} \\ \varepsilon_{int\_DebtGvt} \\ \varepsilon_{gdp} \end{pmatrix} \qquad (2)$$

où ε_{ext}, ε_{er}, ε_{ir}, $\varepsilon_{int\_DebtFin}$, $\varepsilon_{int\_DebtGvt}$ et ε_{gdp} représentent respectivement le choc externe, le choc de demande domestique nominal, le choc d'offre monétaire domestique, le choc financier domestique, le choc fiscal domestique et le choc d'offre réel domestique. On suppose que les différents chocs structurels ne sont pas corrélés entre eux et ont une variance unitaire :

$$E(\varepsilon_t \varepsilon_t^T) = I \qquad (3)$$

I_n est la matrice identité.

Ω est la matrice des variances covariances des innovations canoniques e_t, on a :

$$E(e_t e_t^T) = PE(\varepsilon_t \varepsilon_t^T)P^T = PP^T = \Omega \qquad (4)$$

L étant l'opérateur de retard, nous pouvons écrire le modèle VAR sous cette forme :

$$A(L)\Delta Y_t = e_t \qquad (5)$$

Pour obtenir les réponses aux chocs ainsi que les décompositions de la variance de l'erreur de prévision, il est nécessaire d'écrire le processus sous forme moyenne mobile infinie structurelle. Afin de parvenir à cette forme, nous utilisons le théorème de Wold qui consiste à inverser le modèle VAR canonique pour obtenir sa forme moyenne mobile infinie.

$$\Delta Y_t = C(L)e_t \tag{6}$$

avec $C(L) = \sum_{j \geq 0} C_j L^j$ et $C_0 = I$.

Cette décomposition fait intervenir un nombre infini de paramètres mais toutes les impulsions sont nulles avant la date 0 :

$$\Delta Y_t = \sum_{g=0}^{t-1} C_g \, e_{t-g} \tag{7}$$

où les matrices C_g sont fonction des paramètres du modèles VAR car le modèle VAR a été inversé pour obtenir la décomposition de Wold. Les réponses des séries Y_t aux innovations $e_{j,s}$, $s \leq t$ sont définies à partir des multiplicateurs dynamiques :

$$C_{ij,t-s} = \frac{\partial Y_{it}}{\partial e_{js}} \tag{8}$$

Ces derniers permettent de définir la fonction de réponse correspondante :

$$\forall g \geq 0, g \rightarrow C_{ij,g} \tag{9}$$

Les réponses du système aux impulsions structurelles sont obtenues en évaluant les multiplicateurs dynamiques structurels $\emptyset_{ij,t-s}$ où $\emptyset = C_{t-s}P$, avec P la matrice de passage, car la dynamique peut être caractérisée d'après l'écriture moyenne mobile structurelle :

$$\Delta Y = \sum_{g=0}^{\infty} (C_g P)(P^{-1} e_{t-g}) \tag{10}$$

Comme $\varepsilon_t = P^{-1} e_t$ et $\emptyset = C_{t-s}P$, nous pouvons simplifier :

$$\Delta Y = \sum_{g=0}^{\infty} \emptyset_g \varepsilon_{t-g} \tag{11}$$

Avec L l'opérateur de retard, la forme moyenne mobile structurelle devient :

$$\Delta Y_t = \emptyset(L)\varepsilon_t \tag{12}$$

La matrice $\emptyset_j$représente les fonctions de réponses aux chocs ε_t, à la date t pour les s périodes suivant le choc, des éléments de ΔY_t.

3.2. Choix des données

Pour étudier l'impact des chocs externes sur les économies nous considérons les économies suivantes : Malaisie, Philippines, Indonésie, Thaïlande (uniquement pour la seconde période), Chine, Japon et Corée du Sud. Nous avons choisi d'introduire la Thaïlande dans l'échantillon de la seconde période du fait de la place prépondérante de ce pays au sein de l'Asean en tant que membre fondateur. Nous travaillons sur deux périodes 1993Q3-2003Q3 et 2001Q1-2010Q4, de façon à couvrir une période d'une dizaine d'années pour chacune des deux crises. Nous travaillons en données trimestrielles.[4] Les économies sont décrites par le vecteur des variables endogènes :

$$Y = \begin{pmatrix} ext \\ er \\ ir \\ int\_DebtFin \\ int\_DebtGvt \\ Gdp \end{pmatrix}$$

Ext est la variable externe, le ratio de liquidité bancaire.

Nous nous intéressons au ratio classique de *crédits/dépôts* pour illustrer l'illiquidité grandissante des banques des deux pays concernés, la Thaïlande et les États-Unis. L'étude de l'évolution de ce ratio pour chacun des pays montre qu'à chaque période précédant la crise on observe un pic de ce ratio, largement supérieur à 1 : les dépôts ne couvrent plus les crédits. Plus le ratio augmente plus l'illiquidité grandit pour le pays concerné[5]. Le numérateur du ratio de liquidité bancaire pour les États-Unis comprend les créances du secteur bancaire sur la Banque centrale, les créances nettes sur le gouvernement américain et les créances sur les autres secteurs. Au dénominateur, on retrouve les dépôts transférables et les autres dépôts, le tout inclus dans la définition de la Broad Money. Le numérateur du ratio de liquidité pour la Thaïlande comprend les créances domestiques du secteur bancaire. Le dénominateur comprend les dépôts en monnaie nationale auprès du gouvernement et les dépôts[6]. Nous avons choisi de retenir comme perturbation externe, un choc de liquidité bancaire car la littérature sur la 3ème génération de modèle des crises insiste sur le risque d'illiquidité grandissant des pays dans les périodes précédant les crises (Chang et Velasco, 2001).

er est le taux de change nominal à l'incertain pour les économies asiatiques (nombre d'unités de monnaie pour un dollar US)[7]. ir est le taux d'intérêt nominal du marché monétaire, utilisé comme *proxy* de la politique monétaire. $Int\_DebtFin$ et $Int\_DebtGvt$ représentent respectivement la dette internationale du secteur financier et la dette internationale du gouvernement en Dollar US[8]. Gdp est le PIB réel[9,10].

[4] Les données disponibles ne nous permettaient pas d'effectuer une analyse sur ces mêmes pays en données mensuelles.

[5] Voir détails dans le document de travail correspondant (Coupaud, 2013), Annexe 1.

[6] Toutes ces données ont été extraites de la base Datastream.

[7] Ces données sont extraites de la base IFS du FMI.

[8] Ces données ont été extraites du site de la Bank of International Settlements.

[9] Ces données sont extraites directement de la base IFS du FMI pour les Philippines (2005 prices), le Japon (1995 prices) et la Thaïlande (1988 prices). Les PIB réels de la Corée du Sud et de la Malaisie ont été calculés à partir du PIB nominal et du déflateur (base 2005) disponibles dans la base IFS du FMI. Le PIB de l'Indonésie a quant à lui été calculé à partir du PIB nominal et de l'indice CPI disponible dans la base IFS du FMI. Pour la Chine, nous avons utilisé les données annuelles fournies par les IFS du FMI et nous avons effectué la conversion de la fréquence des données sous Eviews au moyen de la quadratic-match sum.

[10] Les PIB ont été désaisonnalisés selon la méthode Census-X11.

Les variables Gdp, er et ir sont largement utilisées dans la littérature afin d'illustrer la diffusion des chocs monétaires dans une zone économique (Cushman et Zha, 1997 ; Kim et Roubini, 2000 ; Canova, 2005 ; Mackowiak, 2007). Le taux de change nominal nous permet d'étudier l'impact des différents régimes de change entre les deux périodes.

Le niveau de stock de dette du gouvernement est une variable utilisée dans des études plus récentes (Favero et Giavazzi, 2009). La Banque des règlements internationaux (2002) a souligné dans un rapport l'intérêt d'observer ces variables de dettes afin d'en déduire des informations sur l'exposition des économies aux marchés financiers internationaux et les risques qui en découlent. La dette internationale du secteur financier est une variable clef dans la littérature des crises. Une dette internationale d'un montant élevé accroît la vulnérabilité d'un pays face aux changements des anticipations des investisseurs et au phénomène de contagion pure (Masson, 1999). Dans le cas des pays d'Asie, la dépendance des États aux marchés monétaires internationaux est primordiale, rappelons que les gouvernements sont des prêteurs en dernier ressort et leur situation internationale en matière de possibilité d'emprunt est tout aussi importante que celle des institutions financières des pays, notamment pour la Thaïlande.

Le choc externe est représenté par des indicateurs utilisés pour illustrer le problème de liquidité bancaire[11] à l'origine de chacune des deux crises. Ils sont construits d'après le ratio *crédits/dépôts* des banques du pays d'origine de la crise. Pour chaque période, le pays d'origine de la perturbation est différent : la Thaïlande en 1997, rl_th et les Etats-Unis en 2008, rl_us.[12] Nous avons également retenu un choc externe de croissance afin d'analyser la différence de réaction des pays entre deux types de chocs. Pour modéliser ce choc réel, nous avons choisi un choc de PIB pour chacune des périodes : un choc de PIB en provenance de la Thaïlande en 1997 (Gdp_th) et un choc en provenance des États-Unis (Gdp_us) pour la crise de 2008.

Toutes les variables sont transformées en logarithme sauf le taux d'intérêt nominal. Elles sont stationnaires, la plupart en différence première, certaines en niveau et en différence seconde[13]. Un VAR structurel à deux retards pour chaque pays et pour chaque période a été retenu. La définition du nombre de retards ne repose finalement pas sur les critères d'information traditionnels. En effet, ceux-ci suggèrent un nombre de retards différents selon les modèles économétriques. L'objectif d'obtenir des modèles comparables et homogènes entre les pays et entre les périodes (Gossé et Guillaumin, 2010) a conduit à établir un nombre de retards identique pour chaque modèle VAR structurel estimé. De plus, le choix d'un faible nombre de retards apparaît judicieux quant à la périodicité des données (trimestrielles) et à la relative courte durée des périodes étudiées (une dizaine d'années pour chacune) : les modèles estimés avec un nombre plus importants de retards ne donnent pas de résultats significatifs.

[11] Nous verrons ensuite comment nous avons choisi cet indicateur.

[12] *rl* pour ratio de liquidité et *th* pour Thaïlande et *us* pour les États-Unis.

[13] Le détail des tests de racines unitaires est disponible auprès de l'auteur sur simple demande.

Des relations de cointégration sont mises en évidence par le test de Johansen dans les modèles SVAR estimés à partir des variables décrivant les économies de la Malaisie et des Philippines en première période (1993Q3-2003Q3) et dans le modèle SVAR estimé à partir des variables décrivant l'économie japonaise en deuxième période (2001Q1-2010Q4). La cointégration est gérée selon la méthode développée par Enders (1995)[14].

3.3. Restrictions du modèle SVAR

Afin que le modèle soit juste identifié, $n(n\text{-}1)/2$ paramètres de la matrice de passage doivent être posés. Le modèle SVAR que nous étudions comporte six variables, nous avons donc quinze restrictions à poser.

Les variables rl_th et rl_us représentant les variables de liquidité bancaire sont considérées comme des variables externes (Cushman et Zha, 1997), cinq restrictions sont ainsi posées. Cela signifie que les chocs sur ces variables au sein des pays de l'échantillon n'ont pas d'impact dans le court terme sur les variables du modèle.

$$p_{12} = p_{13} = p_{14} = p_{15} = p_{16} = 0$$

D'après Sims et Zha (1999), dont l'étude porte également sur des données trimestrielles, la réponse de la politique monétaire à un choc de production est différée d'un trimestre, un choc de PIB n'influence pas le taux d'intérêt sur une période.

$$p_{36} = 0$$

L'hypothèse d'un retard dans la réponse de l'économie aux perturbations financières nationales et internationales est retenue (Kim et Roubini, 2000). La dette internationale du gouvernement et celle du secteur financier sont soumises aux perturbations financières nationales et internationales dans la mesure où si les marchés refusent de continuer à prêter cela engendrera de graves difficultés économiques dans le pays concerné. La dette internationale du secteur financier et la dette internationale du gouvernement sont les vecteurs de perturbations financières dans l'économie ; pour cette raison, des chocs sur ces variables n'influencent pas de manière contemporaine le PIB.

$$p_{64} = p_{65} = 0$$

Selon l'hypothèse de Kim et Roubini (2000) et Sims et Zha (1995), le délai informationnel ne permet pas à l'autorité monétaire de réagir à un choc de production dans la même période : les chiffres du PIB ne sont pas disponibles en temps réel, par conséquent, les politiques mises en place par les autorités ne se font pas dans la même période. Un choc de PIB n'influence ni le taux d'intérêt ni la dette internationale du gouvernement en un trimestre. De plus, seul le taux de change est considéré comme une variable « forward-looking » (Kim, 2003) ; le choc de PIB n'influence alors pas la dette internationale du secteur bancaire de manière contemporaine.

$$p_{56} = p_{46} = 0$$

[14] Le détail des tests de cointégration est disponible auprès de l'auteur sur simple demande.

La réponse de la politique monétaire, donc du taux d'intérêt nominal, aux perturbations financières nationales et internationales est décalée d'une période (Sims et al., 1995, 1999). La dette internationale du secteur financier, vecteur des perturbations financières internationales, n'influence pas le taux d'intérêt à court terme.

$$p_{34} = 0$$

Selon Gali (1992) et Perotti (2002), un choc sur le taux d'intérêt n'influence pas le PIB à court terme.

$$p_{63} = 0$$

Selon Kim (2003), un choc de taux de change nominal n'influence pas le PIB de manière contemporaine.

$$p_{62} = 0$$

La dette internationale du gouvernement est une donnée de long terme, cette variable représente la politique fiscale ("fiscal policy" en anglais qui désigne la politique budgétaire et la politique fiscale du gouvernement). En effet, nous pouvons considérer la dette externe du gouvernement comme un élément de la "fiscal policy" dans la mesure où elle fait partie des ressources d'un Etat pour équilibrer sa politique budgétaire. La réponse de la politique fiscale aux chocs sur des variables macroéconomiques peut être considérée comme égale à 0 dans l'espace d'un trimestre (Favero et Gianezzi, 2009 ; Blanchard et Perotti, 2002). Un choc sur le taux de change n'influence pas la politique fiscale en un trimestre.

$$p_{52} = 0$$

Giordano et al. (2007) soulignent que le temps que les autorités prennent en compte les changements survenus dans l'économie, en mesurent les conséquences et appliquent des mesures destinées à les contrer en terme de politique fiscale, largement plus d'un trimestre s'est passé. Ainsi, un choc sur la variable de dette internationale du système financier n'impacte pas de manière contemporaine la dette internationale du gouvernement.

$$p_{54} = 0$$

Soit quinze restrictions au total.

4. RÉSULTATS ET ANALYSE DE LA CONTAGION

Les résultats sont délivrés sous forme de graphiques. Notons que la réaction d'une variable à un choc est significative lorsque l'axe des abscisses n'est pas inclus dans l'intervalle de confiance qui encadre la réaction de cette variable. Ces graphiques indiquent la réaction sur six trimestres (abscisses) des variables de chaque pays considéré face à une variation d'un écart-type de la variable externe. Cette réaction peut être positive (négative) : la variable considérée évolue dans le même sens que le choc (dans le sens inverse du choc)[15]. Les tableaux de décomposition de la variance nous permettent d'obtenir le pourcentage de variation de la variable endogène directement lié au choc externe. Ce pourcentage n'est interprété que sur les périodes où l'impact est significatif.

4.1. Contagion de la crise de 1997

La crise bancaire de 1997 trouve son origine en Thaïlande. Nous pouvons nous attendre à ce que les économies d'Asean réagissent par un phénomène de spillover tel que décrit par Masson (1999). Ces pays sont relativement liés commercialement et exportent vers le monde industrialisé. En effet, en 1997, le commerce intra-régional atteint 22% du commerce total en Asean et près de 38% en Asean+3 (Guérin et Sa, 2006). Ces pays bénéficient de l'évolution du commerce international dans la mesure où de nombreuses entreprises y délocalisent une partie de leur production. Les pays d'Asie du sud-est sont au cœur de l'intégration verticale des processus de production dans les années 1990. Ils importent des composants et exportent des produits finis, la part des biens intermédiaires dans le commerce total passe de 25% à la fin des années 1970 à 47% en 2002 (Zebregs, 2004). Nous anticipons une réaction du taux de change visant à dévaluer la monnaie afin de rester compétitif quant à l'exportation de produits finis face au phénomène de crise de change qui fait suite à la crise bancaire en Thaïlande. De même, ces pays dont les économies reposent sur les exportations de biens manufacturés sont susceptibles de voir le PIB affecté par ce type de crise. De plus, la situation de change fixe sur le dollar de tous les pays sauf la Malaisie nous invite à penser que les taux d'intérêt ne seront pas touchés car les pays sont liés par l'impossible trinité de Mundell (1961). Concernant le Japon, on peut s'attendre à des réactions significatives des variables représentatives de l'économie du fait de la forte implication, notamment financière, de ce pays dans les économies d'Asie du sud-est depuis les années 1980[16]. Pour les variables de dettes, des établissements bancaires ou des gouvernements, nous pouvons nous attendre à des réactions significatives de la zone Asie du sud-est étant donné le fort endettement de ces économies sur les marchés internationaux.

En pratique, le choc de liquidité en provenance de la Thaïlande *(rl_th)* touche les pays de manière peu uniforme pendant cette première période (1993Q3–2001Q4). Dans le groupe le plus développé de la zone, des variables de la Corée du Sud et de la Chine réagissent au choc tandis que le Japon n'est pas impacté. Nous observons des mouvements dans la dette internationale du gouvernement pour la Chine (*Ch_Int_DebtGvt*) pour laquelle le choc explique 7,06% de la variance pour la période durant laquelle l'impact est significatif. Durant cette période, ces économies sont encore largement dépendantes des prêteurs internationaux pour faire face aux chocs qui les affectent. Le résultat de la Chine peut sembler surprenant quant à la fermeture de cette économie aux marchés financiers internationaux jusqu'à la fin des années 1990. Le canal fi-

[15] Les graphiques des IRF sont disponibles à la fin du document de travail correspondant, Coupaud (2013).
[16] Voir détails dans le document de travail correspondant (Coupaud, 2013), Annexe 3, Tableau 3.A.

nancier direct peut être avancé pour expliquer la contagion à la Corée du Sud qui avait considérablement investi en Asie du sud-est dès le début de la décennie 1990 (Kim et al., 2001; Kaminsky et al., 2003). Le choc impacte positivement le taux de change[17] (Cs_er) pour 32,21% de sa variance, le taux d'intérêts (Cs_ir) pour 14,49% de sa variance.

Tableau 1. Décomposition de la variance. Choc de liquidité bancaire

	Chine	Corée du Sud	Indonésie	Japon	Malaisie	Philippines
			er			
Période 1	3.66	32.21	13.96	0.00	0.39	2.45
Période 2	2.01	27.24	13.24	0.05	1.01	7.72
Période 3	2.08	27.60	13.69	0.12	6.33	7.52
Période 4	4.86	26.67	14.49	0.12	6.00	8.64
Période 5	4.95	26.88	15.91	0.38	5.96	8.63
Période 6	4.97	27.25	16.59	0.41	7.08	8.57
			ir			
Période 1	9.94	1.09	10.30	3.19	1.64	10.44
Période 2	9.29	14.49	12.55	4.93	1.72	10.82
Période 3	9.21	14.27	18.08	7.57	6.14	7.04
Période 4	11.81	26.42	22.55	9.98	8.06	7.21
Période 5	11.63	29.95	25.05	11.41	8.66	7.68
Période 6	11.54	29.60	24.24	12.02	8.61	7.87
			Int_debtFin			
Période 1	0.94	0.39	0.51	0.20	1.16	5.37
Période 2	0.71	6.47	0.92	0.51	4.72	5.40
Période 3	4.56	10.28	2.05	1.01	10.73	6.42
Période 4	7.47	12.75	2.41	1.07	11.60	6.92
Période 5	8.33	14.34	2.59	1.77	12.25	6.86
Période 6	8.36	15.43	2.65	2.11	12.17	6.84
			Int_debtGvt			
Période 1	7.06	0.82	1.29	0.76	2.15	2.18
Période 2	4.32	1.90	1.27	1.12	18.30	2.78
Période 3	4.18	20.95	1.45	1.09	16.38	3.19
Période 4	7.33	22.81	1.71	1.32	15.35	3.47
Période 5	9.38	23.25	1.73	1.55	14.92	3.49
Période 6	10.59	22.94	1.86	1.60	14.85	3.50
			Gdp			
Période 1	3.01	2.31	2.77	2.44	4.01	1.43
Période 2	5.91	29.62	10.16	2.22	7.49	4.12
Période 3	10.42	32.08	20.94	6.55	5.95	5.77
Période 4	10.16	31.39	24.35	6.54	5.63	5.98
Période 5	10.23	31.42	23.56	6.46	6.88	6.33
Période 6	10.08	32.02	22.55	6.38	7.46	6.41

er est la variable de taux de change, *ir* est la variable de taux d'intérêt, *Int_DebtFin* est la variable de dette internationale du secteur financier, *Int_DebtGvt* est la variable de dette internationale du gouvernement et *Gdp* est la variable de PIB.

[17] On rappelle que dans le cas d'une cotation à l'incertain, une hausse du taux de change correspond à une dépréciation de la monnaie face au dollar.

Tableau 2. Décomposition de la variance. Choc réel

	Chine	Corée du Sud	Indonésie	Japon	Malaisie	Philippines
			er			
Période 1	0.21	32.21	23.05	16.36	36.46	9.99
Période 2	0.41	27.24	27.30	20.46	26.53	7.36
Période 3	4.11	27.60	26.64	19.06	25.49	6.87
Période 4	5.12	26.67	25.89	19.19	25.75	6.41
Période 5	5.46	26.88	27.43	19.42	25.67	6.53
Période 6	5.47	27.25	27.25	19.62	25.54	6.43
			ir			
Période 1	8.43	1.09	14.38	0.81	0.51	1.68
Période 2	8.58	14.49	19.78	0.22	3.28	1.22
Période 3	8.63	14.27	34.78	1.16	7.05	1.26
Période 4	9.37	26.42	49.18	5.27	7.93	1.93
Période 5	9.60	29.95	53.96	8.05	10.64	2.38
Période 6	10.43	29.60	50.90	8.73	11.48	2.37
			Int_DebtFin			
Période 1	0.33	0.39	10.26	13.41	6.65	13.68
Période 2	1.14	6.47	8.62	17.12	7.08	12.76
Période 3	4.76	10.28	8.98	12.81	9.77	11.75
Période 4	8.38	12.75	9.68	13.11	8.97	13.56
Période 5	9.88	14.34	10.12	13.07	8.66	13.48
Période 6	10.07	15.43	10.52	13.19	9.66	13.20
			Int_DebtGvt			
Période 1	1.12	0.82	0.15	1.30	0.84	26.93
Période 2	4.47	1.90	1.72	6.28	0.74	23.83
Période 3	4.15	20.95	2.15	6.24	1.08	23.32
Période 4	6.87	22.81	2.24	7.67	1.14	22.42
Période 5	10.16	23.25	2.78	7.49	1.15	21.66
Période 6	14.06	22.94	2.91	7.29	1.25	21.55
			Gdp			
Période 1	3.61	2.31	3.72	1.90	42.27	14.09
Période 2	4.49	29.62	29.52	1.85	31.52	10.68
Période 3	19.11	32.08	51.90	23.31	27.07	11.20
Période 4	24.76	31.39	50.79	25.46	27.82	11.25
Période 5	27.60	31.42	47.11	24.87	26.99	11.02
Période 6	30.24	32.02	44.53	24.75	26.62	10.92

er est la variable de taux de change, *ir* est la variable de taux d'intérêt, *Int_DebtFin* est la variable de dette internationale du secteur financier, *Int_DebtGvt* est la variable de dette internationale du gouvernement et *Gdp* est la variable de PIB.

En ce qui concerne les économies du groupe Asean originel, aucune variable de l'économie réelle ne réagit significativement au choc financier. Ces résultats permettent de dire que la crise qui s'est propagée de la Thaïlande aux autres pays d'Asie du sud-est s'explique par un phénomène de contagion pure : la sphère réelle ne réagit pas et les investisseurs ont retiré leurs capitaux de ces économies bien que la crise de liquidité thaïlandaise n'ait pas impacté directement leurs fondamentaux essentiels (baisse du PIB). Leur niveau n'a pas évolué directement en fonction de la liquidité bancaire, c'est la perception des investisseurs étrangers par rapport à ces fondamentaux qui a évolué et qui les a poussés à retirer leurs capitaux de ces économies. En se référant à l'article de Kaminsky et al. (2003), nous pouvons ajouter que la présence de prêteurs communs (Japon, Corée du Sud) a contribué à amplifier ce phénomène. Nous sommes dans une situation de contagion pure telle que l'a décrite Masson (1999). Ces résultats rejoignent ceux de Forbes (2000) qui déduit de son étude un phénomène de *wake-up call* de la part des investisseurs étrangers dans les pays d'Asie. Concernant le choc réel en provenance de la Thaïlande (gdp_th) les attentes en termes de réaction des économies sont fortes pour des pays d'Asie du sud-est fortement intégrés commercialement.

Concernant les pays « +3 » de l'Asean, nous nous attendons à une réaction moindre étant donné la relative petite taille de l'économie thaïlandaise par rapport aux économies chinoise, japonaise et coréenne. En effet, les PIB (Gdp) de presque tous les pays réagissent positivement (sauf le Japon), mais nous pouvons identifier un bloc de pays : Indonésie, Malaisie et Corée du Sud où le pourcentage de la variance expliqué par le choc est particulièrement important dans les périodes où son impact est significatif (51,9%, 42,3% et 32,1%). Nous pouvons supposer que c'est le canal commercial qui est en jeu. En effet, ces pays sont intégrés commercialement : 36% des exportations asiatiques se font à destination de l'Asie dont 22 points pour la demande interne en biens de consommation finale (Guérin et Sa, 2006). Ainsi lorsqu'un choc de PIB impacte une de ces économies, les PIB des autres pays de la zone sont également touchés. Ce résultat confirme l'importance de la transmission des chocs par le canal commercial au sein d'une région intégrée commercialement (Gerlach et Smets, 1995; Glick et Rose, 1999). Les Philippines sont aussi impactées mais pour 14,09% de la variance de leur PIB (Gdp). Le choc réel se transmet également à la sphère financière pour le Japon, l'Indonésie et les Philippines : plus de 10% de la variance des dettes internationales du système financier ($Int\_DebtFin$) s'expliquent par ce choc. La dette du gouvernement réagit pour les Philippines ($Ph\_Int\_DebtGvt$) et la Corée du Sud ($Cs\_Int\_DebtGvt$) pour respectivement 26,93% et 20,95% de la variance du choc.

D'une manière générale, les économies réagissent donc beaucoup plus à un choc de croissance du PIB provenant de Thaïlande (Gdp_th) qu'à un choc de liquidité (rl_gdp). Cette réaction s'explique par le moindre développement des marchés financiers dans ces pays pendant cette période. Plus précisément, ces pays sont relativement ouverts pendant cette période dans la mesure où les capitaux étrangers sont libres de circuler. Ces économies entretiennent plus largement des relations avec les pays industrialisés et beaucoup moins entre elles – cette constatation rejoint le résultat de l'étude de Kim et al. (2006) sur le niveau d'intégration financière de l'Asie du sud-est au niveau régional qui apparait encore inachevée. Les chocs se propagent plus facilement par la sphère réelle, les chocs financiers ont un impact par le phénomène de contagion pure accentué par la présence de prêteurs communs (Kaminsky et al., 2003).

4.2. Contagion de la crise de 2008

Les attentes en termes de réaction de ces pays face à un choc de même nature que celui de 1997 sont conditionnées par les décisions prises à la suite de la crise de 1997. Un accord attire particulièrement l'attention, celui de la *Chiang Mai Initiative*, signé en 2000, en vue de contrer une nouvelle occurrence de la crise financière de la fin des années 1990. Cet accord visant à mettre en place un système de swaps de devises et une réserve de devises, signé par l'ensemble des pays que nous considérons nous permet d'anticiper une réaction limitée en terme d'impact sur les taux de change et sur les dettes internationales, les pays étant théoriquement moins dépendants des marchés financiers internationaux pour se financer et moins vulnérables face à une attaque spéculative.

Tableau 3. Décomposition de la variance. Choc de liquidité bancaire

	Chine	Corée du Sud	Indonésie	Japon	Malaisie	Philippines	Thaïlande
				er			
Période 1	17.85	0.30	37.70	18.66	12.14	13.26	15.57
Période 2	17.17	10.99	44.83	22.35	31.83	22.46	33.32
Période 3	20.58	25.23	40.25	26.49	31.12	22.96	33.18
Période 4	20.79	21.70	38.27	26.08	32.13	22.63	32.87
Période 5	21.35	26.59	37.91	25.95	33.17	23.22	32.92
Période 6	21.11	26.01	36.06	26.63	33.61	23.08	32.73
				Ir			
Période 1	12.95	8.34	4.45	28.37	0.22	6.54	2.93
Période 2	10.94	38.91	3.78	20.41	13.77	7.71	5.45
Période 3	16.28	38.28	2.85	19.60	14.44	6.83	5.04
Période 4	17.59	42.69	2.08	21.74	20.43	9.18	5.50
Période 5	17.50	41.90	1.64		18.90	12.69	5.54
Période 6	18.49	41.27	1.46	27.06	19.05	13.42	5.55
				Int_DebtFin			
Période 1	1.18	6.70	0.78	8.08	0.03	4.19	1.23
Période 2	1.25	6.75	13.41	7.71	0.28	11.14	8.03
Période 3	1.23	7.13	12.70	30.53	0.19	11.72	8.18
Période 4	2.18	6.90	12.70	29.88	0.16	12.73	9.56
Période 5	2.36	7.58	12.74	29.37	0.14	15.29	10.37
Période 6	2.64	7.55	12.81	30.34	0.59	15.38	10.32
				Int DebtGvt			
Période 1	10.43	8.82	0.27	14.01	7.72	0.93	5.50
Période 2	9.42	13.70	0.22	31.93	8.44	2.08	4.75
Période 3	9.51	23.42	0.22	48.55	38.74	2.82	4.21
Période 4	12.36	21.92	1.84	46.63	32.55	2.64	9.76
Période 5	12.23	21.86	2.15	48.38	32.35	2.86	9.70
Période 6	13.17	22.28	2.12	48.61	31.59	2.98	9.59
				Gdp			
Période 1	17.20	14.79	0.09	55.91	10.29	3.86	0.48
Période 2	16.07	16.18	0.81	63.29	31.64	12.64	12.00
Période 3	24.38	14.18	2.58	63.27	27.72	22.93	11.54
Période 4	23.15	16.57	2.59	63.50	27.50	22.80	12.80
Période 5	23.54	20.07	2.50	64.00	27.62	19.97	12.33
Période 6	23.10	20.67	2.47	63.73	28.35	20.38	11.36

er est la variable de taux de change, *ir* est la variable de taux d'intérêt, *Int_DebtFin* est la variable de dette internationale du secteur financier, *Int_DebtGvt* est la variable de dette internationale du gouvernement et *Gdp* est la variable de PIB.

Tableau 4. Décomposition de la variance. Choc réel

	Chine	Corée du Sud	Indonésie	Japon	Malaisie	Philippines	Thaïlande
				er			
Période 1	22.21	11.43	24.00	20.12	20.20	10.25	8.33
Période 2	20.86	7.10	35.74	20.68	21.79	10.84	13.50
Période 3	20.09	6.50	33.78	19.41	22.48	10.62	13.27
Période 4	19.99	8.11	36.50	20.67	22.46	10.62	13.25
Période 5	20.92	9.23	37.18	20.56	22.38	10.52	13.22
Période 6	20.72	10.84	36.21	20.54	22.12	10.66	13.14
				ir			
Période 1	6.77	0.50	14.38	25.56	0.63	3.46	11.31
Période 2	24.97	3.60	19.48	25.32	23.75	3.09	22.54
Période 3	23.07	4.93	18.97	24.67	41.80	6.33	24.38
Période 4	21.83	9.17	17.06	22.07	42.61	13.79	26.69
Période 5	22.19	13.56	14.35	21.95	39.23	19.33	27.65
Période 6	22.73	15.19	12.61	21.15	38.26	22.45	27.65
				Int_DebtFin			
Période 1	2.62	0.66	8.33	0.26	1.16	6.96	1.84
Période 2	7.77	1.76	8.14	1.83	1.96	12.10	1.19
Période 3	7.96	6.65	7.65	4.23	4.65	10.58	1.49
Période 4	8.50	6.57	8.10	7.47	6.76	12.99	2.34
Période 5	9.09	6.65	10.11	7.94	6.58	12.92	2.89
Période 6	9.68	6.65	10.61	9.88	5.99	15.29	3.32
				Int_DebtGvt			
Période 1	12.11	7.58	1.57	0.41	0.24	2.97	6.96
Période 2	27.21	0.34	1.34	25.15	0.20	2.67	8.07
Période 3	24.71	8.80	6.98	46.69	8.56	3.47	6.96
Période 4	23.44	8.94	6.93	46.76	15.30	3.18	7.07
Période 5	22.75	9.74	8.45	45.29	16.48	3.17	7.16
Période 6	23.30	10.41	8.47	45.97	17.09	3.52	7.08
				Gdp			
Période 1	16.32	0.07	1.55	61.92	21.03	0.98	2.93
Période 2	13.81	0.07	4.48	64.96	30.95	0.90	25.28
Période 3	13.55	0.20	4.09	64.53	31.55	38.19	16.72
Période 4	13.39	0.22	3.99	58.46	30.70	38.75	17.66
Période 5	15.30	0.64	3.78	59.23	30.01	37.14	15.40
Période 6	15.16	0.64	4.27	57.57	30.01	36.34	14.99

er est la variable de taux de change, *ir* est la variable de taux d'intérêt, *Int_DebtFin* est la variable de dette internationale du secteur financier, *Int_DebtGvt* est la variable de dette internationale du gouvernement et *Gdp* est la variable de PIB.

On observe des réactions significatives de la part des pays les plus développés de cette zone à la suite d'un choc de liquidité américain: Japon, Corée du Sud et Chine. Les pays réagissent tous de la même façon en termes de PIB (*Gdp*) et de taux d'intérêt (*ir*). Ces pays sont beaucoup plus intégrés financièrement et sont de grandes puissances mondiales ayant des relations commerciales très approfondies. La Corée du Sud, le Japon, la Chine et les États-Unis sont très liés commercialement[18]. L'ouverture financière et commerciale de la Chine est récente, mais la vitesse de son développement économique en fait un pays important sur la scène internationale, notamment pendant la deuxième période étudiée (2001-2010). Notons néanmoins que cette ouverture est très partielle : la convertibilité du yuan est en effet autorisée à des fins commerciales mais non pas financières. Les dettes internationales des gouvernements du Japon ($Jap\_Int\_DebtGvt$) et de la Corée du Sud ($Cs\_Int\_DebtGvt$) réagissent de manière significative, soulignant l'importance des marchés internationaux pour se procurer des financements. Leurs variations sont expliquées par le choc respectivement à 48,55% et 23,42%. La contagion peut être qualifiée de fondamentale dans le cas de ces trois pays : elle passe par le canal commercial et le canal financier pour se propager à la sphère réelle.

À l'exception de la Malaisie, les pays les moins développés de la zone (Indonésie, Thaïlande et Philippines) ont une réaction similaire face à un choc de liquidité en provenance des États-Unis. Seule la variable taux de change (er) réagit mais il n'est noté aucun impact significatif sur les autres variables. Cette réaction s'explique par la faible intégration financière de ces pays qui limite leur exposition aux perturbations financières internationales, l'effet richesse reste limité dans le cas d'un choc financier américain (Allegret et al., 2012).

Ces résultats rejoignent ceux de Mackowiak (2007). Il n'y a pas d'effet Mousson à proprement parler (Masson, 1999), les perturbations financières en provenance des États-Unis ne se répercutent pas directement dans la sphère économique réelle des pays d'Asie du sud-est. Le taux de change réagit positivement : face à une hausse de l'illiquidité des banques américaines, comme cela s'est produit en 2008, le taux de change (er) augmente provoquant une dépréciation de la monnaie. Les monnaies des pays cités précédemment sont moins demandées par les investisseurs qui se débarrassent de ces monnaies même si le choc n'a pas impacté directement les fondamentaux de ces économies. C'est, à proprement parler, un phénomène de contagion pure telle que définie par Masson en 1999 : la crise se propage sur le marché des changes de ces pays sans avoir auparavant affecté les fondamentaux. Ce phénomène est amplifié par la présence de prêteurs communs, comme en 1997[19]. Il faut cependant noter que l'inutilité d'une attaque spéculative a été comprise par les spéculateurs qui n'envisagent pas d'attaquer la monnaie car le taux de change, même s'il réagit, est seulement impacté sur une courte période. Nous noterons l'absence de réactions des variables de dette internationale ($Int\_DebtGvt$ et $Int\_DebtFin$) de ces pays que ce soit du système financier ou du gouvernement, en comparaison de la première période : il semble que ces pays soient moins dépendants des marchés financiers internationaux pour se financer. De ce point de vue-là, si l'on se réfère aux résultats obtenus dans cette étude, certaines leçons de la crise

[18] Voir détails dans le document de travail correspondant (Coupaud, 2013), Annexe 3, Tableaux 3.B et 3.C.

[19] Voir détails dans le document de travail correspondant (Coupaud, 2013), Annexe 3, Tableau 3.A.

de 1997 ont été comprises : les systèmes financiers des pays semblent plus solides et les institutions ont limité leurs dettes externes.

Dans le cas du choc réel de croissance américain (Gdp_us), nous obtenons des réactions significatives des pays les plus développés. En Chine et en Corée du Sud, les taux de change (Ch_{er}) et (Cs_er) sont impactés et réagissent de manière inverse à un choc réel de PIB (Gdp_us) américain. Le taux de change de la Corée du Sud (Cs_er) réagit de manière très brève en tout début de période et seulement 11,43 % de la variance est expliquée par le choc. La réaction est brève également pour la Chine mais la décomposition de la variance montre que 22,21% de la réaction est expliqué par le choc américain. L'explication se trouve dans les forts liens commerciaux de ces pays avec les États-Unis : si le PIB de cette économie subit un choc négatif, le taux de change (à l'incertain) de l'économie augmente, la monnaie est moins demandée (notamment pour les échanges commerciaux) et se déprécie.

Les PIB chinois et japonais (Ch_Gdp) et (Cs_Gdp) réagissent dans le même sens qu'un choc réel, avec une décomposition de la variance de respectivement 16,32% et 61,92%. Ces résultats s'expliquent par les forts liens commerciaux entre la Chine, le Japon et les États-Unis (Glick et Rose, 1999).

De leur côté, certains pays d'Asie du sud-est sont affectés dans leur sphère réelle. La Malaisie et la Thaïlande voient leur PIB (Gdp) réagir positivement à ce type de choc. Les économies de ces pays suivent dans le même sens les fluctuations réelles de l'économie américaine. De plus, les taux de change (er) ont une réaction uniforme sauf pour la Thaïlande : ils réagissent inversement au choc. Les liens commerciaux avec les États-Unis constituent une solide explication de ces phénomènes : les économies de ces pays s'appuient fortement sur les biens manufacturés échangeables et donc tout choc touchant l'économie d'un important partenaire commercial entraîne des modifications dans la demande de ce type de biens et par conséquent sur la demande de monnaie domestique.

C'est le canal commercial qui est en jeu dans la contagion du choc en provenance des Etats-Unis.

5. CONCLUSION

Cette étude montre que la contagion pure joue un rôle important dans la transmission des crises financières en Asie du sud-est et dans les pays asiatiques plus développés lors des deux épisodes de crise, en 1997 et en 2008. Nous pouvons en conclure que la crédibilité de ces économies notamment en matière de gestion des crises n'est pas encore assez forte pour maintenir la confiance des investisseurs en cas de perturbation de portée internationale.

Les recommandations qui peuvent être faites à cette zone économique pour assurer sa stabilité concernent notamment son système financier et s'inscrivent dans la lignée des mesures qui ont été conseillées à la suite de la crise de 1997. Tout d'abord, réduire le problème d'aléa moral du système financier en mettant systématiquement en place un système d'assurance des dépôts (par exemple) et non plus un système de garantie totale qui incite les banques à prendre des risques inconsidérés. La Thaïlande est un exemple d'économie qui a mis en place au lendemain de la crise asiatique un tel système. Les Philippines ont, de manière générale, mieux résisté à la crise et ce pays avait déjà un système similaire dès 1990. Ensuite, les innovations financières sont aujourd'hui la clef du développement financier. Encore une fois, la Thaïlande, à la suite de 1997, avait préconisé l'introduction d'investisseurs étrangers dans la gestion des banques afin d'augmenter le niveau de technologie des produits financiers. Cependant, la crise de 2008 montre le potentiel nuisible d'outils trop complexes dont le risque devient indétectable. Une troisième recommandation consiste en la diversification des acteurs des marchés financiers afin d'éviter les comportements mimétiques qui mènent à la forte volatilité des actifs : développer l'implication des investisseurs institutionnels sur le marché des actions et développer la part des investisseurs particuliers dans le marché des obligations afin d'en assurer la liquidité. D'après les résultats, il semble que les pays d'Asean soient moins vulnérables en matière de dette externe : les gouvernements et les systèmes financiers ne s'exposent plus aux marchés financiers internationaux dans les mêmes proportions à court terme, c'est une caractéristique que ces pays doivent conserver afin de stabiliser leur économie. L'accumulation des réserves de change semble avoir joué son rôle de protection contre les attaques spéculatives en temps de crise durant la seconde période.

Les réactions similaires en deuxième période face au choc de liquidité des pays d'Asean semblent constituer un point positif dans la perspective d'une union monétaire : les pays subissent tous un impact sur leur taux de change mais celui-ci est de courte période et les fondamentaux ne sont pas affectés. Les économies semblent répondre de manière uniforme et efficace aux chocs externes. Les avancées effectuées au fil des accords signés semblent se concrétiser au sein de l'Asean offrant ainsi de nombreuses perspectives de recherche.

REFERENCES

Ackermann, A., 2008, « The subprime crisis and its consequences », *Journal of Financial Stability*, Vol. 4, pp. 329-337.

ADB, Asia Regional Integration Center.

http://www.aric.adb.org/initiativetable.php?iid=69&ssid=2&title=South%20East%20Asia,%20New%20Zealand,%20Australia%20(SEANZA).

Akerlof, G-.A., 1970, « The market for "lemons": quality uncertainty and the market mechanism », *The Quarterly Journal of Economics*, Vol. 84, pp. 488-500.

Allegret, J-P., Couharde, C., Cyriac G., (2012), « The impact of external shocks in East Asia: lessons from a structural VAR model with block exogeneity », *International Economics*, 132, pp. 35-89.

Artus, P., Betbèze, J-P., De Boissieu, C., Capelle-Blancard, G., 2008, « La crise des subprimes », *Conseil d'Analyse Économique*, Rapport n°78.

ASEAN Organisation, http://www.Aseansec.org/18757.htm

Balassa, B., 1961, « The theory of economic integration », *Irwin, Homewood*, Illinois pp. 304.

Banque des règlements internationaux, 2002, « Comparison of creditor and debtor data on short-term external debt », BIS Papers n°13.

Blanchard, O., Perotti R., 2002, « An empirical characterization of the dynamic effects of changes in government spending and taxes on output », *Quarterly Journal of Economics*, Vol. 117, pp. 1329-1368.

Brunnermeier, M., 2009, «Deciphering the liquidity and credit crunch 2007–2008», *Journal of Economic Perspectives*, Vol. 23, pp. 77-100.

Calvo, G., 1998, « Capital market contagion and recession: an explanation of th Russian virus », College Park, Maryland, University of Maryland.

Calvo, G., Mendoza, E., 2000, « Rational contagion and the globalization of securities markets », *Journal of International Economics,* Vol. 51(1), pp. 79-113.

Canova, F., 2005, « The transmission of US shocks to Latin America », *Journal of Applied Econometrics*, Vol. 20, pp. 229-251.

Chang, R., Velasco, A., 1998, « The Asian liquidity crisis », *National Bureau of Economic Research*, Working Paper n°6796.

Chang, R., Velasco, A., 2000, « Banks, debt maturity and financial crises », *Journal of International Economics*, Vol. 51, pp.169-194.

Chang, R., Velasco, A., 2001, « The 1997-98 liquidity crisis: Asia Versus Latin America », *Working Papers Central Bank of Chile 120*, Central Bank of Chile.

Couharde, C., Guillaumin, C., 2011, « Chocs externes et perspectives d'union monétaire en Asie de l'est: les enseignements d'un modèle VAR Structurel », *Cahiers de Recherche du CREG*, n°2011-01.

Coupaud, M., 2013, « Contagion des crises de 1997 et 2008 en Asean+3 : un modèle VAR struturel », *Document de travail du LAREFI*, CR13-EFI/06.

Cushman, D.O., Zha, T., 1997, « Identifying monetary policy in a small open economy under flexible exchange rates », *Journal of Monetary Economics*, vol. 39(3), pp. 433-448.

Davane, O., 1998, « Instabilité du système financier international», *Conseil d'Analyse Economique*, Rapport n°14.

Eichengreen, B., Rose, A., Wyplosz, C., 1996, « Contagious currency crisis », *Scandinavian Economic Review,* Vol. 98(4), pp. 463-484.

Enders, W., 1995, *Applied Econometric Time series*, USA, John Wiley and Sons.

Esquivel, G., Larrain, F., 1998, « Explaining currency crisis », *International Development.*

Favero, C., Giavazzi, F., 2009, « Debt and the effects of fiscal policy », *Working Papers 317, IGIER,* Bocconi University.

Forbes, K., 2000, « The Asian flu and Russian virus: firm-level evidence on how crises are transmitted internationally », *NBER Working Paper, n°* 7808.

Gali, J., 1992, « Does the IS-LM model fit us postwar data? », *Quarterly Journal of Economics,* Vol. 152, pp. 708-738.

Gerlach, S., Smets, F., 1995, « Contagious speculative attacks », *European Journal of Political Economy*, Vol. 11, pp. 5-63.

Gimet, C., 2007, « L'impact des chocs externes dans les économies du Mercosur: un modèle VAR Structurel », *Economie Internationale,* 2/2007 (n°110), pp. 107-136.

Gimet, C., 2009, «The spread of international financial shocks to Asean countries», GATE Working Paper N°09-28.

Giordano, R., Momigliano, S., Neri, S., Perotti, R., 2007, « The effects of fiscal policy in Italy: Evidence from a VAR model », *European Journal of Political Economy*, Vol. 23 (3), pp. 707-733.

Glick, R., Rose, A.K., 1999, « Contagion and trade: why are currency crises regional? » *Journal of International Money and Finance*, Vol. 18(4), pp. 603-617.

Gossé, J-B., Guillaumin, C., 2010, « L'impact des chocs externes sur et à l'intérieur de la zone euro : les enseignements d'un modèle vectoriel autorégressif structurel », *Economie & prévision*, n° 195-196, pp. 15-33.

Guérin, J., Sa, S., 2006, « Les progrès de l'intégration monétaire et financière en Asie », *Revue de la stabilité financière* 8, Banque de France, pp. 117-35.

Guglietta, J., Sgard, J., 1998, « Thaïlande : de la crise de croissance à la crise monétaire », *Economie internationale*, n°76.

Guillaumin, C., 2008, « (A)symétrie et convergence des chocs macroéconomiques en Asie de l'Est : une analyse dynamique », *Economie internationale*, 114, pp. 29-68.

Kaminsky, G., Reinhart, C., 2000, « On crisis, contagion, and confusion », *Journal of International Economics*, Vol. 51(1), pp. 145-168.

Kaminsky, G.L., Reinhart, C.M.,Vegh, C.A., 2003, « The unholy trinity of financial contagion », *Journal of Economic Perspectives*, vol. 17(4), pp. 51-74.

Kim, D., 2007, « An East Asian currency union? The empirical nature of macroeconomic shocks in East Asia », *The Journal of Asian Economics,* Vol. 18(6), pp. 847-866.

Kim, S., 2003, « Monetary policy, foreign exchange intervention, and the exchange rate in a unifying framework », *Journal of International Economics*, Vol. 60(2), pp. 355-386.

Kim, S.H., A. Kose, Plummer M-G., 2001, « Understanding the Asian contagion», *Asian Economic Journal,* 15(2), pp. 111-138.

Kim, S., Lee, J.W., Shin, K., 2006, « Regional and Global Financial Integration in East Asia », *Discussion Paper Series 0602*, Institute of Economic Research, Korea University.

Kim, S., Roubini, N., 2000, « Exchange rate anomalies in the industrialized countries: a solution with a structural VAR approach », *Journal of Monetary Economics,* Vol. 45, pp. 561-586.

Kodres, L., Pritsker, M., 2002. « A rational expectations model of financial contagion », *Journal of Finance,* Vol. 27(2), pp. 769-800.

Lütkepohl, H., Krätzig, M., 2004, *Applied time series econometrics*, Cambridge Books, Cambridge University Press.

Ma, G., Remolona, E-M., 2005, « Opening markets through a regional bond fund: lessons from ABF2 », *BIS Quarterly Review*. http://ssrn.com/abstract=1884913.

Mackowiak, B., 2007, « External shocks, U.S. monetary policy and macroeconomic fluctuations in emerging markets », *Journal of Monetary Economics*, vol. 54(8), pp. 2512-2520.

Masson, P., Mussa, M., 1995, « The role of the fund financing and its interactions with adjustement and surveillance », *Pamphlet series N°50*, IMF.

Masson, P., 1999, « Contagion: macroeconomic models with multiple equilibria », *Journal of International Money and Finance*, Vol. 18 (4), pp. 587-602.

Mundell, R., 1961, « Optimum Currency Areas », *American Economic Review*, Vol. 51, pp. 509-517.

Radelet, S., Sachs, J., 1998, « The onset of the East Asian financial crisis », *NBER Working Paper*, No. 668.

Sarno, L., Taylor,P., 1999, « Moral hazard, asset price bubbles, capital flows, and the East Asian crisis: the first test », *Journal of International Money and Finance*, Vol. 18(4), pp. 637-657.

Sato, K., Zhang Z., 2006, « Real Output Co-movements in East Asia: Any Evidence for a Monetary Union? », *The World Economy*, 29(12), pp.1671-1689.

Shleifer, A., Vishny, R.W., 1997, «The limits of arbitrage », *Journal of Finance*, vol. 22, pp. 35-55.

Sims, C.A., Zha, T., 1995, « Does monetary policy generate recessions? Using less aggregate price data identify monetary policy », *Working paper Yale University*, CT.

Sims, C.A., Zha, T., 1999, « Error bands for impulse responses », E*conometrica*, Vol. 67, pp. 1113-1155.

Takatoshi, I., 2000, « Capital Flows in Asia», in: Capital Flows and the Emerging Economies: Theory, Evidence, and Controversies », *National Bureau of Economic Research*, pp. 255-298.

Turner, P., 1998, « La crise financière en Asie : risques de marché et risques de politique Economique », *Economie Internationale*, n° 76.

Zebregs, H., 2004, « Intra-regional trade in emerging Asia », *Fonds Monétaire International*, n° 04/01.

Zivot, E., Andrews, D., 1992, « Further evidence on the great crash, the oil-price shock, and the unit-root hypothesis », *Journal of Business and Economic Statistics*, American Statistical Association, vol.20 (1), pp. 25-44.

CONTAGION OF THE 1997 AND 2008 CRISES IN ASEAN+3: A STRUCTURAL VAR MODEL

Abstract - *The crises of 1997 and 2008 provide a resourceful environment to study the impact of monetary and real shocks in Asean economies. The paper aims at analyzing the reaction of the Asean+3 member states facing international disturbances and at identifying the contagion mechanisms in action during the crisis periods. The main objective is to provide policy recommendations in order to increase these countries' economic stability to contemplate a monetary union in the medium term. We use a Structural VAR to highlight phenomenon of pure contagion in the spread of the crises among the countries. We also witness a positive evolution in the shock responses of the Asean+3 member states, especially when they face international financial disturbances.*

Key words - STRUCTURAL VAR, CONTAGION, LIQUIDITY CRISIS, ASEAN, MONETARY UNION

OUTPUT VOLATILITY AND FDI TO MIDDLE EAST AND NORTH AFRICAN COUNTRIES: A CLOSE-UP ON THE SOURCE COUNTRIES

Dalila NICET-CHENAF[*], **Eric ROUGIER**[**]

Abstract - *Macroeconomic determinants of FDI are seldom analysed from the perspective of source countries, priority generally being given to host country characteristics. Using a gravity model, we analyse FDI flows from a sample of European and non-European countries to MENA economies. We find that European investment to our chosen MENA host countries is higher the higher the source country output volatility, thus lending support to the existence of a substitution effect for European transnational corporations. We also find that the 1995 Barcelona agreement has reinforced MENA countries' vulnerability to European short- and medium-term macroeconomic cycles. Regional integration of MENA economies and the emergence of new sources of FDI for MENA economies is not necessarily a positive development since investment to MENA countries coming from the Mediterranean periphery of Europe is affected by a revenue effect, with FDI flows being reduced when macroeconomic volatility increases in the zone. Our results are robust with respect to various changes in estimator, sample composition and measurement of instability.*

Key words - INFLATION, FDI, GRAVITY MODEL, EUROPEAN UNION, MENA

JEL classification - F21, F43, F44

[*] LAREFI – Bordeaux Université ; dalila.nicet-chenaf@u-bordeaux.fr
[**] GREThA – Bordeaux Université ; eric.rougier@u-bordeaux.fr

1. INTRODUCTION

Whereas the domestic determinants of what attracts foreign direct investment (FDI) have been extensively studied[1], the empirical literature has, until very recently, tended to disregard external macroeconomic conditions. Those conditions need, however, to be considered as crucial determinants of FDI inflows since, every time there is a global financial crisis, economists and policymakers are abruptly reminded of just how volatile financial flows can be. Loayza, Rancière, Servén and Ventura (2007) have expressed that need, stressing the fact that the role of trade and FDI flows as absorbers or amplifiers of shocks has not yet been fully established.

Undoubtedly, external shocks tend to trigger Gross Domestic Product (GDP) volatility for developing economies (Martin and Rey, 2006), the impact of those shocks on activity and employment being channelled, *inter alia*, by huge variations in foreign investment flows (Lensink and Morrissey, 2007). As an illustration, global FDI flows dropped severely in 2009 when western economies and firms were hit by the 2008 financial crisis and the ensuing drastic credit restriction (UNCTAD, 2009). Even though global crises are important in explaining brutal swings in FDI inflows to developing economies, we claim in this paper that it would be also fruitful to take external instability into account at the more disaggregated source country level. Source-related macroeconomic determinants of FDI have, so far, not been studied properly or explicitly in the literature on the determinants of FDI inflows to developing economies. Since they generally explain FDI inflows to developing economies without considering their origin, the majority of the studies that are found in the literature are constrained by their framework to use a single average measurement of external conditions, thereby failing to address source-related determinants of FDI[2].

In sharp contrast to this literature, the present paper tests the sensitivity of FDI levels to source country GDP instability in a gravity model. The gravity model is generally seen as a relevant approach to explaining bilateral trade flows (Evenett and Keller 2002; de Mello-Sampayo 2009), and this model has also been used recently to explain bilateral flows of FDI (Frenkel et al. 2004; Bevan and Estrin, 2004; Desbordes and Vicard, 2009; Busse et al. 2010). This framework allows the FDI effect of host countries' characteristics to be differentiated according to the degree of instability of the source country, while controlling for a series of distance-related factors. A couple of recent papers have used this gravity model in order to identify the specific effects on bilateral FDI flows of various sources of macroeconomic volatility. Cavallari and D'Addona (2012) have examined the role of host and source country nominal and real volatility, but their study is limited to bilateral FDI flows among 24 OECD economies. Levy-Yayeti et al. (2007) are closer to our concerns since they address North-South FDI more explicitly. They focus, however, on the source level, and they do not explicitly address the host country determinants of the

[1] See Bloningen (2005) for an overview of that literature.
[2] A recent illustration is Méon and Sekkat (2012) who proxy external macroeconomic volatility using an aggregate ratio of world FDI to world GDP.

corresponding FDI inflows that are received by developing economies because of their high level of output volatility.

Our paper focuses on North-South investment and aims at identifying the simultaneous effect on FDI of both source and host country output instability by studying the impact of European countries' macroeconomic instability on FDI flowing to the Mediterranean economies of the Middle East and North Africa (MENA)[3]. There are several reasons why this model has been chosen. First, as in many other parts of the world, Mediterranean MENA countries have progressively reformed their institutions and opened up their economies to foreign trade and investment over the last two decades (Mina, 2012). However, although MENA countries have enjoyed a steep increase in FDI inflows since the mid-1990s, they have failed to reap the benefits of their efforts in terms of their share of world FDI. They have also suffered from the marked instability of those incoming investment flows during the last decade (UNCTAD, 2009). Second, the sensitivity of FDI to macroeconomic performance is of vital concern for all those highly age-dependent, labour-exporting MENA economies that are particularly dependent on sources of foreign investment. As such, they tend to be extremely vulnerable to economic fluctuations in source countries, with dramatic consequences on their own output volatility (Koren and Tenreyro, 2007). Third, since the mid-1990s, Mediterranean MENA economies have been more closely associated with the European Union via the bilateral Euro-Med trade and exchange agreements, which has made their economies more exposed to external sources of instability[4].

Table 1 shows that, since 1995, FDI instability has been significantly higher for Southern and Eastern Mediterranean countries than for other developing regions in the world. The Mediterranean MENA countries have become much more subject to instability coming from Europe, without benefitting from structural transfer flows like those that sustained Central and Eastern European economies during their accession to the European Union. Fourth, GDP volatility is traditionally strong in MENA economies, which has significantly reduced domestic investment (Aysan, Pang and Veganzonès-Varoudakis, 2009)[5].

[3] The Mediterranean MENA countries considered are Morocco, Algeria, Tunisia, Libya, Egypt, Jordan, Lebanon, Syria and Turkey. In the econometric part of our work, we have focused on the five biggest recipients of FDI as our host country sample: Morocco, Tunisia, Egypt, Lebanon and Turkey. Algeria is not included in our host country sample since inward FDI is highly concentrated on oil. MENA Gulf countries are considered neither as host nor as source countries in our analysis, because they are not as closely associated with European trade and investment as the Mediterranean ones.

[4] They have also increased regional integration by adopting various free trade agreements (UMA, GAFTA).

[5] Aysan et al. (2009) also report a significant adverse effect of external instability, as measured by the debt burden, on the formation of private capital in the region. They estimate that a more stable external environment would have increased the number of decisions to invest on average by 8.4% in Morocco and 10% in Egypt in the 1980s and by 3.9% in Morocco and 2.6% in Tunisia in the 1990s. Chan and Gemayel (2004) also found that the instability of ICRG scores for political, financial and economic risks has an adverse effect on the quantity of FDI entering MENA economies, but they do not explicitly address macroeconomic instability.

Table 1: FDI level and variability: Before and after 1995

FDI inflows (M $ US)	1987-1995		1996-2009	
Countries	Annual average levels	Coefficient of variation	Annual average levels	Coefficient of variation
Egypt	863.221	0.425	3,689.557	1.112
Morocco	287.908	1.602	1,540.046	2.663
Tunisia	301.774	0.085	1,086.767	1.102
Turkey	622.111	0.020	6,666.500	0.211
Lebanon	10.452	9.530	2,281.927	0.728
Southern and Eastern Mediterranean Countries	2,613.595	0.316	25,062.096	0.857
Asia	36,913.603	0.670	196,046.140	0.545
Latin America and Caribbean	14,889.762	0.589	102,751.060	0.455

Source: UNCTAD - Author's calculations.

In line with Cavallari and D'Addona (2012) and Levy-Yayeti, Panizza and Stein (2007) which recently found that investors tend to substitute foreign investment for domestic investment when domestic macroeconomic conditions worsen, we find that FDI to Mediterranean MENA economies is marked by a substitution effect, i.e. transnational corporations (TNCs) tend to increase their foreign investment when macroeconomic instability increases in their domestic market. This effect is especially strong for the TNCs originating in the most developed core European countries. On the contrary, FDI coming from the periphery of Europe exhibit revenue effects since it is the lowest for the most volatile source country. As a consequence, Mediterranean MENA economies are not equally vulnerable to macroeconomic fluctuations in source countries through their impact on FDI.

The remainder of this paper is organized in four sections. Section 2 discusses the effects of several kinds of macroeconomic instability (internal/external) on FDI inflows. Section 3 presents the indicators of macroeconomic stability (internal/external) retained in the empirical study, as well as the model and the estimation strategy. In Section 4, we first present and then discuss the results of our gravitational model panel data estimation, paying specific attention to source countries and the possibility of cumulative effects. Section 5 shows the results of our estimation when source countries are differentiated according to their level of development. Section 6 develops a series of robustness checks, and Section 7 concludes.

2. FDI AND MACROECONOMIC VOLATILITY: OVERVIEW OF THE LITERATURE

Though the nominal sources of volatility, essentially price and exchange rate fluctuations, have been frequently analysed since the early 1990s, real output volatility, especially external, has been somewhat downplayed by empirical studies of macroeconomic stability[6]. The theoretical effect of output volatility on the flow of FDI to developing countries is far from straightforward, especially when one considers both host and source macroeconomic instability.

As for host country volatility, it undoubtedly increases the entry costs associated with investing abroad, thereby leading to a reduction in FDI. This is particularly true when high levels of real instability indicate a host country's excessive vulnerability to domestic or external macroeconomic shocks. Uctum and Uctum (2011) show, for example, that in the case of Turkey, FDI reacts significantly and adversely to crises in the host country, whereas portfolio investment is most strongly affected by source country instability. But FDI may also be attracted towards highly volatile economies insofar as they also tend to grow rapidly. In this case, foreign investment is driven towards highly volatile countries by market opportunities. A marked depreciation of the exchange rate, or a fall in the value of stocks in host economies may equally increase investment by those foreign firms that are looking for merger opportunities (Krugman 2000; Aguiar and Gopinath 2005). A recent illustration can be provided by the waves of sector-based consolidations that have been reported in the oil and gas, mining, and automobile industries or in financial services (UNCTAD 2009), in years of sharp decrease in global FDI flows: 2008 (-15 %) and 2009 (-30%). Hence, host country volatility may theoretically have either a negative or positive effect on FDI inflows. In the case of European investment in MENA economies, we may reasonably expect that the positive effects will be prevalent, insofar as vertical, green field forms of FDI - less sensitive to output volatility than to exchange rate instability - tend be dominant[7].

Source country output instability may also have either a negative or a positive effect on FDI flows. When business cycles in the source and host countries are synchronised, TNCs may react to the anticipated fall in their profits and to rising financial costs by holding back on investment projects, and by disinvesting abroad (Aizenman, 2003; Wang and Wong, 2007). Hence, source country volatility may reduce FDI outflow because firms are subject to an adverse revenue effect. Conversely, when business cycles in the source and host countries are not synchronized, with, for example, the host country undergoing a bust while the source country benefiting from a boom, substituting FDI for domestic investment may become attractive for firms subject to high volatility in their original market. In that case, a positive substitution effect may well be identified, with higher levels of volatility in the source country increasing FDI flows

[6] Frenkel, Funke and Stadtmann (2004), Apergis and Katrakilidis (1998) or Garibaldi *et al.* (2001) have studied the effects of domestic inflation on FDI inflows. As for exchange rate volatility effects on FDI inflows, see Froot and Stein (1991), Bénassy-Quéré, Fontagné and Lahrèche-Révil (2001), Bechri (1999), Kiyota and Urata (2004), Frenkel, Funke and Stadtmann (2004), Schmidt anjd Broll (2009), Calderón and Didier (2009), Lederman (2011) and Takagi and Shi (2011).

[7] In non-oil MENA countries, the ratio of the number of Greenfield operations to the number of M&A is four to five times higher than the world average, and three times higher than that of developing economies [Authors' calculations based on UNCTAD (2009)].

to other countries. This is the case in Cavalleri and D'Addona (2012) who find FDI between OECD countries to increase when the source country has higher output volatility. They argue that such behaviour of investors with respect to host and source country volatility is consistent with the view that investors choose between investment options at home and abroad on the basis of the volatility differential between the source and host economies. By estimating a gravity model of North-South FDI, Levy-Yeyati, Panniza and Stein (2007) found a similar substitution effect, with FDI flows tending to be countercyclical with respect to output cycles in the US and Europe, thereby reflecting investors' arbitrage among different investment opportunities. They concluded by arguing that, contrary to what is usually claimed, recessions in industrial countries are likely to increase FDI flows to developing countries, particularly to those with close ties with the U.S. and Europe. This is the substitution effect. Thus, output volatility in source countries may have both a negative and a positive effect on FDI flows to developing economies, with this effect being highly conditional to the relative magnitude of those income and substitution effects.

Of course, the effect of source instability on FDI flows to developing countries might well be amplified by bad internal macroeconomic performance in the host country (Eichengreen 2000; Kose, Prasad, Rogoff and Wei, 2009). If host country's output growth or exchange rate[8] turns out to be less stable, it is likely that the source country's volatility positive effects on FDI will be weaker (Kaminsky, Lizondo and Reinhart 1998). Thus there is less chance of a country attracting higher FDI flows when an external shock is combined with bad domestic macroeconomic performance (Ishii *et al.* 2002)[9]. Méon and Sekkat (2012) found that FDI flows to developing economies tend to be reduced in times of global symmetrical economic crisis, with generalized bad external macroeconomic conditions tending to outweigh the domestic institutional or structural factors that might attract or repel FDI. FDI flows tend, however, to react quite differently to increased macroeconomic risks depending on whether those investments are sourced in countries whose firms traditionally invest abroad or in economies where foreign investment is less common. Andrès, Busse and Nunnenkamp (2012) have, for example, recently found that non-traditional sources of FDI are less risk-averse than traditional ones.

The next section explains the method used in order to identify which one of these two effects dominates in the case of Euro-Mediterranean FDI flows.

[8] For a recent study of the contrasted effects of exchange rate instability on FDI inflows, see Schmidt and Broll (2009).

[9] As the decision to set up a subsidiary abroad is generally justified by the intention of obtaining long-term profits from the selected location (Caves, 1996), the odds are, however, that the corresponding sunk costs (especially for greenfield projects) will make the FDI less reactive than other forms of capital to a transitory deterioration of source or host countries' macroeconomic conditions. This assumption has received empirical support in Fernandez-Arias and Hausman (2001), Levchenko and Mauro (2007) for host country volatility, and in Levy-Yeyati, Panizza and Stein (2007) for source country volatility.

3. MODEL, VARIABLES AND METHODS

In order to identify the sensitivity of FDI inflows to the host and source country's instability, we use a gravity model that links thirty-two countries that were sources of investment to the five largest recipient countries in the MENA region (Egypt, Lebanon, Morocco, Tunisia and Turkey), during the period 1987-2009[10]. The standard expression of the gravity model adapted to bilateral flows of FDI can be written as:

$$FDI_{ij} = A\frac{Y_i^{\beta_1} Y_j^{\beta_2}}{D_{ij}^{\beta_3}} \quad (1)$$

where FDI_{ij} is the annual flow of FDI from source country i to host country j, Y_i and Y_j are the annual GDP levels of the source and host countries, D_{ij} is an indicator of the distance between the two countries, and A, β_1, β_2 and β_3 are the parameters to be estimated. When Equation (1) is log-linearized, it becomes:

$$Ln(FDI_{ijt}) = \alpha + \beta_1 Ln(GDP_{it}) + \beta_2 Ln(GDP_{jt}) - \beta_3 Ln(D_{ijt}) + \beta_4 Macro_{ijt} + \beta_5 Controls_{jt} + u_{ij} + v_t + \varepsilon_{ijt} \quad (2)$$

where, FDI_{ijt} represents the value in dollars of the inflows of FDI from a country i (source country) entering country j (host country) at time t. In order to control for the multilateral resistance terms identified by Anderson and Wincoop (2003), we have chosen to introduce bilateral country-pair fixed effects u_{ij} since, as stressed by Bergstrand and Egger (2007), sources of multilateral resistance appear to move only slowly, and country-pair fixed effects reduce the omitted variable bias associated with unobserved time-invariant pair-specific heterogeneity[11].

If we now consider the right-hand side of equation (2), $Ln(GDP_{it})$ and $Ln(GDP_{jt})$ stand for the natural logarithm of GDP levels of the source and host countries respectively, and β_1 and β_2 take a positive sign if there is a "mass" effect operating in determining bilateral direct investment flows. By extension, higher host country GDP is generally considered to increase horizontal FDI, as the size of the local market is worth being served by a multinational firm's production subsidiary. The *Difference in GDP* per capita (in log form) between the two countries is used as a proxy for the differences in factor endowments or in the level of economic and technological development in each country. The coefficient takes a positive sign if FDI is attracted by low labour costs, and a negative sign if the FDI-related labour requirements are more skill-intensive. D_{ijt} is the vector of the various concepts of distance controlling for the most typical

[10] The country list is given in the Appendix. Algeria is excluded because of the size of the FDI related to energy. Turkey is also treated as a source country for FDI because of its proximity to the European Union.

[11] Random effects enable time-invariant factors such as distance or common border to be controlled for. The time dimension is accounted for by random effects because it enables all kinds of dyadic events, not specified in equation (2), such as bilateral trade or investment treaties, to be controlled for.

sources of transaction and transport costs involved in an investment moving from one country to another. The physical bilateral distance (*Distance*) corresponds to the distance between the countries' capitals[12]; FDI is generally taken as being inversely proportional to the distance between the two countries involved. However, when the host country shares a common border, language, or a former colonial link with the source country, it is generally considered that FDI will be higher. *Adjacency* and *Common language* take the value 1 if the source and host countries respectively share a common border or have a common language; they take the value 0 otherwise[13]. The variable *Past colonial links* takes value 1 if the source country had colonized the host country, and 0 otherwise[14].

$Macro_{ijt}$ is a vector of macroeconomic determinants of FDI inflows concerning either source country *i* or host country *j*, including source and host country characteristics in terms of output volatility (respectively *Volatility source* and *Volatility host*). The expected sign of the *Volatility source* coefficient has been discussed in the previous section. It may be positive or negative, conditional on the dominance of substitution or income effect. As for *Volatility host* coefficient, its sign may also be a priori undetermined. On the one hand, FDI inflows tend to be reduced when the short- and medium-term growth potential of the host economy is afflicted by instability. This point is particularly true in relation to market-led FDI, but is also the case for other categories of foreign investment: investors always seek out a stable macroeconomic environment. On the other hand, financial difficulties imposed on host country domestic firms by a high degree of growth instability can favour opportunity-led investments of a fire-sale type. In that case, FDI inflows should increase in proportion to the host country's growth volatility. From what precedes, we can anticipate that the coefficient for *Instability host* can be either negative or positive, but the opportunity-driven positive effect seems to be plausible for MENA economies, given the nature of the foreign investments they tend to attract.

For each time period, the standard deviation of GDP growth has been calculated for both host and source country. Mean and standard deviation values at time *t* have been computed as a three-year moving average over *t-2*, *t-1* and *t*. We have supposed that investors observe short-term past volatility and compare it for different potential destinations. In order to avoid a null average value, we

[12] Stein and Daude (2007) have also recently shown that differences in time zones have an adverse effect on the location of investment because time distance increases the transaction costs associated with activities necessitating real-time communication and interaction. Given the concentration of our sample on a limited array of time zones, that aspect has not been included in our model.

[13] The influence of former colonial links on the institutional, linguistic and cultural proximities that facilitate the creation of international networks is considered by Bénassy-Quéré, Coupet and Mayer (2007) and Abderrezak (2008) to be a determinant in explaining trade or FDI flows.

[14] It should be noted that *Past colonial links* is a good proxy for legal origin, which appears to be significant in explaining bilateral portfolio investment flows (Lane and Milesi-Ferretti 2008) as well as bilateral FDI flows (Stein and Daude 2007).

have chosen to compute absolute values of standard deviations, and, then, to express them in logarithmic form[15].

Controls$_{jt}$ is a vector of additional determinants of bilateral FDI flows. As it is expected that openness to trade will either tend to increase inflows of efficiency-led FDI by lowering export costs for TNCs, or tend to decrease market-led FDI motivated by tariff-jumping, we control for the degree of openness to trade ($Openness_{jt}$), measured by the ratio of exports to GDP at time t for the host country j. Dummies for membership of a common regional trade agreement are also included, since integration spurs FDI (Daude, Levy-Yeyati and Stein, 2003), especially that of a North-South nature (Stein and Daude, 2007). As our study uses a sample of both MENA and European countries, we explicitly introduce controls for membership of three regional trade agreements (*GAFTA*, *UMA* and Euro-Med, noted as *MED*). Medvedev (2012) has provided evidence that there is a positive correlation between the size of any two economies bound by a Free Trade Agreement and their mutual FDI flows. Similarly, it has also been found that bilateral investment treaties have positive effects on FDI inflows to developing economies in general (Desbordes and Vicard, 2009), and to MENA economies in particular (Mina, 2012). Here, we focus exclusively on bilateral trade agreements, as they are often associated with increased export processing FDI. Equally, since investment decisions made by TNCs generally use a global evaluation of host country property rights (Ali, Fiess and MacDonald, 2012), any empirical assessment of FDI flows requires the introduction of a variable to control for institutional quality[16]. The comprehensive indicator that is used here, *Investprofil*, is particularly suitable for capturing the impact of business regulation and property rights enforcement on FDI, since it combines ratings of contract viability, risks of expropriation, repatriation of profits and delays in payments[17]. It is also worth remarking that the VIF test reported in Annex1, table A3 does not reject the assumption of no multi-collinearity between our variables.

4. FDI AND SOURCE COUNTRY VOLATILITY: BASELINE ESTIMATIONS

Insofar as our model takes a logarithmic form, it is necessary to deal with the issue of zero value FDI flows. Several alternatives are used in the panel gravity

---

[15] Although *volatility source* is not likely to be endogenous to FDI levels, volatility host may theoretically be affected by the contemporary level of incoming FDI. To limit this risk, *volatility host* is computed as a three-year moving average including the year t-1 and t-2. Out the three measurements of GDP growth included in the standard deviation computation, one only (that in time t) may be affected by contemporaneous FDI levels. Moreover, FDI to MENA are modest relative to MENA GDP. Furthermore, we have tested our model with *host country* lagged one-year (computed over time t-3, t-2 and t-1) with respect to FDI inflows in time t, with no significant change on the estimated coefficients.

[16] Anderson and Marcouiller (2002) have previously shown that omitting indexes of institutional quality biases typical gravity model estimates of trade.

[17] The definition, source and descriptive statistics of the variables are reported in the Appendix.

model literature. The Eichengreen correction, coupled with Random Effect estimation, is the most commonly used approach in order to circumvent the problem of the zero for dependent variables. It consists of using a simple transformation of the form *ln*(1+FDI), which enables the coefficient to be interpreted as elasticity when the value of *ln*(1+FDI) is approximately equal to *ln*(FDI), which is accepted as a reasonable assumption (Eichengreen and Irwin, 1998). Since the dependent variable is censored, however, the model may also be estimated by using the Tobit method, which presents the advantage of dealing with the problem of zeros, corresponding to null FDI flows, without excluding them. Explicitly accounting for zero FDI flows increases the variation of the dependent variable, thereby producing higher values and significance for the estimated coefficients of the various determinants of FDI. The Tobit Random Effect model, based on maximum likelihood estimation, is considered as a robust approach when dealing with censored data concerning the dependent variable (Eaton and Tamura, 1994; Wei, 2000; Head and Ries, 2008). Our baseline model Random Effect estimations, with the Eichengreen correction, and by the Random Effect Tobit estimator are reported in Table A4.

When the model does suffer from heteroscedasticity, however, the gravity model Poisson estimation is to be preferred, as shown by Santos Silva and Tenreyro (2006). The tests reported in the lower panel of columns A4.1 and A42 (Table A4) show that we cannot reject the hypothesis of heteroscedasticity in our case. Our preferred estimator is thus the Poisson Pseudo-Maximum Likelihood, with estimation results being reported in the first two columns of Table 2.

The baseline regression (Column 2.1) is in accordance with the results of the existing literature. *GDP source* has the expected positive influence on FDI flows. If *GDP host* is not significant *per se*, the difference between it and *GDP source* significantly increases FDI flows, meaning that the greater the technological distance, the greater the investment flow. This confirms that FDI to MENA countries may be more vertical than horizontal. The two variables controlling for cultural distance have contrasted impacts on FDI flows. Whereas a common language seems to slightly increase FDI flows between two countries, signalling a reduction in transaction costs, the existence of past colonial links has no effect. This result is confirmed by the positive and significant impact of the quality of institutions (*InvestProfil*) in host countries, which confirms that minimizing transaction costs is an objective of European firms when they invest in the Mediterranean periphery.

As for the two variables assessing transport costs, *Adjacency* and *Distance*, they are not significant, suggesting that geographical distance does not explain the location of FDI as far as the five MENA economies in our sample are concerned. Although this result would be surprising if obtained on the basis of a worldwide sample, it is more understandable in the context of our sample. Since all source countries are geographically close to the five receivers, there is very low observable heterogeneity in the geographical distances. Although trade openness has no effect on FDI levels to MENA economies, regional integration has a positive influence, since *GAFTA* and *AMU* both show a positive and significant coefficient. The significant effect of the Euro-Med dummy (*MED*), moreover, confirms that the reduction of both the institutional distance and trade barriers increases FDI flows for European firms, irrespective of the particular colonial history of the source and host countries.

Having first examined the standard determinants invoked in the empirical analyses of bilateral FDI flows, we can now proceed to consider the simultaneous effects of our specific variables that focus on macroeconomic instability: host and source country output instability.

Table 2: FDI levels: Baseline Poisson estimation, with GDP instability and war (Student *t*)

	2.1	2.2	2.3
Openness	-.180 (-3.28)***	-.101 (-1.77)*	-.0874 (-1.51)
MED	.166 (5.26)***	.173 (5.43)***	.183 (5.70)***
AMU	.947 (4.94)***	.593 (2.67)***	.605 (2.72)***
GAFTA	.317(4.83)***	.275 (3.81)***	.290 (3.99)***
InvestProfil	.090 (12.27)***	.091 (11.66)***	.090 (11.57)***
GDP source	.481 (11.96)***	.373 (8.71)***	.374 (8.72)***
GDP host	.032 (0.92)	.050 (1.38)	.229 (0.59)
Difference in GDP per capita	.170 (6.42)***	.163 (6.06)***	.160 (5.96)***
Distance	-.293 (-1.31)	-.229 (-1.00)	-.216 (-0.94)
Adjacency	-.264 (-1.01)	-.253 (-0.97)	-.257 (0.99)
Past colonial links	.096 (0.17)	.253 (0.47)	.255 (0.45)
Common language	.492 (1.77)*	.351 (1.25)	.327 (1.17)
Volatility source	-	.035 (5.38)***	.035 (5.36)***
Volatility host	-	-.309 (-2.03)**	-.080 (-0.44)
War	-	-	-.490 (-2.68)***
Post War	-	-	-.002 (-0.02)
Constant	-6.866 (-3.89)***	5.863 (-3.20)***	-5.572 (-3.84)***
Log likelihood	6832.770	6394.726	6390.425
LRTest	χ^2 = 4451.83***	χ^2 =4259.38 ***	χ^2= 4219.55***
Wald χ^2	2321.92***	1799.86***	1800.14***
AIC	13693.54	12821.45	12817.12
BIC	13779.28	12985.93	12925.85

*Notes: *, **, *** significant at 10%, 5% and 1% risk.*
*Number of observations: 3375; Number of years: 23; Number of country-pairs: 27*5=135.*

The negative sign of Volatility host in column 2.2 shows that host countries exhibiting more GDP instability attract significantly lower FDI. This result seems somewhat contradictory with the fact that MENA economies attract vertical rather that horizontal FDI. The hypothesis cannot be rejected, however, that this result could be driven by the particularities of Lebanon during both wartime and post-war periods. The wartime period necessarily exacerbated GDP instability in Lebanon, while FDI nose-dived, thereby possibly producing an adverse relationship between host GDP volatility and FDI inflows. As for the post-war reconstruction period, from 1991 onwards, with its context of high GDP growth variation springing from growth and FDI recovery, it may have induced a positive relationship between GDP host and FDI inflows. As the net effect of the Lebanese war on the estimated impact of GDP volatility on FDI might be contradictory, a war dummy, taking the value 1 for the Lebanon between 1987 and 1991 and 0 otherwise, and a post-war dummy taking value 1 for the Lebanon from 1992 to 1995, and 0 otherwise were simultaneously introduced into Equation 2. Column 2.3 shows that the coefficient for host GDP growth volatility is no more significant when the two dummies are introduced as additional controls[18]. When the particular characteristics of the Lebanese wartime and post-war periods are controlled for, FDI is no longer dependent on macroeconomic conditions in MENA countries, which is more consistent with the type of investment that traditionally flows to this region. As mentioned above, FDI to our five MENA economies is generally resource-based and vertical, with little likelihood of sensitivity to macroeconomic conditions in host countries (Sadik and Bolbol, 2001; Nicet-Chenaf and Rougier, 2011).

As far as output volatility in source countries is concerned, we find that it significantly increases FDI towards our sample of MENA economies (Columns 2.2 and 2.3). This result suggests that, in response to source country output volatility, the investors in our sample may well arbitrate between investment options at home and abroad, thereby lending support to the substitution view put forward by Levy-Yayeti, Panizza and Stein (2007) or Cavallari and D'Addona (2012). As our indicator of output instability does not allow us to differentiate between boom and bust cycles, FDI cannot be considered as being strictly counter-cyclical relative to the source country and pro-cyclical relative to the host country.

5. VOLATILITY, TRADITIONAL AND NON-TRADITIONAL SOURCES OF FDI

Focusing on source country macroeconomic characteristics, it could be argued that the estimated positive effect of GDP instability on FDI levels is driven by a selection bias. Firms from more stable countries might invest more in MENA countries because they are more internationalised than those from more unstable economies. One reason for this could be that less stable economies, those located at the periphery of Europe in our sample, are less developed. This means that their firms are further from the technological frontier than those from more stable and developed economies and this distance limits their capacity to invest at an international level. The positive coefficient of *Volatility source* might thus simply reflect the fact that more developed economies are also more stable, and that their firms invest more in less developed countries than is the case for firms from less stable economies.

In order to test this hypothesis, the set of source countries has been separated into two subsets in terms of average GDP level. The first subset, labelled *Central*, is composed of the most developed Western European economies which are also the traditional sources of investment to MENA economies[19]. The sec-

[18] Since *Post war* has never entered significantly into the explanation of FDI levels, it has been withdrawn from subsequent estimations. We checked that our main findings remain unchanged when *Post war* is removed (Column 3.1 in Table 3).

[19] This subset includes members of the European Union before the accession of Eastern and Central European countries, plus Switzerland and Norway.

ond group, labelled *Peripheral*, includes less developed and stable economies located in the periphery of Europe[20]. They are non-traditional sources of FDI to MENA economies in the sense that their firms have only started investing abroad very recently. The standard deviation of GDP growth, computed over the whole period for the *Central* group, is about half (.001435) that of the *Peripheral* group (.002887): these mean values are statistically different. Hence, the *Central* group of source countries is significantly less volatile than the peripheral one. Two separated estimations of Equation 2 were carried out, one for each subset (*Central* and *Peripheral),* and a Chow test was performed to check the hypothesis that FDI behaviour might be differentiated according to the type of source country. The results of these estimations are reported in columns 3.1 and 3.2 of Table 3.

Column 3.1 of Table 3 shows a positive and significant FDI effect of *Volatility source* for the *Central* subgroup of source countries. In addition, the positive sign of the *Volatility host* coefficient suggests that FDI from traditional Western European sources tends to be lower when volatility is higher in our MENA host countries. Conversely, column 3.2 shows that, although FDI from more unstable *Peripheral* economies increases in response to host country output volatility, it tends to be reduced when domestic output volatility is higher since the coefficient of *Volatility source* is negative. The Chow test reported in the lower panel of Columns 3.1 and 3.2 confirms that the two estimations have significantly different coefficients.

Thus, our results for the whole sample may be driven by the behaviour of the core European firms, with those of the European periphery having adopted very different behaviour with respect to host country instability. This finding suggests that the substitution effect found for the whole sample was essentially due to the more developed core European economies. TNCs from the less stable *Peripheral* economies tend, on the contrary, to reduce their investment abroad in times of higher domestic instability, thereby being subject to a revenue effect. FDI is therefore reactive to volatility in the host country, with different patterns of reaction being observed for traditional and non-traditional sources. Since the estimated coefficients for *Volatility host* are different across the two subgroups, our findings also highlight the fact that FDI sensitivity to host country volatility is significantly different according to the country of origin of TNCs. Although firms from the core European market tend to invest less in the more volatile MENA host economies, those from the periphery of Europe tend to be more attracted by those volatile economies. Hence, not only do our results confirm the finding published recently by Andrès, Busse and Nunnenkamp (2012) that FDI from traditional sources (developed economies) exhibits different sensitivity to host country conditions than FDI from non-traditional sources, but our results also generalize this differentiation in the sensitivity to the volatility of the source country.

---

[20] Eastern and Central European (Hungary), Mediterranean (Malta) and MENA countries (Egypt, Morocco, Tunisia, Turkey, Lebanon, Syrian Arab Republic, Jordan, Mauritania).

Table 3: Estimations of FDI levels: Chow tests (Student *t*)

	3.1	3.2	3.3	3.4
N=3375	First group *Central*	Second group *Peripheral*	First group 1987-1995	Second group 1996-2009
Openness	-.251 (-4.02)***	.739 (3.87)***	.092 (0.70)	-.160 (-1.98)**
MED	.212 (6.24)***	.281 (1.66)*	-	.384 (7.33)***
AMU	-	.278 (1.14)	.632 (2.66)**	1.075 (1.79)*
GAFTA	-	.052 (0.54)	-	.300 (1.91)**
InvestProfil	.080 (9.62)***	.153 (6.10)***	.119 (6.44)***	.079 (8.29)***
War	-.362 (-2.11)**	-22.521 (-0.01)	-.297 (-1.32)	-
Volatility source	.059 (7.60)***	-1.211 (-3.06)***	.0189 (0.05)	.028 (2.55)**
Volatility host	-.316 (-1.74)*	2.061 (3.26)***	-.589 (-1.69)*	.202 (0.91)
GDP source	.560 (8.47)***	.069 (0.82)	.757 (7.26)***	.226 (4.32)***
GDP host	-.056 (1.21)	.421 (3.32)***	-.043 (-0.37)	.093 (2.06)**
Difference in GDP p.c.	.064 (2.07)**	.227 (4.70)***	.159 (2.00)**	.129 (4.59)***
Distance	-.776 (-2.59)***	.086 (0.21)	-.332 (-1.07)	-.040 (-0.13)
Adjacency	-.308 (-1.13)	-.555 (-0.84)	-.536 (-1.54)	-.196 (-0.71)
Past colonial links	.2161 (0.13)	1.747 (1.28)	.232 (0.30)	.608 (1.00)
Common language	-.079 (-0.23)	1.304 (2.01)**	1.480 (3.65)***	.026 (0.06)
Constant	2.370 (0.96)	-11.727 (-3.50)***	-11.370 (3.75)***	-4.954 (2.42)**
Log likelihood LR test	-4664.617 χ^2)= 2153.89 Prob>χ^2=0.0000	-1628.036 χ^2)= 1112.85 Prob>χ^2=0.0000	-1787.328 χ^2)= 4366.37 Prob>χ^2=0.0000	-4011.767 χ^2)= 3607.37 Prob>χ^2=0.0000
Wald χ^2 test	Waldχ^2(14)=230Pr ob>χ^2=0.0000	Waldχ^2(16)=547 Prob > χ^2 = 0.0000	Waldχ^2(15)=284.3 Prob > χ^2 = 0.0000	Waldχ^2(14)=470 Prob>χ^2=0.0000
Instability source Instability host	χ^2(2)=13.21 Prob > χ^2 = 0.0001		χ^2(2)=44.07 Prob > χ^2 = 0.000	
Group	χ^2(3)=29.68 Prob > χ^2 = 0.0001		χ^2(3)=18.22 Prob > χ^2 = 0.00010	
GDP source GDP host	χ^2(2)=74.06 Prob > χ^2 = 0.0000		χ^2(2)=24.06 Prob > χ^2 = 0.0000	
Group	χ^2(3)=74.40 Prob > χ^2 = 0.000		χ^2(3)=45.27 Prob > χ^2 = 0.0000	

*Notes: *, **, *** significant at 10%, 5% and 1% risk.*

A related issue is whether our results are driven by a specific sub-period. It is likely that the determinants of European FDI flows to MENA countries changed after the 1995 Barcelona agreement. We test this assumption by estimating Equation 2 for the two periods before and after 1995, and perform a Chow test. As assumed, our estimations, reported in columns 3.3 and 3.4 (and in the lower panel for the Chow test), show a structural break for 1995 in the empirical model used to explain FDI levels to MENA economies. That particular year corresponds to the Barcelona agreement that eased trade and investment between European Union and MENA countries. Columns 3.3 and 3.4 show that our main results are driven more by the post-1995 period, opening with the Barcelona agreement, than by the pre-1995 period, which, moreover, includes both the Lebanese war and post-war reconstruction. Equally, column 3.3 shows that, prior to 1995, host country instability and the existence of a common language were critical factors for attracting FDI to our MENA countries. The results reported in column 3.4 show that it is only after 1995 that source country output volatility became so significant in explaining FDI levels. In a sense, the 1995 Barcelona agreement reinforced MENA countries' vulnerability to European short- and medium-term macroeconomic cycles. By the same token, after the Barcelona agreement, economic governance and cultural proximity became less significant, whereas MENA-European Union trade agreements became more significant in explaining both FDI levels.

6. ROBUSTNESS CHECKS

In this section, we address several issues related to the robustness of our results.

The first issue is that focusing on such country-level indicators of macroeconomic instability as standard deviation of GDP growth could entail a misspecification bias arising from the fact that the real volatility that reduces FDI flows to MENA economies may be global instead of being related to source country characteristics. Méon and Sekkat (2012) have recently provided convincing evidence that global waves of increase in FDI can outweigh the most prominent domestic determinants of attractiveness to FDI. In our initial model, waves of FDI were not controlled for. However, as that might have led to an overestimation of the impact of source country macroeconomic characteristics, an indicator of global FDI waves, similar to that of Méon and Sekkat (2012) was subsequently introduced[21], leaving the coefficients for source country and host country instability unchanged (Table 4). Insofar as FDI instability tends to be as important as FDI levels to explain economic development (Lensink and Morissey, 2006; Choong and Liew, 2009), we also tested our gravity equation with three-year moving average standard deviations of FDI inflows as the dependent variable[22]. The estimation results, reported in columns 4.2 and 4.4 of Table 4, show that although MENA countries do not attract more foreign investment when world FDI increases, FDI waves tend to reduce FDI volatility, with likely positive effects on future economic growth.

The second issue is that focusing on three-year moving averages might lead to overestimating the coefficients used to measure the effect of host and source country GDP volatility on FDI. Column 5.2 of Table 5 shows that when an alternative computation of GDP instability (five year-moving standard deviation) is used, our main findings remain unchanged. The coefficients estimated for *Volatility source* and *Volatility host* are, thus, robust to a change in the measurement of output volatility.

---

[21] The World FDI wave indicator consists of the annual value of world FDI outflows; similarly, the European FDI wave is computed as the annual value of European FDI outflows.

[22] So as to limit any reciprocity bias, GDP volatility is lagged by one year in these two estimations.

Table 4: FDI levels and FDI waves (Student *t*)

	4.1 FDI Levels	4.2 FDI volatility	4.3 FDI Levels	4.4 FDI volatility
Openness	-.083 (-1.44)	.382 (3.98)***	-.082 (-1.42)	.386 (4.01)***
MED	.1915 (5.65)***	.074 (1.22)	.191 (5.55)***	.070 (1.12)
AMU	.605 (2.72)***	-.009 (-0.04)	.603 (2.71)***	-.007 (-0.03)
GAFTA	.299 (4.07)***	-.053 (-0.54)	.300 (4.05)***	-.057 (-0.57)
InvestProfil	.093 (10.74)***	.021 (1.32)	.093 (10.74)***	.0142 (0.89)
War	-.475 (-2.68)***	.684 (2;97)***	-.474 (-2.66)***	.701 (2;98)***
Europe FDI wave	-.016 (-0.75)	-.167 (-4.30)***	-	-
World FDI wave	-	-	-.0178 (-0.64)	-.100 (3.87)***
Volatility source	.036 (5.41)***	.0001 (0.01)	.036 (5.39)***	.001 (1.69)*
Volatility host	-.086 (-0.50)	-1.540 (-5.12)***	-.091 (-0.52)	-1.598 (-5.29)***
GDP source	.378 (8.70)***	.351 (6.14)***	.378 (8.76)***	.353 (6.12)***
GDP host	.034 (0.84)	.832 (12.43)***	.037 (0.87)	.866 (11.62)***
Diff. in GDP p.c.	.162 (6.01)***	-.054 (-1.75)*	.162 (5.99)***	-.057 (-1.84)**
Distance	-.220 (-0.97)	-.269 (-1.14)	-.222 (-0.97)	-.280 (-1.17)
Adjacency	-.255 (-0.98)	-.287 (-1.03)	-.255 (-0.98)	-.289 (-1.03)
Past colonial links	.255 (0.45)	.123 (0.22)	.255 (0.45)	.121 (0.22)
Common language	.341 (1.21)	.728 (2.46)*	.343 (1.22)	.737 (2.46)*
Constant	-5.421 (-2.95)***	-16.209 (-7.97)***	-5.418 (-2.94)***	-16.375 (-7.93)***
Log likelihood	-6390.275	-4287.048	-6390.350	-4290.267
LR test	$\chi^2 = 4067.55$ Prob>χ^2=0.0000	$\chi^2 = 1336.71$ Prob>χ^2=0.0000	$\chi^2 = 4004.60$ Prob > χ^2 = 0.0000	$\chi^2 = 1341.60$ Prob>χ^2=0.0000
Wald χ^2 test	Wald χ^2 (16)= 1791.28 Prob>χ^2=0.0000	Wald χ^2 (16)= 815.85 Prob>χ^2=0.0000	Wald χ^2 (16)= 1791.35 Wald χ^2= 0.0000	Wald χ^2 (16)= 802.61 Prob>χ^2=0.0000
AIC	12816.55	8610.097	12816.7	8616.535
BIC	12925.28	8718.83	12925.44	8725.269

*Notes: *, **, *** significant at 10%, 5% and 1% risk.*
Number of observations: 3375; Number of years: 25; Number of country-pairs: 140.

The third issue concerns the indicator of volatility. The value of a distribution's standard deviation is proportional to the value of its arithmetic mean. It might thus be argued that, because they operate in more dynamic domestic markets, firms from more volatile source countries tend to invest more abroad because their revenues are higher. The positive coefficient estimated for source country volatility would therefore reflect revenue rather than a substitution effect.

In order to test the robustness of our results with respect to the indicator of volatility, while checking the assumption of a revenue effect, we computed a coefficient of variation using the following formula:

$$Cv_{jt} = \frac{\sigma_{GDP_{jt}}}{Mean_{GDP_{jt}}} \quad (3)$$

where, σ_{GDPjt} is the standard deviation of the GDP growth rate for country *j* at period *t*, and $Mean_{GDPjt}$ is the average rate of growth of the GDP for country *j* over the same period *t*. The standard deviation is thus corrected for the GDP growth size effect. The results of the regressions of FDI levels on three-year and five-year moving coefficients of variation are reported in Table 5.

Table 5: Regressions of FDI levels: 5 year-moving standard deviations, 5 year-moving and 3 year-moving coefficients of variation (Student *t*)

	5.1 5-year moving standard deviations	5.2 5-year moving standard deviations	5.3 3-year coefficients of variation	5.3 5-year coefficients of variation
Openness	-.156 (-2.82)***	-.077 (-1.08)	-.091 (-1.16)	-.077 (-1.20)
MED	.170 (5.39)***	.167 (4.63)***	.175 (5.47)***	.162 (4.55)***
AMU	.957 (4.99)***	1.050 (1.83)*	.619 (2.79)***	1.049 (1.83)**
GAFTA	.325 (4.54)***	.279 (3.77)***	.311 (4.31)***	.276 (3.74)***
InvestProfil	.087 (11.71)***	.078 (9.14)***	.089 (11.48)***	.077 (9.03)***
War	-.450 (2.84)***	-.134 (-0.75)	-.476 (-2.63)***	-.135 (-0.75)
GDP source	.487 (12.11)***	.386 (8.86)***	.426 (10.15)***	.389 (8.94)***
GDP host	.017 (0.49)	.087 (1.76)*	.008 (0.23)	.089 (1.89)**
Diff. in GDP p.c.	.171 (6.45)***	.135 (5.08)***	.151 (5.67)***	.136 (4.11)***
Distance	-.285 (-1.28)	-.171 (0.73)	-.251 (-1.12)	-.175 (-0.75)
Adjacency	-.267 (-1.02)	-.254 (-0.98)	-.252 (-0.97)	-.253 (-0.98)
Past colonial links	.086 (0.15)	.292 (0.2)	.144 (0.26)	.287 (0.51)
Common language	.487 (1.75)*	.251 (0.83)	.397 (1.42)	.260 (0.86)
Volatility source	-	.045 (3.53)***	.510 (3.65)***	.714 (3.53)***
Volatility host	-	-.331 (-1.81)*	-1.79 (-0.58)	-6.764 (-2.14)**
Constant	-6.848 (-3.90)***	-7.122 (-3.73)***	-5.992 (-3.33)***	-7.165 (-3.78)***
Log likelihood	-6828.250	-5929.180	-6397.902	-5928.500
LR test	χ^2= 4366.37 Prob>χ^2=0.0000	χ^2= 4036.30 Prob>χ^2=0.0000	χ^2= 4217.74 Prob>χ^2=0.0000	χ^2= 4032.34 Prob>χ^2=0.0000
Wald χ^2 test	Wald χ^2 (13)= 2315.20 Prob>χ^2=0.0000	Waldχ^2(14)= 1341.26 Prob>χ^2=0.0000	Wald χ^2(14)= 1765.64 Prob > χ^2 = 0.0000	Wald χ^2(14)= 1342.26 Prob>χ^2=0.0000
AIC	13686.51	13676.62	12829.81	11891
BIC	13778.37	13758.28	12932.5	11992.1

*Notes: *, **, *** significant at 10%, 5% and 1% risk.*
*Number of observations: 3775; Number of years: 21; Number of country-pairs: 28*5=140.*

Columns 5.3 and 5.4 show that the coefficient of *Volatility source* keeps its positive sign when measured by a coefficient of variation (instead of a standard deviation) and remains significant. This is especially the case when instability is measured by 3-year moving coefficients of variation. It should also be noted that when computed as 5-year moving coefficients of variation, the adverse effect of *Volatility host* becomes significant, even when the effect of the Lebanese war on FDI is controlled for. Since the coefficient of *Volatility source* remains positive even after controlling for the size effect, the positive impact of the standard deviation of GDP growth is not driven by the fact that the most volatile countries are also those where the growth rates of aggregate income and corporate revenues are the highest. Thus rejecting the revenue effect reinforces the conclusion that there is a substitution effect.

The fourth and final issue concerns the influence of host country nominal instability on our core results. Although our paper focuses on the impact of real volatility on FDI flows to MENA countries, nominal sources of instability, notably affecting domestic prices or exchange rates, may also be relevant to explaining the attraction of FDI. We tested the impact of price instability and exchange rate fluctuations on FDI to MENA countries and checked whether or not it changed our basic results with respect to real volatility. We first tested the impact of host country inflation on FDI. Whereas inflation may reduce FDI inflows, it could also explain the impact of host country GDP volatility on FDI flows in the case where GDP volatility is mainly provoked by price variations. Column 6.1 of Table 6 shows that although inflation reduces FDI inflows, it does not change the estimated value and significance of our core GDP volatility variables.

The assumption that exchange rate volatility may increase fire-sale FDI in developing MENA economies has also been tested. According to Kaminsky, Lizondo and Reinhart (1998), an exchange rate crisis is typically a situation in which a speculative attack leads to a sharp depreciation of the local currency and to considerable losses in exchange reserves, especially in the case of fixed or pegged regimes. Although exchange rate crises are expected to have a negative impact on FDI, especially vertical FDI, they may foster fire sale investments attracted by low-price Merger & Acquisition opportunities in times of high frequency exchange rate crises (Krugman 2000; Aguiar and Gopinath 2005). Our indicator of exchange rate volatility takes the value 1 if the country has experienced a large variation in the value of the real exchange rate or of its foreign currency reserves, and 0 otherwise. The algebra of the indicator is reported in Annex 2.

Table 6: FDI levels and nominal instability (Student *t*)

	6.1	6.2
Openness	-.087 (-1.52)	-.075 (-1.31)
MED	.174 (5.43)***	.173 (5.41)***
AMU	.622 (2.80)***	.6393 (2.88)***
GAFTA	.310 (4.29)***	.309 (4.27)***
InvestProfil	.089 (11.38)***	.083 (10.03)***
GDP source	.429 (10.19)***	.441 (10.44)***
GDP host	.007 (0.19)	-.020 (0.51)
Difference in GDP p.c.	.148 (5.55)***	.1535 (5.73)***
Distance	-.253 (-1.12)	-.242 (-1.09)
Adjacency	-.254 (-0.98)	-.261 (-1.01)
Past colonial links	.137 (0.24)	.107 (0.19)
Common language	.396 (1.42)	.373 (1.34)
Volatility source	.0384 (3.60)***	.038 (3.64)***
Volatility host	-.1438 (-0.78)	-.048 (-0.28)
War	-.456 (-2.55)***	-.528 (-2.99)***
Exchange rate crisis	-.029 (-1.36)	-
Inflation	-	-.037 (-2.62)***.
Constant	-6.000 (-3.34)***	-5.772 (-3.21)***
AIC	12830.13	1771.60
BIC	12938.86	12933.87
Log Likelihood	-6397.062	-6394.566
Likelihood ratio test	$\chi^2 = 4205.90$ ***	$\chi^2 = 4227.83$ ***
	Wald $\chi 2$= 1767.44***	Wald $\chi 2$= 1771.60***

*Notes: *, **, *** significant at 10%, 5%, 1% risk. N. of observations: 3220; N. of years: 23; N. of country-pairs: 28*5=140.*

Our estimations, reported in column 6.2 of Table 6 show that real exchange rate crises have no effect on the FDI levels received by our five MENA economies, suggesting that fire sales, or Mergers & Acquisitions driven by price opportunities, are not the dominant form of foreign investment in the countries in our sample. It does not modify the estimated value of our core GDP instability variable coefficients. This result is consistent with the significantly higher proportion of green-field investment in total FDI, which differentiates MENA economies from those in other developing regions.

7. CONCLUSION AND POLICY ISSUES

In the present paper, we analyse the impact of output volatility on FDI location in Middle Eastern and North African countries within the framework of a gravity model. As such a model allows the reduction of risks and costs associated with distance (geographical, linguistic and legal) to be controlled for, this enables the impact of macroeconomic sources of risks and costs on FDI to be differentiated from other sources of risks and costs. Additionally, since the gravity model allows the effect on FDI of various determinants concerning source countries to be assessed, our paper has been able to pay special attention to the impact of source country output volatility on FDI. We could therefore consider output volatility in both source and host countries, and find evidence of opposing impacts on FDI flows for these two variables, when controlling for bilateral and host country characteristics such as economic and political risk, trade openness and distance.

More specifically, we first show that FDI to MENA countries increases with the level of output volatility in the source country, therefore supporting the assumption of a substitution effect between domestic and foreign investment for our sample source countries. Second, we find that MENA countries with a higher level of output instability tend to attract less FDI, but this result is sensible to the control for Lebanon war. We also found that after the introduction of the Euro-Med agreement, institutional or cultural distances started to fall, with short-term macroeconomic factors of attraction also becoming less important in explaining European investment in MENA economies. Third, we show that FDI from non-traditional sources (in our sample essentially least-developed non-European Mediterranean countries) tends to have adopted radically different patterns of reaction to economic fluctuations in both the source and host countries than FDI originating from traditional sources (the most highly-developed Western European countries). Although FDI coming from central European countries is higher when volatility is higher in source and lower in host MENA countries, FDI sourced from countries located at the Europe periphery (mostly non-European Mediterranean countries) is lower when volatility is higher in source and lower in host MENA countries. Hence, our results confirm recent finding that FDI from traditional and non-traditional sources exhibits different sensitivity to host country conditions (Andrès, Busse and Nunnenkamp 2012), by focusing on macroeconomic volatility rather than on institutional quality. Furthermore, our findings extend this differentiation to the FDI sensitivity to home country volatility.

As for the policy issues raised by our findings, there are two of them. First, although regional integration increases levels of FDI to developing economies via the reduction of microeconomic transaction costs, it also tends to raise the macroeconomic costs associated with volatility. When business cycles are synchronised in the different peripheral economies of our sample, FDI coming from non-traditional sources (other MENA economies and countries of the European periphery, such as Malta or Hungary) is more prone to be pro-cyclical and transmit source country instability than FDI coming from more traditional (Western Europe) sources. Thus, deepening integration to central European economies, via association agreements, would be more beneficial to MENA economies than increasing purely regional integration since it could reduce the risks related by pro-cyclical FDI behaviour. Second, our results challenge the currently widely-held idea that, because FDI is less pro-cyclical than the other forms of financial inflow, it is a more stable source of external finance for developing economies (Fernandez-Arias and Hausmann 2001; Calderón and Didier 2009). Developing economies, like those of MENA countries, that are dependent on foreign investment, can finally suffer from external sources of macroeconomic instability that are not global but, instead, related to the countries whence the FDI comes.

Consequently, although diversifying FDI sources towards non-traditional investors is necessary for MENA countries, especially by increasing regional trade and value chain integration, MENA countries should find new partners outside the MENA region. Trying to increase their attractiveness to Asian investors could be a very positive development for the countries of the region. A good policy would be to diversify the portfolio of FDI sources so that pro-cyclical and counter-cyclical effects could compensate, with limited effect on the level of FDI flowing to MENA economies.

REFERENCES

Abderrezak, A. 2008. "Foreign direct investment in the MENA region: Is there a colonisation memory effect?". *The Journal of North African Studies* 13, no. 2: 219-226.

Aguiar, M., and G. Gopinath. 2005. "Fire-sale foreign direct investment and liquidity crises". *The Review of Economics and Statistics* 87, no. 3: 439-452.

Ahluwalia, P. 2000. "*Discriminating contagion: An alternative explanation of contagious currency crises in emerging markets*". IMF working paper WP/00/14, The International Monetary Fund, Washington D.C.

Aizenman, J. 2003. "Volatility, employment and the patterns of FDI in emerging markets". *Journal of Development Economics* 72, no. 2: 585-601

Ali, F.A., N. Fiess, and R. MacDonald. 2010. "Do institutions matter for Foreign Direct Investment?". *Open Economies Review* 21, no. 1: 201-219.

Anderson, J.E., and D. Marcouiller. 2002. "Insecurity and the pattern of trade: An empirical investigation". *The Review of Economics and Statistics* 84, no. 2: 342-352.

Anderson, J. E., and E. van Wincoop. 2003. "Gravity with gravitas: A solution to the border puzzle". *American Economic Review* 93, no. 1: 170-192.

Andrés M. S., P. Nunnenkamp, and M. Busse. 2012. *"What drives FDI from non-traditional sources ? A comparative analysis of the determinants of bilateral flows"*. Kiel Institute for the World Economy Working Papers No. 1755. Kiel Institute for the World Economy, Kiel, Germany.

Apergis, N., C. Katrakilidis. 1998. "Does inflation uncertainty matter in foreign direct investment decisions? An empirical investigation for Portugal, Spain and Greece". *Rivista internazionale di Scienze economiche e commerciali* 45, no. 4: 729-744.

Aysan, A., G. Pang, and M.-C. Véganzonès-Varoudakis. 2009. "Uncertainty, economic reforms and private investment in the Middle East and North Africa". *Applied Economics* 41, no. 11: 1379-1395.

Bechri, M. 1999. *"Institutional obstacles, reform uncertainty and Tunisia's integration with the European Union"*. ERF/OECD/World Bank: The Dynamics of New Regionalism in MENA: Integration, Euro-Med Partnership Agreements & After, Cairo, February 6th and 7th of 1999.

Bénassy-Quéré, A., L. Fontagné, and A. Lahrèche-Révil. 2001. "Exchange-rate strategies in the competition for attracting foreign direct investment". *Journal of the Japanese and International Economies* 15, no. 1: 178-198.

Bénassy-Quéré, A., M. Coupet, and T. Mayer. 2007. "Institutional Determinants of Foreign Direct Investment". *The World Economy* 30, no. 5: 764-782.

Bergstrand, J. H., and P. Egger. 2007. "A knowledge-and-physical-capital model of international trade flows, foreign direct investment, and multinational enterprises". *Journal of International Economics* 73, no. 2: 278–308.

Bevan, A.A., and S. Estrin. 2004. "The determinants of foreign direct investment into European transition economies". *Journal of Comparative Economics* 32, no. 4: 775-787.

Bloningen, B. 2005. "A review of the empirical literature on FDI determinants." NBER *Working Paper No. 11299*. National Bureau of Economic Research, Cambridge, MA.

Busse, M., J. Königer, P. Nunnenkamp. 2010. "FDI promotion through bilateral investment treaties: more than a bit?".*Review of World Economics* 146:147-177.

Calderón, C. and T. Didier. 2009. "Will FDI be Resilient in this Crisis?" *Mimeo.* The World Bank, Washington D.C.

Cavallari L. 2010. "Exports and FDI in an endogenous-entry model with nominal and real uncertainty". *Journal of Macroeconomics* 32, no. 2: 300-313.

Cavallari, L., S. D'Addona. 2012. *"Nominal and real volatility as determinants of FDI." Mimeo.* University of Roma 3.

Chan, K. K., and E. R. Gemayel. 2004. "Risk instability and the pattern of FDI in the MENA region". IMF *Working Papers WP/04/139*. Washington D.C.

Choong, C.-K., and V. K.-S. Liew. 2009. "Impact of foreign direct investment volatility on economic growth of ASEAN-5 countries". *Economics Bulletin* 29, no. 3: 1829-1841.

Daude, C., E. Levy-Yeyati, and E. Stein. 2003. "Regional Integration and the Location of FDI". *Working Paper 492*. Inter-American Development Bank.

Demekas, D,G, B. Horváth, E. Ribakova, and Y. Wu. 2007. "Foreign direct investment in European transition economies: The role of policies". *Journal of Comparative Economics* 35, no. 2: 369-386.

De Mello-Sampayo, F. 2009. "Competing-destinations gravity model: an application to the geographic distribution of FDI". *Applied Economics* 41, no. 17: 2237-2253.

Desbordes, R., and V. Vicard. 2009. "Foreign Direct Investment and bilateral investment treaties: An international political perspective". *Journal of Comparative Economics* 37, no. 3: 372-386.

Head, K., and J. Ries. 2008. "FDI as an outcome of the market for corporate control: Theory and evidence". *Journal of International Economics* 74, no. 1: 2-20.

Eichengreen, B. J. 2000. "Taming capital flows". *World Development* 28, no. 6: 1105-1116.

Eichengreen, B. J., and D.A. Irwin. 1998. "The role of history in bilateral trade flows". In *The Regionalization of the World Economy*, ed. J. A. Frankel. Cambridge, Mass: National Bureau of Economic Research.

Evenett, S.J., and W. Keller. 2002. "On theories explaining the success of the gravity equation". *Journal of Political Economy* 110, no. 2: 281-316

Fernandez-Arias, E., and R. Hausmann. 2001. "Is Foreign direct investment a safer form of financing?". *Emerging Markets Review* 2, no. 1: 34-49

Frenkel, M., K. Funke, and G. Stadtmann. 2004. "A panel analysis of bilateral FDI flows to emerging economies". *Economic Systems* 28, no. 3: 281-300.

Ishii, S., K. Habermeier, B. Laurens, J. Leimone, J. Vadasz, and J.I. Canales-Kriljenko. 2002. "Capital account liberalization and financial sector stability". IMF Occasional Paper 211. Washington D.C.: The International Monetary Fund.

Kaminsky, G., S. Lizondo, and C. Reinhart. 1998. "Leading indicators of currency crises". *IMF Staff Papers* 5, no. 1: 1-48.

Kiyota, K., and S. Urata. 2004. "Exchange rate, exchange rate volatility and foreign direct investment". *The World Economy* 27, no. 10: 1501-1536.

Koren, M., and S. Tenreyro. 2007. "Volatility and development". *The Quarterly Journal of Economics* 122, no. 1: 243-287.

Kose, M. A., E. Prasad, K.S. Rogoff, and S.-J. Wei. 2009. "Financial Development: A reappraisal". *IMF Staff Papers* 56, no. 1: 8-62.

Krugman, P. 2000. Fire-sale FDI. "In *Capital Flows and the Emerging Economies: Theory, Evidence, and Controversies*", ed. S. Edwards. Chicago, Ill.: The University of Chicago Press for the NBER.

Lane, P., and G. M. Milesi-Ferretti. 2008. "International Investment Patterns". *Review of Economics and Statistics* 90, no. 3: 538-549.

Lederman, D. 2011. Large devaluations, foreign direct investment and exports: A speculative note. *Policy Research Working Paper 5619*, Washington D.C., The World Bank.

Lefilleur, J., M. Maurel. 2010. “Inter- and intra-industry linkages as a determinant of FDI in Central and Eastern Europe”. *Economic Systems* 34, no. 3: 309-330.

Lensink, R., O. Morrissey. 2006. “Foreign Direct Investment: Flows, volatility and the impact on growth”. *Review of International Economics* 14, no. 3: 478-493.

Levchenko, A., P. Mauro. 2007. “Do some forms of financial flows help protect against “sudden stops”?” *The World Bank Economic Review* 21, no. 3: 389-411.

Levy-Yeyati, E., and F. Sturzenegger. 2001. “Exchange rate regimes and economic performance”. *IMF Staff Papers* 47, no. 1: 62-98.

Levy Yeyati, E., U. Panizza, and E. Stein. 2007. “The cyclical nature of north-south FDI flows”. *Journal of International Money and Finance* 26, no. 1: 104-130.

Loayza, N.V., R. Rancière, L. Servén, and J. Ventura. 2007. “Macroeconomic volatility and welfare in developing countries: An introduction”. *The World Bank Economic Review* 21, no. 3: 343-357.

Medvedev, D. 2012. “Beyond trade: The impact of Preferential Trade Agreements on FDI inflows”. *World Development* 40, no. 1: 49-61.

Méon, P.-G., and K. Sekkat. 2012. “FDI Waves, waves of neglect of political risk”. *World Development* 40, no. 11: 2194-2205.

Mina, W. M. (2012). “The institutional reforms debate and FDI inflows to the MENA region: The “best” ensemble”. *World Development* 40, no. 9: 1798-1809

Nicet-Chenaf, D., and E. Rougier. 2011. “New exports matter: FDI, export discoveries and growth in MENA countries”. *Journal of International Trade and Economic Development* 20, no. 4: 507-533.

Petri, P.A. 2012. “The determinants of bilateral FDI: Is Asia different?”. *Journal of Asian Economies* 23, no. 3: 201-209.

Sadik, A., and A. Bolbol. 2001. “Capital flows, FDI and technology spillovers: Evidence from Arab countries”. *World Development* 29, no. 12: 2111-2125.

Santos Silva, J., S. Tenreyro. 2006. “The log of gravity”. *The Review of Economics and Statistics* 88, no. 4: 641-658.

Stein, E., C. Daude. 2007.” Longitude matters: time zones and the location of foreign direct investment”. *Journal of International Economics* 71, no. 1: 96-112.

Takagi, S., and Z. Shi. 2011. “Exchange rate movements and foreign direct investment: Japanese investment in Asia, 1987-2008”. *Japan and the World Economy* 23, no. 4: 265-272.

Uctum, M., and R. Uctum. 2011. “Crises, portfolio flows, and foreign direct investment: A application to Turkey”. *Economic Systems* 35, no. 4: 462-480.

UNCTAD. 2009. *World Investment Report 2009*. Geneva: United Nations Conference on Trade and Development.

Wang M., and S. Wong S. 2007. “Foreign direct investment outflows and business-cycle fluctuations”. *Review of International Economics* 15, no. 1: 146-163.

Wei, S.-J. 2000. “How taxing is corruption on international investors?”. *Review of Economics and Statistics* 82, no. 1: 1-11.

ANNEX 1.

Table A1: Data sources and definitions

Variables	*Description*	*Data Source*
FDI_{ij}	The value in thousands of US dollars of flows of foreign direct investment (FDI) from a country *i* (source country) towards the country *j* (host country) at time *t*	OECD, UNCTAD FDI/TNC database Balance of payments of Morocco, Central Bank of Tunisia
GDP host	GDP in thousands of US dollars	CEPII, CHELEM database
GDP source	GDP in thousands of US dollars	
Difference in GDP per capita	Difference in GDP per capita (thousands of US dollars) between source country *i* and host country *j*	Population data used to measure per capita GDP is collected from IMF International Financial statistics
Distance	Distance in kilometers between source and host capitals	CEPII, Geo dataset
Adjacency	Common Border between country *i* and *j* (takes the value 1 if the two countries share a common border, and 0 otherwise)	CEPII, Geo dataset
Common language	Common official language for country *i* and *j* (takes the value 1 if the two countries share a common language, and 0 otherwise)	CEPII, Geo dataset
Common colonial power	Common colonizer for country *i* and *j* (takes the value 1 if the two countries had a common colonizer, and 0 otherwise)	CEPII, Geo dataset
Past colonial links	Country *j* is colonized by county *i* (takes the value 1 if the country *j* was colonized by country *i*, and 0 otherwise)	CEPII, Geo dataset
Investprof	Score of the risk to FDI not covered by other political, economic and financial risk components. It includes ratings of contract viability, risks of expropriation, profit repatriation and payment delays. Highest score equates X very low risk.	ICRG database
Openness	Ratio of trade openness of country *j*	Export and import data collected from IMF
Inflation	Inflation rate of country *j*	World development indicators (WDI)
Exchange rate crisis	Index of crisis exchange of host country (takes the value 1 if the country has experienced a large variation in the value of its real exchange rate or foreign currencies reserves, and 0 otherwise)	Authors' calculations on the basis of IMF data
Volatility host and Volatility source	Volatility of GDP growth for host or source country *j* reflecting the coefficient of variation of growth	Authors' calculations CHELEM database

War	Dummy variable takes the value 1 for Lebanese war years (1987-1991) and 0 from 1992 onwards	Authors' calculations
Post_War	Dummy variable takes the value 1 for Lebanese post-war years (1992-1996) and 0 for other years	Authors' calculations
World FDI wave	World levels of FDI flows in value	UNCTAD
Europe FDI wave	European Union (UE25) levels of FDI flows in US Dollar	UNCTAD
Central	Dummy variable takes the value 1 if the country belongs to the European core (UE15) in 2009, and takes null otherwise.	Authors' calculations
Peripheral	Dummy variable takes the value 1 if the country does not belong to the European core (UE15) in 2009, and null otherwise.	Authors' calculations

TABLE A2: List of countries in the sample

Algeria	Germany	Libya	Romania
Austria	Great Britain	Malta	Spain
Belgium-Luxembourg	Greece	Mauritania	Sweden
Czech Republic	Hungary	**Morocco**	Switzerland
Denmark	Ireland	Netherlands	Syria
Egypt	Italy	Norway	**Tunisia**
Finland	Jordan	Poland	**Turkey**
France	**Lebanon**	Portugal	Ukraine

Note: the five main MENA host countries are reported in bold.

TABLE A3: Multicolinearity VIF tests

	VIF	1/VIF
Openness	1.69	0.592556
AMU	1.28	0.780349
GAFTA	1.69	0.590143
InvestProfil	2.03	0.491424
GDP source	1.85	0.541074
GDP host	187	0.536023
Difference in GDP p.c.	2.28	0.439394
Distance	1.25	0.801524
Adjacency	1.44	0.695449
Past colonial links	1.19	0.839594
Common language	1.65	0.606727
Volatility source	1.33	.0.749694
Volatility host	1.29	0.777782
Mean VIF	**1.63**	-

Table A4: FDI levels: Eichengreen correction and Tobit RE estimations (Student *t*)

Estimator	Eichengreen's correction RE estimator		Tobit RE estimator	
	2.1	2.2	2.3	2.4
Openness	.7566 (3.55)***	.489 (2.16)***	.753 (3.54)***	.481 (2.13)***
MED	1.433 (9.00)***	1.316 (8.16)***	1.437 (9.05)***	1.324 (8.24)***
AMU	2.206 (4.54)***	1.944 (3.29)***	2.191 (4.47)***	1.882 (3.11)***
GAFTA	-.424 (-1.85)*	-.4182 (-1.79)*	-.413 (-1.81)*	-.392 (-1.66)*
InvestProfil	.145 (4.31)***	.233 (6.23)***	.145 (4.32)***	.236 (6.30)***
GDP source	1.261 (11.8)***	1.153 (10.08)***	1.256 (11.39)***	1.118 (9.07)***
GDP host	.489 (4.26)***	.445 (3.54)***	.485 (4.14)***	.441 (3.40)***
Diff. in GDP pc	.014 (0.17)	.038 (0.42)	.014 (0.17)	.041 (0.44)
Distance	-.631 (-2.03)**	-.655 (-1.99)**	-.6294 (-1.93)**	-.648 (-1.42)*
Adjacency	-.2851 (-0.63)	-.3842 (-0.87)	-.2890 (-0.66)	-.403 (-0.85)
Past col. links	.653 (0.74)	1.056 (1.13)	.667 (0.72)	1.141 (1.12)
Common lang.	1.188 (2.78)***	1.103 (2.41)	1.178 (2.64)***	1.063 (2.15)**
Volatil. source	-	.0430 (1.23)	-	.0457 (1.31)
Volatil. host	-	2.588 (5.29)***		2.646 (5.41)***
Constant	-28.40 (-8.43)***	-25.2041 (-6.88)***	-28.220 (-8.14)***	-24.539 (-6.34)***
R^2 within	0.24	0.22		
R^2 Between	0.61	0.60		
R^2 Total	0.45	0.44		
Tests	Fisher Test : MCO vs individual FE $F(134,3233)=21.32$ $Pr>F=0.000$ Hausman test $\chi^2 = 83.03$ $Pr>\chi^2 = 0.000$ $Wald\chi^2=1293.53$***	Fisher Test : MCO vs individual FE $F(134,3233) = 22.16$ $Pr>F=0.000$ Hausman test $\chi^2 = 1036$ $Pr>\chi^2 = 0.000$ $Wald\chi^2=1073.11$***	AIC = 16771.74 BIC = 16863.6 Loglikhd=8370.867 $Wald\chi^2=1270.80$***	AIC = 15401.82 BIC = 15504.51 Loglikhd=7683.9077 $Wald\chi2=1035.11$***
Breush Pagan $\chi^2_{(1)}$ test	$\chi^2 = 179.00$ $Pr>\chi^2 = 0.000$	$\chi^2 = 130.34$ $Pr>\chi^2 = 0.000$		

*Notes: *, **, *** significant at 10%, 5% and 1% risk. Number of observations: 3375; Number of years: 23; Number of country-pairs: 27*5=135).*

ANNEX. 2

Exchange rate crisis indicator

In line with Ahluwalia (2000), we implement for each host country an ex-post identification of the periods during which they were affected by such a crisis. To this end, an index combining variations of nominal exchange rates and variations in foreign exchange reserves has been computed. Equation (3) shows that the indicator consists of a weighted average of the variations of nominal exchange rate and exchange reserves.

$$IND = \left(\frac{\frac{1}{\sigma^2_{TCN}}}{\left(\frac{1}{\sigma^2_{TCN}} + \frac{1}{\sigma^2_{RES}} \right)} \right) * \Delta TCN + \left(\frac{\frac{1}{\sigma^2_{RES}}}{\left(\frac{1}{\sigma^2_{TCN}} + \frac{1}{\sigma^2_{RES}} \right)} \right) * (-1) * \Delta RES \tag{3}$$

These two variables, computed as quarterly variations on the basis of monthly average levels, are respectively named ΔTCN and ΔRES. The weights respectively measure the shares of the variance of the exchange rate and of the foreign exchange reserves in the sum of these variances.

This index, designed to reflect the intensity of the pressures that a national currency undergoes during an episode of balance of payments crisis, enables the severity of those periods of external instability to be measured. It should be noted that the negative sign allotted to the average monthly variation of the foreign exchange reserves makes it possible to obtain the highest level of the index when the crisis is imminent (Ahluwalia, 2000). In order to identify whether a country *j* is affected by a crisis at date *t*, we need to establish a threshold above which the value of IND can be considered as a crisis peak. This threshold is defined on a country-by-country basis and not for the whole sample. It is obtained by considering both the average level ($Mean_{IND}$) and the standard deviation (σ_{IND}) of IND. A crisis is detected when IND is superior or equal to $Mean_{IND} + \sigma_{IND}$. That definition of the crisis threshold corresponds to the minimal bound found in the literature. A higher threshold ($1,5^*\beta_{IND} + \sigma_{IND}$) would have resulted in an insufficient variation in the variable. Subsequently, the effect on FDI is taken into account by introducing into the econometric estimates a binary variable *Crisis* of the type: Crisis = 1 if IND $\geq Mean_{IND} + \sigma_{IND}$ and 0 otherwise. In order to transpose these quarterly crises data into annual impacts, we made the commonly admitted assumption that any episode of crisis lasting for more than three months will have effects on the current year, which means that the crisis could be regarded as annual. In order to avoid reverse causality with FDI inflows, a crisis in year *t* has been imputed in estimation as a determinant of FDI inflows in $t+1$.

STABILITÉ DE LA CROISSANCE DES PAYS INVESTISSEURS ET FLUX D'IDE DANS LES PAYS D'AFRIQUE DU NORD ET DU MOYEN-ORIENT

Résumé - *Si les déterminants macroéconomiques des flux d'IDE ont beaucoup été analysés du point de vue du pays hôte et de ses caractéristiques, ils l'ont plus rarement été du point de vue du pays source. A l'aide d'un modèle gravitaire nous analysons les déterminants des IDE entrants des pays MENA en focalisant notre attention sur la stabilité macroéconomique d'un ensemble de pays investisseurs (européens et non européens). Notre analyse en panel montre que les investissements européens dans les pays MENA sont d'autant plus élevés que la stabilité macroéconomique des pays source est faible ce qui confirmerait pour les firmes transnationales européennes, l'existence d'un « effet de substitution ». Nous trouvons également que les accords de Barcelone de 1995 ont renforcé la vulnérabilité des pays MENA aux cycles européens tant à court qu'à moyen terme. Nous montrons également que l'intégration régionale des pays MENA et l'émergence de nouvelles sources d'IDE en provenance de pays méditerranéens à la périphérie de l'UE n'ont pas nécessairement eu des effets positifs sur les flux d'IDE à destination des MENA. Nous pouvons en effet observer un « effet revenu » par lequel les flux d'IDE en provenance des pays périphériques à l'Europe diminuent lorsque leur croissance est plus instable. Nos résultats sont robustes lorsque nous testons notre modèle avec différents estimateurs, différents échantillon et différentes mesures de l'instabilité.*

Mots-clés - IDE, MODÈLE DE GRAVITÉ, UNION EUROPÉENNE, MENA, INFLATION

COMPTE RENDU

Jean-Paul Carrière, Christophe Demazière, Rodica Petréa et Luminita Filimon (dir.), ***La mise en œuvre du développement territorial durable : déclinaisons franco-roumaines*****, L'Harmattan, Paris, 2013, 275p.**

Cet ouvrage réunit un ensemble de contributions de chercheurs français et roumains qui explorent le croisement entre les analyses sur le développement territorial et celles sur le développement durable. Les premières sont tirées des travaux sur les districts industriels et les systèmes productifs locaux et ont été enrichies, par la suite, par une série de contributions d'économistes, d'aménageurs et de géographes qui cherchent à comprendre la dimension territoriale des processus de croissance économique et de développement. Les secondes sont issues des réflexions et des recherches développées à partir du rapport Brutland et de l'intégration des principes de la préservation de l'environnement, de la précaution d'utilisation des ressources et de l'équité intergénérationnelle, dans la conception de l'action publique.

Les différentes contributions qui composent cet ouvrage sont le résultat d'une série d'échanges entre les chercheurs de l'Université de Tours et de l'Université d'Oreada et s'inscrivent dans le prolongement d'un projet de recherche sur les « *Taris* » roumains en tant que territoires de projet et modèles de développement territorial, à l'image des « *Pays* » français. Ces contributions se focalisent plus particulièrement sur les expériences de développement comparées en France et en Roumanie. Le fil conducteur reste fortement pluridisciplinaire, en privilégiant des analyses d'économistes, d'aménageurs, d'urbanistes et de géographes.

L'ouvrage s'organise en trois parties : la première partie, d'ordre théorique, est dédiée à l'aménagement du territoire face au défi de la durabilité et permet de mesurer la convergence de différentes approches vers ce que l'on pourrait qualifier de développement durable à l'échelle méso-territoriale. La deuxième partie est dédiée à l'étude des politiques territoriales mises en œuvre en France et en Roumanie et à la façon dont elles intègrent la durabilité. Enfin, la troisième partie de l'ouvrage est consacrée aux rapports entre développement territorial et questions environnementales.

L'intérêt de l'ouvrage réside dans trois aspects. En premier lieu, il réunit deux séries d'analyses – celles sur l'économie territoriale et celles sur l'aménagement durable qui se sont parfois développées de façon parallèle sans véritablement se confronter ou se rencontrer dans une même perspective de recherche. En deuxième lieu, l'ouvrage reste fortement teinté d'un caractère pluridisciplinaire, ce qui le rend abordable à un grand nombre de lecteurs, y compris des décideurs et des praticiens du développement durable territorial. Enfin, en troisième lieu, il permet de donner un aperçu des dynamiques du développement territorial en Roumanie.

Comme tous les ouvrages collectifs, celui-ci souffre évidemment de certaines asymétries, selon les chapitres, dans l'utilisation des concepts et des théories sous-jacentes à ces thématiques mais aussi dans les méthodologies utilisées pour les études empiriques. En ce qui concerne les expériences de développement roumaines, elles sont détaillées mais mériteraient une meilleure tentative de théorisation. Enfin, pour les chercheurs français, il manque quelque peu une partie introductive permettant de cadrer les évolutions roumaines en général et les évolutions particulières en matière de développement régional et territorial. Ces remarques ne diminuent cependant, aucunement, l'intérêt de cet ouvrage.

Michel Dimou
LEAD, Université de Toulon

REVUE RÉGION ET DÉVELOPPEMENT

Site Web : www.regionetdeveloppement.org

Recommandations aux auteurs

La Revue Région et Développement publie en français ou en anglais des articles originaux, des notes et documents et des comptes rendus de lecture. Pour soumission à publication, l'auteur doit adresser à la rédaction de la revue le texte par courrier électronique ou le manuscrit dactylographié en deux exemplaires. La présentation des chapitres, des références bibliographiques et des notes de bas de page doit être conforme à celle de la revue. Les articles doivent être accompagnés d'un résumé en français et en anglais d'une dizaine de lignes, des mots-clés correspondants et de la classification du JEL. Le nom de l'auteur, l'institution à laquelle il appartient et l'adresse complète doivent figurer en page de garde.
Les articles proposés à la revue Région et Développement sont évalués par le Comité de rédaction puis soumis de manière anonyme à un ou deux referees. L'auteur reçoit un rapport d'évaluation, lui aussi anonyme, concluant à publication, révision ou refus.
Après avis favorable à la publication dans la revue, il sera demandé à l'auteur un envoi par mail du texte en Word (y compris figures, tableaux et formules mathématiques compatibles avec Word 2010).

Les propositions d'articles doivent être adressées à la rédaction de la revue :

Professeur Maurice Catin
Revue Région et Développement
LÉAD - Faculté de Sciences Économiques et de Gestion
Université de Toulon
70 Avenue Roger Decouvoux
83000 Toulon

Tél. : 04 83 36 63 18
Mail : maurice.catin@univ-tln.fr

Secrétaire général de la rédaction : Christophe Van Huffel
Mail : vanhuffel@univ-tln.fr

BULLETIN D'ABONNEMENT

Revue "Région et Développement"

- **Je désire souscrire un abonnement pour l'année 2014 (deux numéros) :**

☐ France, DOM-TOM : 37 € ☐ Étranger : 40 €

- **Règlement :**

☐ CCP ☐ Chèque bancaire ☐ Mandat international

Pour l'étranger, merci d'effectuer un virement en euros sur le ***CCP 23 625 44 N Paris*** ou bien un règlement par chèque bancaire en euros sur une banque domiciliée en France ou par carte de crédit internationale.

N° de la carte : ☐☐☐☐☐☐☐☐☐☐☐☐☐☐☐☐

Date d'expiration : |__|__|__|__|__|__|__| Banque : ....

Nom et Prénom : ....
Adresse : ....
....
Code Postal : .... Ville : ....
Pays : ....

Date :

Signature :

Ce bulletin d'abonnement à la Revue "Région et Développement" et votre règlement sont à retourner à :

Éditions L'HARMATTAN - 7, rue de l'École-Polytechnique, 75005 PARIS
Tél. : 01 40 46 79 14 - fax : 01 43 29 86 20 - site web : www.librairieharmattan.com

Abonnement annuel : 2 numéros
France, DOM-TOM : 37 €
Étranger : 40 €

L'HARMATTAN ITALIA
Via Degli Artisti 15; 10124 Torino

L'HARMATTAN HONGRIE
Könyvesbolt ; Kossuth L. u. 14-16
1053 Budapest

L'HARMATTAN KINSHASA
185, avenue Nyangwe
Commune de Lingwala
Kinshasa, R.D. Congo
(00243) 998697603 ou (00243) 999229662

L'HARMATTAN CONGO
67, av. E. P. Lumumba
Bât. – Congo Pharmacie (Bib. Nat.)
BP2874 Brazzaville
harmattan.congo@yahoo.fr

L'HARMATTAN GUINÉE
Almamya Rue KA 028, en face
du restaurant Le Cèdre
OKB agency BP 3470 Conakry
(00224) 657 20 85 08 / 664 28 91 96
harmattanguinee@yahoo.fr

L'HARMATTAN MALI
Rue 73, Porte 536, Niamakoro,
Cité Unicef, Bamako
Tél. 00 (223) 20205724 / +(223) 76378082
poudiougopaul@yahoo.fr
pp.harmattan@gmail.com

L'HARMATTAN CAMEROUN
BP 11486
Face à la SNI, immeuble Don Bosco
Yaoundé
(00237) 99 76 61 66
harmattancam@yahoo.fr

L'HARMATTAN CÔTE D'IVOIRE
Résidence Karl / cité des arts
Abidjan-Cocody 03 BP 1588 Abidjan 03
(00225) 05 77 87 31
etien_nda@yahoo.fr

L'HARMATTAN BURKINA
Penou Achille Some
Ouagadougou
(+226) 70 26 88 27

L'HARMATTAN SÉNÉGAL
10 VDN en face Mermoz, après le pont de Fann
BP 45034 Dakar Fann
33 825 98 58 / 33 860 9858
senharmattan@gmail.com / senlibraire@gmail.com
www.harmattansenegal.com

L'HARMATTAN BÉNIN
ISOR-BENIN
01 BP 359 COTONOU-RP
Quartier Gbèdjromèdé,
Rue Agbélenco, Lot 1247 I
Tél : 00 229 21 32 53 79
christian_dablaka123@yahoo.fr

Achevé d'imprimer par Corlet Numérique - 14110 Condé-sur-Noireau
N° d'Imprimeur : 119488 - Dépôt légal : juin 2015 - *Imprimé en France*

www.ingramcontent.com/pod-product-compliance
Lightning Source LLC
LaVergne TN
LVHW021216061026
849535LV00008B/2757
* 9 7 8 2 3 4 3 0 6 4 3 6 9 *